Calculating Soul Connections

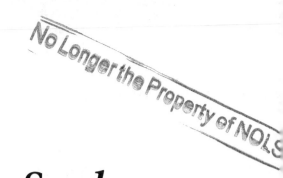
Calculating Soul Connections

A Deeper Understanding of Human Relationships

Tom Blaschko

Pine Winds Press
Enumclaw, WA
360-825-7797

An imprint of Idyll Arbor, Inc.

paper ISBN 9780937663189
e-book ISBN 9780937663356

Library of Congress Cataloging-in-Publication Data

Blaschko, Thomas M.
  Calculating soul connections : a deeper understanding of human relationships / Tom Blaschko.
      pages cm
  Includes bibliographical references and index.
  ISBN 978-0-937663-18-9 (alk. paper)
  1. Soul. 2. Interpersonal relations--Miscellanea. 3. Vital force. 4. Religion and science--Miscellanea. I. Title.
  BF1999.B651455 2013
  128'.1--dc23

                                                    2013001786

From the point of view of basic physics, the most interesting phenomena are of course in the *new* places, the places where the rules do not work — not the places where they *do* work. That is the way in which we discover new rules.

— Richard Feynman

Contents

Acknowledgements ix

I. Introduction 1
   1. Background 3
   2. Wishes 9
   3. Life Force: Energy and Information 11

II. Soul Structure 19
   4. Structure of Souls 21
   5. Chakra Structure Basics 67
   6. Chakra Storage 75
   7. External Chakra Connections 101
   8. Internal Chakra Connections 139
   9. Soul Integration 157

III. Simple Soul Connections 165
   10. Ordinary and Non-Ordinary Connections 167
   11. Sending and Sensing 179
   12. Building Connections 199
   13. Ordinary Reality and Connection 221
   14. Sending a Message 237
   15. Extremely Powerful Life Force 247

Part IV. Complex Soul Connections 251
   16. Soul-Body Connections 253
   17. Soul Interactions 265
   18. Non-Living Interactions 277
   19. Wrapping Up, Moving On 281
   20. Apologies 285
   Appendix 1. The Heraclean Ego 289
   Appendix 2. Operators and Variables 293
   Endnotes 297
   References 301
   Index 311

Acknowledgements

Many people have contributed to this book in many different ways. Without them I would never have found or thought of all the ideas that I have put together here. In an approximate time sequence here are the people and groups who have personally helped me on this journey.

To my parents: My father, Oliver Blaschko, was a good and honest man who saw the good in people and still understood their realities. I've tried to learn that skill. My mother, Margaret MacLeod Blaschko, loved me even when she couldn't understand me. She typed final drafts of papers for me in high school, usually the night before they were due. If she were still around, this book might have been written sooner. Only in retrospect do I understand how fey the MacLeod part of my heritage was and is. My thanks to Malcolm, Eva, Pat, and Jake for allowing me to be myself. I've seen the Fairy Flag at Dunvegan.

Richard Feynman, who came to the Summer Science Program at Thacher School in Ojai, California, and shared a physics problem along with his philosophy of how to solve it. I got more out of the philosophy.

At Caltech and to the present day these people have been sources of inspiration: Steve Bankes, Phil Morgan, Jeff Ross, Manfred Chiu, and John Heuman.

Seven friends that I met through karate have been especially influential in my life. They are Caylor Adkins, Burk Dowell, Nancy Weller, Mike Panian, Pam Logan, Jerry Bentler, and Jay Boyer. There are many other people in my karate practice, both seniors and juniors, whom I want to thank for helping me understand ki. They include Tsutomu Ohshima, Ron Thom, Randy McClure, Carol Baker, Hugh Glaser, John Todderud, Jesse Schulte, and Mike Vance. I also learned from brief encounters with Master Shigeru Egami, Master Tadao Okuyama, and

Master Kisshomaru Ueshiba. Some of them taught me and others forced me to understand ki better so I could explain it to them. There are many other people in Shotokan—Ohshima who shared wonderful practices with me. Thanks to you all.

My brother Bill and his wife Melody, who let me stay at their cabin in the mountains and spend serious time writing. For the many conversations we shared. For finding a reason why I really needed to go to Scotland. For living near a hot springs.

Mark Lawrence. We travel through the world on the edge of science and the realms where science only thinks it understands what is going on.

joan burlingame for Manressa Castle, founding Idyll Arbor, and helping me work through my thoughts about ghosts and other spirits.

Phyllis Rodin who told me to get busy and write. It took much longer than either of us expected.

My son, Will, who listens and understands. My daughter, Chris, who hears me when I think loudly.

Patrick Harpur who provided the field guide for my journey through the otherworld. I freely admit to straying off the path, but there are always adventures off the beaten trail.

Diane Steinbach, one of the few people I know who has always done what I write about.

Gary Craig, who gave the world EFT, and David MacKay, PhD, who made sure it continued to be available.

Sand Swenby, my partner. The small but sturdy rock that strengthens the foundation I stand on and gives me perspective on my life in ways no one else could. This book would not have been completed without her support.

Those who read the book and helped make it better (yes some of the names are repeats): Sand Swenby, Mark Lawrence, Will Blaschko, Patrick Harpur, Deborah Byron, Perry Edwards, Joseph Drumheller, Bill and Melody Blaschko, Doug Anderson, and Mike Panian.

I. Introduction

...philosophers have said before that one of the fundamental requisites of science is that whenever you set up the same experiment, the same thing must happen. This is simply *not true*, it is *not* a fundamental condition of science.

— *Richard Feynman*

Here we look for ways to discuss souls and their connections.

1. Background

Loyalty to petrified opinion never yet broke a chain or freed a human soul.

— *Mark Twain*

Exploring the connections between souls is what this book is all about. We will be looking at the structure of the soul and the life force that connects one soul to another. Understanding souls and how they are connected makes the world a very different place.

We will start by looking at the basic concepts of life force, life energy, and information. All of these are ways a soul communicates within itself and are what is transferred when two different souls communicate.

Part II takes a look at a model of a soul by dividing it into seven parts (chakras) and then looking at the basic structure of each chakra, the chakra's connections to the outside world, the chakras connections within a soul, and how each chakra remembers its experiences.

In Part III we will study the connections between souls: how we can measure the connection, what increases and decreases the connections, and how messages are sent between souls.

Part IV puts all of the pieces together to show how our souls connect with our bodies and how souls interact with other souls.

Along with the explanations, there will be equations and testable predictions. If you are not mathematically inclined, you can skip the equations. Everything the equations say is in the text — just not as precisely. When we are finished, I hope we will have a better understanding of ourselves and our connections with others.

Let's start with the basic question, what is a soul?

I think we are all pretty clear on what a body is. Humans usually have one with two arms, two legs, a head, and a torso. There usually is a face with all the eyes, ears, and such. We expect some way to process food. Our blood system moves energy throughout the body. There are a few organs scattered around that have some sort of function that experts kind of understand. The brain may or may not do some thinking, but it almost always controls things like perception and movement. Given that there are several billion people in the world, we can suspect that reproduction happens.

And, oh yeah, the body can be alive or dead.

That alive or dead part moves us into the realm of the soul.* Alive means that the body and soul are together. A dead body means that they have come apart. This doesn't describe what a soul is, but it leads us in the direction of seeing that the body and soul have some responsibility to connect into a functional system. Before looking at that connection, let's take a moment to discuss a few other alternatives.

There are those who can't believe in souls. Can't believe there is anything beyond the physical. Can't believe that science has anything major left to discover. If you are one of those people, you might as well put the book down and go do something else. There's nothing for you here. There's another book coming along called *We All Have Souls and I Think I Can Prove It* that will give you a lot more to scoff at. This book simply makes the assumption that souls exist and rolls on from there.

Some believe souls are our connection with God. I agree that that's part of what souls do. I'm going to be a little more detailed in how the connection happens than many standard religious texts, but I don't think you will find that part offensive. You might be concerned that I allow for

---

* I understand that some people don't believe the soul is required for life. This is because we are alive and they are convinced the soul doesn't exist. If that was my point of view, I would have written a book titled *Trying to Explain All the Ways People Are Connected Without Including the Idea of a Soul*. I prefer the current approach, which seems far simpler.

something like a soul in creatures besides humans, but that really isn't important in developing the calculations. If it bothers you, please consider the idea of non-human souls a defect in my understanding and assume what I say applies only to humans and angels and God.

Some see souls or things our souls can connect with in everything. That's where I stand. Some of these people are rather adamant that we can't understand these connections through calculations. They should be very amused to read on and see whether I succeed or not.

For the rest of you who are waiting for me to say something with substance, I guess it's time to move on.

In this book I suggest that the soul has a structure that interacts with the body in a relatively complicated way. Body and soul do need to work together, after all. The best model I have found so far is the concept of chakras, multiple energy centers in the soul that are loosely associated with particular parts of the body.

I also suggest that there is a fifth force in our universe, which I call the life force. The Chinese use the word chi (or qi), as in Tai Chi or Qigong. Japanese use ki, as in Reiki and Aikido. Christians have the related concept of grace. Hindus use the term prana. Except on the fringes, Western science hasn't found out about this force yet, so I'm performing a formal introduction between science and the life force here in this book.

We'll take a look at life force and the structure of souls, but the real purpose of this book is to look at how to calculate the interactions of souls. Even more, this book is a way to discuss how souls and life force act in our world. I'll try hard to amuse myself and you as we develop the relevant equations. I'm glad you decided to come along for the ride.

Before we get started, I want to talk about the roadmaps we will need for the journey we are taking. There are some concepts that you may be hearing for the first time. If you already use these words, I want to make sure you have some idea of how I am applying them. I'm not quite as bad as the caterpillar in *Alice in Wonderland*, but sometimes I use ideas a little differently than the mainstream definition.

Reality

I propose that there are (at least) two types of reality: ordinary reality and soul reality. To move along we need to understand why we need to consult a roadmap for each.

Ordinary reality is what we see all around us, buildings, roads, plants, computers, books (or e-readers), refrigerators. Most writers who discuss more than one reality prefer the term ordinary. Some choose physical reality instead. This is the world our bodies interact with and it is the world that Western science studies. Most of us understand the roadmap of this kind of reality pretty well.

Soul reality takes on many names. Carlos Castaneda calls it non-ordinary reality. Patrick Harpur calls it daimonic reality, where daimonic comes from the Greek word *daimones*, which means messengers between God (gods) and men. Shamans, kahunas, mediums, and similar folk work in this reality much of the time. I believe we, usually ordinary, folk also visit soul reality a lot, although we don't often recognize that we have. I chose to use the term soul reality because soul is in the title of the book and because I think soul reality captures the essence of our daily, intimate connection with something besides ordinary reality better than the other choices. The roadmap for soul reality is something we will develop in this book.

Senses

We need different senses to read the roadmaps in each of these realities. There are two concepts that I want to borrow from Elizabeth Lloyd Mayer:[1] daytime eyes and nighttime eyes. Although Mayer speaks about eyes, I believe her concept of daytime eyes includes all the senses we use to perceive ordinary reality. Nighttime eyes are the senses we use to perceive soul reality. Mayer suggests that we can't use both types of eyes at the same time, but I think she is underestimating our abilities. She is correct, though, that each type of eye perceives something very different. What is really important to realize is that we need to use both to understand the totality of our reality.

Mathematical Equations

As I said earlier, there are mathematical equations in this book. You may ignore them. They are there for people who want to rigorously test what I have written. For everyone else, the text says the same thing as the equations, just not as formally. I hope you will give the book a try and not worry about the equations. All of the math has a gray background, so you will know what to skip.

2. Wishes

The Curious Mind naturally cultivates a certain
level of necessary detachment...
— *Joseph Drumheller*

Here is what I hope you will learn from what I discovered while
writing this book.

There are delightful, exciting, and unexpected insights into many
areas that interest me. Insights from other people that I found useful have
become more useful when I place them in this soul model. Ideas that
didn't make sense now fit in. Places where there are ongoing
controversies — it must be either this or it must be that — seem to have a
place for both once we get away from the idea of having just a brain and
add a soul to the mix.

I believe anyone who studies energy healing, martial arts,
psychology, human relations in small groups such as families or large
groups such as countries will benefit from the insights in this book.
Talking about the uses of this model is not the purpose of this book, but I
would like to give a few examples to show what I am talking about.

I believe the biggest benefit will be for people who know life energy
exists in a particular specialty field. They often face skepticism from
others who are locked into ordinary reality. Unfortunately, soul reality is
hard to prove in terms of ordinary reality. It may, in fact, be impossible in
particular areas of study. What this model does is join many of the views
of soul reality into a common system. When one area of study supports
all the other areas, all of them become easier to accept. Areas that will

benefit are as varied as shamanism, ghost research, and paranormal experiments.

There are many variations on energy healing. One set (including arts like Qigong and Reiki) speaks specifically about using life energy to do the healing. The other main set (including Eye Movement Desensitization and Reprocessing or EMDR and Emotional Freedom Techniques or EFT) is less specific about the interaction between the techniques and life energy. The model I'm proposing offers insight into the conditions that are required for the techniques to work, including what is required from both the client and the practitioner. In some cases the model provides information about how a technique works.

Psychologists, sociologists, and anyone else who studies the way people act will have a richer model of human behavior to work with. Some of the questions about nature versus nurture are easier to frame. There is a place for behaviorists and, at the same time, there is a place for Freudians and Jungians and cognitive-behavioral therapists and social psychologists (and more). It's not that any of them are right or wrong. Each is looking at part of the system. What the ideas in this model offer is a view of the system as a whole and how all the pieces fit together.

Those who study relationships between people will find new vocabulary and new ways to think about interaction processes. Being able to speak more directly about the use of power or to separate love from lust or to describe a senior-junior relationship (in the martial arts sense of the relationship between an instructor and a student) makes discussing changes and solutions easier.

Many people already have the insights that are in this model. In fact, a large portion of how I wrote this book was to look at something someone did exceptionally well and ask, how the heck did he or she do that? A little of it is my own invention (or handed to me by whatever muse inspired this book). Most is taking the genius of others and tying it together in a way that makes sense. With that I believe we are ready to begin our journey with a look at the life force.

3. Life Force: Energy and Information

Einstein's audacity is breathtaking. Having discarded Newton's absolute space and absolute time with almost no experimental justification, he was now inclined to discard Newton's enormously successful law of gravity, and with even less experimental justification. However, he was motivated not by experiment, but by his deep, intuitive insight into how the laws of physics *ought* to behave.

— *Kip S. Thorne*

This chapter will introduce the concept of life force, which is the basis for calculating how souls connect. A force is something that causes a change.* In the physical world there are four fundamental forces:

---

* More technically a force is a vector quantity defined by the rate of change in the momentum of an object. It may be experienced as a lift, a push, or a pull. The actual change in momentum is determined by doing a vector sum of all of the forces acting on the object to get a net force. When we are dealing with objects larger than a point, the forces may be different on different parts of the object causing rotations and deformations. Momentum in a soul is more complex than momentum in a physical object.

gravity, electromagnetic, strong nuclear, and weak nuclear.* The life force I am proposing is also a force, but it is different from these, and its interactions with the physical world raise some very difficult questions. Why do we need a life force? Because things happen that can't be explained by any of the currently accepted forces.

A newly accepted force opens up a wide range of possibilities and explains many phenomena that can't be easily explained with the four physical forces. We need to understand that the life force transfers both life energy and information.

Life energy is part of how the life force affects objects it acts on. Life energy is interesting because it can be included in the energy total when we are adding up all the energy in a system. There are observations that can't be explained without adding energy that follows a non-physical path.

Information transfer is the second aspect of life force. Information is not vital to studying the four physical forces until you get to the realm of quantum mechanics. When it comes to life, communication between souls is something that is of the utmost importance. In fact, it is the transfer of information that provides some of the strongest evidence that we need to study life force in addition to the four physical forces.

Energy

Energy is a measure of something. In 1963 Richard Feynman, a physics professor at the California Institute of Technology, wrote, "It is important to realize that in physics today, we have no knowledge of what energy is."[2] This has changed some. Modern physics talks about energy in terms of vibrational frequency. Higher frequencies mean higher energy. However, many people still look at the more sensation-based concept of energy, which comes in many forms: gravitational, kinetic,

---

* "Force was first mentioned by Archimedes in the 3rd century BC but only mathematically defined by Isaac Newton in the 17th century. Following the development of quantum mechanics it is now understood that particles influence each another through fundamental interactions, making force a redundant concept. Only four fundamental interactions are known: strong, electromagnetic, weak (unified into one electroweak interaction in 1970s), and gravitational (in order of decreasing strength)." (Force, 2007)

electrical, chemical, radiant, nuclear, mass, and more. For each of the forms of energy we have non-vibrational formulas to calculate how much energy we have. It is a strange thing that we can calculate how much of something we have without knowing exactly what it is, but there you have it. That's just the way it works.

I want to add one more type of energy to the list: life energy. By life energy I do not mean the chemical energy that supports physical life. I am proposing a kind of energy that exists in things and provides the energy to power the soul. Luckily I don't have to explain what this energy is or try to figure it out in vibrational terms. All I have to do is provide the equations to calculate it and show how it is transformed into and back from other types of energy. Calculating life energy really is the crucial issue because the one thing we know about energy is that it is conserved. As Richard Feynman said:

> There is a fact, or if you wish, a *law*, governing all natural phenomena that are known to date. There is no known exception to this law — it is exact so far as we know. The law is called the *conservation of energy*. It states that there is a certain quantity, which we call energy, that does not change in the manifold changes which nature undergoes. That is a most abstract idea, because it is a mathematical principle; it says that there is a numerical quantity which does not change when something happens. It is not a description of a mechanism, or anything concrete; it is just a strange fact that we can calculate some number and when we finish watching nature go through her tricks and calculate the number again, it is the same.[3]

When a force acts on an object, it changes its energy. We know from conservation of energy that the energy of the total system does not change, so we can also say that, within a system, force moves energy from one object or one place to another.

Gravity, for example, always pulls objects together. In our case (unless you are one of the rare people who walked on the moon) gravity is always pulling us down to the earth. When we are high above the earth, say we are jumping out of an airplane, we have a lot of potential energy. Gravity (one of the four physical forces) acts between us and the earth to pull us together. We lose the potential energy from being high over the earth, but it turns into kinetic energy (energy from motion) as our speed toward the earth increases.

Falling bodies reach terminal velocity. That means that gravity isn't making them go any faster. So what is happening? The potential energy is decreasing, kinetic energy isn't increasing, so there must be some other kind of energy being created. In this case it's mostly thermal energy. Our bodies heat up and the air heats up from the air molecules hitting our body. (In space, where there is no air, there is no terminal velocity, but relativity makes the calculations a lot more interesting.*) The parachute that should be opening about now slows our velocity by increasing the thermal energy more and giving off a certain amount of sound energy (an organized wave through air molecules). When we hit the ground, we transmit the last of our kinetic energy to the earth, which hardly notices it.

So how do we explain St. Teresa of Avila? She described the moments she felt closest to God by saying, "…the Lord catches up the soul…and carries it right out of itself…and begins to show it the features of the Kingdom He has prepared for it."[4]

While these were significant spiritual moments, there was something physical that went with them. It wasn't just her soul that was swept off the ground. Her whole body was lifted up, too. The other nuns tried, and usually succeeded, in holding her down, but this conduct was so extraordinary that her confessor made her write down her experiences to make sure they weren't the work of the devil. This was a real effect witnessed by dozens of people at a time. She wasn't alone in levitating; more that 100 Catholic saints have been said to have had the experience[5] and other, non-Christian traditions have similar stories. (D. D. Home, who was observed in the mid-1800s, is one of the best known and most extensively documented.[6])

---

* Mass increases as velocity increases. According to the physics of relativity we never move faster than the speed of light. It's all explained in Wikipedia under "Special relativity."

Gravity doesn't let you float off the ground. Neither do the other currently accepted forces.* Conservation of energy makes it clear that something else is involved to increase the levitators' potential energy. If we want to explain what happen to St. Teresa (and all of the others who have defied gravity), we're going to need some other force. I'm calling it the life force.

There are two other concepts related to force that will be relevant to this discussion: fields and radiation. A physical field is a way of representing the value of a force at every point in space. There is the classical picture of a magnet and iron filings, as shown in Figure 1. Each point in space can be assigned a

Figure 1: Iron filings show the lines of force in a magnet. The iron filings line up along the lines of force.[7]

strength and direction for the force. A gravitational field is even simpler. The field always points toward the object and its strength is a function of the distance, getting weaker as we move farther away from the object. (It is actually proportional to the inverse square of the distance, for those who remember such things from their physics classes.)

Related to the concept of a field is the concept of radiation. When electrons are jiggled, they produce photons. Depending on the frequency of the jiggling, the photons may be radio waves, light, x-rays, or some other part of the electromagnetic spectrum. The important thing about

---

* Actually electromagnetic force might let a person float, if you can explain how the earth and the person both suddenly added (or lost) a bunch of electrons. Now explaining where the energy to move the electrons might have come from is the issue that is unexplainable without life force.

radiation is that the effects stay stronger at large distances than the field effects of a static (non-moving) electron. Radiation falls off as $1/r$ while field effects fall off as $1/r^2$. Lasers take this one step better. If we could make a perfect laser, the coherent light it produced wouldn't change at all because of distance. The only thing that stops the photon group in a perfect laser is running into something. I believe communication between a pair of souls can approach the efficiency of a perfect laser in that distance does not affect the quality of the soul signal.

Information

The information that is passed by the life force has many levels of complexity. At its most basic level, the information can be as simple as the desire to be alive. For us that would be heartbeat and breathing. Simpler life forms, such as bacteria, would have their own equivalents. Other desires, such as eat, drink, connect, are also pretty basic messages.

I think these desires are best described by single verbs, but the information itself doesn't have the symbolism that words imply. What is being transmitted is the desire itself, not the word I write to explain it.

More complex messages might include the actions that are required to fulfill the desires and the hoped-for situation after the desires have been met. These are still wordless. One of the terms we apply to this kind of information is emotional. The feeling comes through, but the sender does not need to form words to express the feeling. The interactions between pets and owners usually fall into this range of information complexity.

Beyond this, we get into the range of symbols. Words are one kind of symbol, but information is also conveyed in non-verbal sounds, images, facial expressions, and gestures. The symbols can range from the very simple to as complex as anyone can understand. We can understand much more by using symbols than we can by using raw information, but learning the symbology can take years of training. To understand the symbology of field theory in physics seems to take about six years of concentrated study.*

Information is one of the things that exists in both ordinary reality and soul reality. It's not the information itself that defines whether an information transfer is ordinary or non-ordinary. What matters is how the information is transferred.

Different parts of the soul are capable of handling different types of information. Some parts are really good at handling energy, but not so good at handling information. Other parts do well with information, but not so well with energy. We'll talk more about that when we look at the parts of the soul.

Life Force

My concept of the life force is that it contains both energy and information. The life force is a force that comes from living things, including you and me, angels, God, and anything else that is alive. I think that souls receive it and souls send it out again.

It seems to affect non-living things, too. Whether we want to speculate that all things have souls or propose a way the life force can affect things without souls is something we will look at later.

The life force is useful (and probably required) for explaining the "strange" stuff like knowing something is going to happen before it actually does and knowing that you really need to talk to a friend because something is wrong. It is also important when we study energy exchanges that determine the outcome of martial arts matches.

I am including information along with energy in the life force because getting information causes us to change the direction (momentum, if you will) of our lives. A force does that, so I am using that rationale to include information in the life force. It would also be possible to say life force causes only the energy exchange and use another term for the information transfer. The transfer is fundamental. The symbology we use to express it is arbitrary as long as it makes

---

* The first person to use the symbology started with a blinding flash of inspiration. Then it took years to work with the inspiration to get it to a point where others could understand it, too.

accurate predictions. Combining the two in the life force simplifies discussions later in the book.

As an example of the life force, we'll be talking about Rupert Sheldrake's experiments on knowing that you are being stared at. (Sheldrake calls it "extended mind."*) I think the life force also provides a way to understand ghosts and angels, ESP and ki, and a lot of other stuff. (A friend of mine, who is a hunter, told me that when he was walking in a forest, he could tell that a deer was looking at him. "I just looked back over my shoulder and there he was."[8] Life force can explain that, too.)

It is a force, not gravitational, not electromagnetic, and not either of the nuclear, that moves between us and connects us with the world. It may have some similarities to the other forces, but, with the concept of a transfer of information, it has some significant differences. I think it interacts with the physical world, because an interaction seems to be required for us to experience it in our brains. There may be more questions than answers about the life force in this book, but I promise amusing insights along the way.

Exploring what happens if there is a life force is the heart of this book. We can propose a system of connections between souls using the life force. The connections can be turned into calculations, leading to testable predictions about the soul. In the end we understand ourselves and our relations with others better — which I think is a worthwhile goal.

---

* One problem that seems to plague Sheldrake's extended mind and the related idea of morphic resonance is that Sheldrake suggests that they are fields that have no energy, but still affect the physical world. His ideas work much better when we allow a life force and corresponding life energy that can interact with the physical world. I make that change when I am thinking about his work, but it is not in agreement with *his* thinking at the time I am writing this book.

II. Soul Structure

But what is the source of knowledge? Where do the laws that are to be tested come from? Experiment, itself, helps to produce these laws, in the sense that it gives us hints. But also needed is *imagination* to create from these hints the great generalizations — to guess at the wonderful, simple, but very strange patterns beneath them all, and then to experiment to check again whether we have made the right guess.

— *Richard Feynman*

Let me start by explaining what I want to do. I want to establish a system that can be used to calculate the interactions of souls and the life force. That will allow us to set up situations and predict what the results will be. I'm aiming for the same level of understanding that Isaac Newton had regarding gravity or James Maxwell had about electromagnetism. The life force seems to be more complicated than either of those, which is part of the reason why people with any sense avoid the kind of analysis I am attempting.

In this part of the book we will look at a model of the soul. I am proposing a soul made up of seven parts called chakras. Each chakra has particular functions that it performs as part of the system. Chakras connect to one another inside the soul and also form connections between souls. The concept of chakras is useful for explaining what we find when we study the interactions of people in both ordinary reality and soul reality.

4. Structure of Souls

The soul is so far from being a monad that we
have not only to interpret other souls to ourself
but to interpret ourself to ourself.

— *T. S. Eliot*

To get a deep understanding of the soul, I suggest we divide it into parts. This is not a particularly new idea. In fact it's an ancient concept (as humans measure ancient). For centuries, Hinduism and Buddhism have talked about the concept of energy centers in the body, which they call chakras.

The model I like is almost identical to the chakras found in these disciplines. Each of the centers has a different purpose. The combination of centers, including the energy and information that is present in each, makes up a complete soul. The model goes a long way toward explaining how we function in the world.

The most commonly described sets of chakras have seven, nine, ten, or thirteen centers. In systems with more than seven chakras, there are clusters of chakras near the throat, two chakras at the heart, and two separate chakras above the head. (One is just above the head and the top one is higher.) The diagram on the inside of the back cover shows their location in the body. Table 1 has a list of the chakras with the names I prefer.

Table 1: Chakras in the Soul

- Spirit Chakra (7)
- Mind Chakra (6)
- Communication Chakra (5)
- Heart Chakra (4)
- Will Chakra (3)
- Desire Chakra (2)
- Chaos Chakra (1)

One question that often comes up at this point asks whether chakras are part of the body, part of the soul, or part of the even more mysterious spirit body. Most of the modern thoughts about chakras seem to suggest that the chakras are part of the physical body. The folks at Spirit + Self say they are tied to major nerve ganglia.[9] Third Eye Health says they are tied to the endocrine glands.[10] Some suggest they are non-physical energy reservoirs attached to parts of the body. Others believe they are more soul-like and less a part of the physical world.

Goswami, in the more authoritative book, *Layayoga*, says that yogis who meditate on the chakras do not connect them with the physical body. In fact he says,

> The yogi utilizes the knowledge of the chakras in his yoga practices; and to do this no anatomical knowledge of the chakras is really necessary. But a person who has a knowledge of anatomy and physiology, as well as a correct understanding of the chakras, and utilizes his knowledge of chakras in his yoga practice, finds that there cannot be any real identification of the chakras with the nerve plexuses. But this lack of identification does not interfere with his yoga practice.... The yogis, in absorptive concentration, when the outer world and along with it their own bodies are completely forgotten, experience a new inner world in each chakra. To them the chakras are inner power phenomena; they are vivid and "seen." It will not serve any purpose of theirs to identify the chakras with nerve plexuses.[11]

My observations suggest that the most practical model is a soul that is a collection of chakras and a body that coexists with the soul, much like Goswami suggests. I don't think the idea of chakra points is useful. I prefer to say that the soul has chakra regions that correspond with regions of the body. In the final analysis I think the body is what the soul uses to amplify its ability to do things when it's in the physical world. So I see the chakras as aspects of the soul that hook up with parts of the body, sort of like an Xbox player hooks up to the avatar through the Kinect sensor.

One major difference between my model and the Hindu model is that I think the body has some things it can do independent of the soul. I include some kinds of thought processes in this category. That is based on my belief that souls developed bodies so they could manipulate the physical world and so they could think about what they were doing (or how things fit together or something like that). But that's a bigger question that I want to postpone until after we look more closely at the structure of the soul.

What I want to do first is talk about the chakra regions. I discuss my interpretations and I also include some of the literally and figuratively flowery descriptions from the Hindu studies. (They use a flower to describe each chakra.) When we look at the chakras as a whole, the ancient descriptions provide some useful insight into the complete system.

Most people number the chakra regions from bottom to top. It seems that there is an implication that the chakras go from simpler to more complex as we move up the body. I believe the bottom chakra is actually the most interesting one, so I will keep the numbering, but start at the top and move down.[12]

For each chakra region I'll provide several pieces of information: the usual Western name for the chakra and the associated color, the Narayana name and structure, the Waidika name and structure, and the Tantric name, color, and structure. There are often similarities between the various schools of thought, but the differences are also instructive.

The chakras are often described as flowers with some number of petals. Usually, for small numbers of petals, each petal is given a meaning (mercy or gentleness, for example). As with the chakra regions in general, the meanings tend to imply that the best parts of a human are in the top chakras. The mind region, near the top, deals with things like deep spiritual love. The sacral chakra contains pitilessness and delusion. I don't put a lot of stock in this idea of higher chakras being responsible for the better parts of humans. *All* of the aspects handled by the soul are part of being human. Our task is to integrate our whole soul, the parts that are in the light and the parts that are in shadow.

You'll notice that the Western colors cleverly range through the visible light spectrum from violet for the top chakra to red for the bottom chakra, just like a rainbow. Similarly, many Western discussions of chakras talk about the musical tones associated with the chakras, ranging from middle C at the bottom to B at the top (in the key of C)[13]. I think this orderly interpretation is probably a choice made by the observers, not something that is intrinsic to the chakras themselves.

The other traditions also speak of colors, but there is no orderly progression from top to bottom. These traditions also talk about the number of petals on the flower of the chakra. Again there is no orderly progression. The Tantric tradition that I include here has several chakra regions where they believe there is a cluster of chakras. I think the chakras in the cluster all serve similar purposes, and I'm not sure if there is an advantage to dividing a region into several chakras. In general, I will consider the region as performing a single set of functions.

Chakras are not a clearly defined concept. Even traditions that have studied them for thousands of years have not settled on completely consistent definitions. After the wisdom from serious researchers, I'll offer some of my own thoughts.

One important aspect, which gets a section all its own, is the progression in how each chakra handles the life force. The top chakras are very good at handling the information component, but they are not good at handling energy. As we move down the chakras we find that each chakra handles less complex information and more energy than the chakra above it. The top chakra is almost all information and the bottom chakra is almost all energy. As we look at each chakra, I'll explain the kinds of energy and information that each chakra is able to process.

This chapter does not lend itself to the kind of mathematical equations we will be using in later chapters. For now I will ask you to make a subjective judgment about the relative openness of each chakra in your soul. At the end of the descriptions, I'll ask you to rate how important each of the chakras are in your life. Just to practice thinking about your attitude toward each chakra, I will ask you about your relations with the things the chakra is connected to.

For the top chakra, we'll look at your connection to the divine.

For the middle five chakras, I suggest you think about your culture. If you want to look at more situations, think about how the chakra is involved in your relationship with a significant other, your family, your work or school, your interaction with a particular clerk in a particular store, or any other situation that comes to mind. The situations can be quite general or very specific.

For the bottom chakra, your connection to universal energy is the major concern.

We will be using that information later in the book when we look at the math that describes the connections between the parts of souls that belong to two different people.

Let's take a look at the chakras.

Spirit Chakra (7)

Traditional observations

Western tradition calls this the crown chakra with the color violet. The Narayana tradition says there are two chakras here: nirvana and sahasrara. The Waidika tradition also has two chakras. Sahasrara is above the head with 1000 petals and represents the supreme void. It is represented by the god Purnagiri. The other chakra, nirvana, is at the top of the skull with 100 petals of subtle smoky light. The Tantric tradition has three chakras: sahasrara in the region above the head (as the upper part of the guru chakra) with 1000 petals in 20 layers of 50 petals (white, red, golden, changing

colors of white, red, yellow, black, and green); guru also in the region above the head with 12 white petals; and nirvana at the top of the head just inside the skull with 100 petals of shining white.

My interpretation

The top chakra (above the head) is the soul's connection to the spiritual. Perhaps it's a connection to God. Maybe it is the way people speak with angels. The theosophists* talk about the akashic records.† Scientists speak of blinding flashes of inspiration, and so do poets. Musicians hear the music of the spheres through this chakra. All of these can be what I

---

* For more information of the theosophists and their place in the world of spiritualism and other aspects of the soul, see Judge (1971).

† Akasha is a Sanskrit word meaning "sky," "space," or "aether," so these would be records of past occurrences that are kept somewhere in the space around us. The belief is that we can access these records through a spiritual channel. I believe there may be something to this idea. With this and the blinding flash of inspiration discussed next, the connection seems to be through this chakra.

would call spiritual. I see the times we reach into this chakra and access information from it as a brief and very difficult to reach understanding of how a small part of the universe functions. We are not capable of understanding with our minds all the information that is available up here.

The Brahman traditions place great emphasis on this chakra. Perhaps it is related to their emphasis on castes. The highest caste (which is what the leaders of the traditions believe everyone wants to be) is associated with spiritual and intellectual matters. What I get from that is that they believe the "higher" chakras are more important than the lower. It looks to me like they would, if possible, choose to live in the higher chakras while discarding any connection with the lower chakras. There are Western traditions that have similar beliefs: Christians, for example, often suggest that the ideal is to be one with God, while giving up all earthly desires. Other traditions seem to choose a more balanced approach to the aspects of the soul, as we will see later.

Usually people think of this chakra as a connection to the divine. I agree but still have a question about what we mean by divine. The Hindu religion has many gods. Some are associated with building up, but others are associated with tearing things back down. The Norse gods (and most of the other systems with a pantheon of gods) have a trickster (Loki) who works hard to undo the efforts of the other gods. In monotheistic religions, such as Christianity, there is usually a devil who is responsible for the same kind of destruction.

Some might think that this chakra is the connection to the good spirits and the bottom chakra is the connection to the evil spirits. After all, God is in heaven above and the devil is in hell below. I think this model is mistaken. The lower chakra in my model has a completely different function. I suggest that the spirit chakra is responsible for our communication with both gods and demons.

One important question is whether this chakra exists at all. It is, after all, above the head. Does the soul extend outside the body? How far above the physical body does it go? The Tantric tradition has three related chakras ranging from the top of the skull up into the areas above the head. Whether the soul "controls" this very top chakra or whether the top part is simply a connection to spirits and not within the control of the individual's soul is something that different traditions disagree about. In the end it may not matter. To believe we control our access to God is usually a dangerous assumption. Given the chance, you might ask Mother Teresa for her opinion.* Believing we can deal with the devil seems to lead to even more problems.

Life force processing

For humans the spirit chakra is all about information. When we connect with something through this chakra, it's usually tenuous and fleeting. When we get an inspiration, it then takes a lot of energy to translate the inspiration into something that we can hold in our mind, and even more energy to turn the understanding into something we can communicate to others. Thomas Edison's famous quote speaks to that: "Genius is one percent inspiration and ninety-nine percent perspiration."

There is much more information available through the spirit chakra than we can handle. If we work hard at understanding something, we can tap into a small part of what is available, but we will never see the big picture. This explains why visions one person has of the divine do not match up with visions other people have. Each is seeing only a small part of the whole.

When I think of the energy of the spirit chakra, I think of gods and lightning bolts. There is a lot of energy in a lightning bolt. The best number I could find was five billion Joules.[14] Gods have the reputation of being able to generate that amount of energy on a regular basis. We are not gods, however. I think that humans are unable to send or receive any energy through the spirit chakra. For humans the connections made with this chakra are all information and no energy.

---

* Mother Teresa is reported to have heard Jesus for a few weeks in 1946 when she was 36 years old. She dedicated her life to doing what she thought of as God's work based on that encounter (Scott, 2005). She never spoke to God again and died feeling despondent about her work and betrayed. Of course, if you get the chance to ask her how she feels about all of that now, you may find that she has settled up with God and has a different opinion than she did while she was alive.

Measuring openness

This chakra has to do with our connection with a deity or deities, whether they are good or evil, or a connection that gives us insight into the workings of the universe that are usually too complex for us to understand. The scales here look at the openness of our connections with our deity, but you can also answer the questions as they relate to your availability to access universal insights.

Mark one statement in the outward set point and one statement in the inward set point that comes closest to expressing how you experience your connection with your deity. Also mark the external set point and internal set point statements that describe the kinds of actions you seek from your deity.

Outward Set Point

_____ Very open. I pray to my deity and ask it to act for me whenever I seek understanding of what is happening or see a need for a change on this earth.

_____ Balanced. Sometimes I pray to my deity for action, but usually I am looking for guidance about what I should do.

_____ Very Closed. No deity listens to me. There may be no deities.

Inward Set Point

_____ Very open. I hear my deity speaking in everything I experience.

_____ Balanced. Sometimes I hear my deity, but other times I'm more tuned in to the sounds of the world around me.

_____ Very Closed. No deity, even if one exists, speaks to me.

External Set Point

_____ Building. I interact with my deity with the intention of increasing his or her ability to influence what happens on the earth.

_____ Neutral. My deity understands more than I do and is perfectly capable of making decisions without my input. Also pick neutral if you don't believe in a deity but it's all right if other people do.

_____ Destroying. I want my deity to do less of what I ask it to do or I don't believe in a deity and work to show other people the foolishness of religious or spiritual faith.

Internal Set Point

_____   Building. I want more and deeper understanding of my deity and the interactions of all creation.

_____   Neutral. I think my contact with my deity is about what it should be. Also pick neutral if you don't believe in a deity but it's all right if other people do.

_____   Destroying. I want less contact with my deity and have no desire for bursts of inspiration.

Mind Chakra (6)

Traditional observations

Western tradition often calls this the third eye with a color of indigo. Narayana has ajna with 12 petals. Waidika and Tantric traditions have three chakras in this region: ajna, indu, and manas. Both traditions put ajna in the eyebrow region with two petals. The Tantric tradition sees the petals as lightning-like with radiations of power going upward and downward. Both traditions put the manas just above the ajna. The Tantric tradition says there are six petals that are white,  but show up with colors when senses operate and are black when the person is sleeping. Above the manas, in the forehead region, is the indu. Both traditions say there are 16 petals. The Waidika talk about deathless substance while the Tantric say the petals are moon-white and represent mercy, gentleness, patience, non-attachment, control, excellent-qualities, joyous mood, deep spiritual love, humility, reflection, restfulness, seriousness, effort, controlled emotion, magnanimity, and concentration.

My interpretation

The mind chakra, which is connected with most of the head (especially the brain), is a combination of sensing and intellect. That's the ability to see and hear the world, to make sense of things, sort them out, and figure out how they all fit together. The Tantric and Waidika traditions both divide this region into three parts. In the Tantric system the top chakra of the three seems to deal with positive emotional states and the middle one is concerned with the senses. My best thought for the lowest, two-petal chakra in the set is that it is concerned with the regulation of energy flowing to and from the mind.

Western interpretations of this chakra seem to focus on the intuition aspect of the third eye. When New Age thought began to consider the possibilities of Eastern thought, the idea of mystically understanding the "deep connectedness between all things" was a striking concept. The mystery of using the eyes to see, the ears to hear, or the skin to feel was somehow looked on as less wonderful. I think the difference is that the senses were viewed as one of those mundane physical things while the "third eye" was seen as totally spiritual and, somehow, more special. I suggest that all the senses are special and represent aspects of our souls.

Some traditions, including Zen Buddhism, say that the consciousness is actually a sixth sense organ. Peter Fox[15] says

> In yogic understanding, our senses radiate out and know things where they are. Our consciousness goes out and collects data rather than coming in to our senses. Manas [consciousness — the organizer of the senses] goes out, collects the raw data, sorts it and then passes what is useful on.

If we accept this point of view, it is clear why this chakra contains at least some aspects of what we call mind.

I believe that the other important aspect of this chakra, beyond the five or six senses, is that it is involved in the more complicated process we call thought. We have a very powerful physical brain, which we have worked for billions of years to evolve.* In addition, we have the part of the soul many people call the mind that connects the soul with the physical brain. Western belief is that memories are stored in the brain. Scientists do a lot of hand waving about ideas like holographic fields and neural networks to explain how memories are stored. People who have created artificial neural networks are extremely dubious of any claims that the physical brain and/or the neural connections in it are responsible for memories.

For example, Mark Lawrence, who wrote the programs used in every neural network chip ever made, described an experiment with caterpillars and butterflies.[16] Caterpillars were taught to avoid a particular odor. When the caterpillars turned into butterflies, the butterflies avoided the same odor. When Mark sent out his newsletter, several people responded with comments about how amazing it was that the caterpillars could store

---

* Or God gave us. Or both.

that kind of information in their nervous system as they became butterflies. The only problem is that there is no nervous system when the change happens. Everything is broken down into some very primitive compounds and there isn't enough physical structure left to store memories. It's one of several places where biology based on only the physical world is running into serious problems. If we allow butterflies to have a butterfly soul (Rupert Sheldrake uses the term morphic resonance), there is a place to store memories.

A fair question at this point is, how does the soul store memories? But there actually is a better question: Why are we concerned with memories in the mind chakra? Do we believe that only the mind chakra stores memories? I think the answer is a clear no. Chakras store information that works with the kinds of energies they process. We'll talk about memories in more detail later.

This is the chakra where many of us, intellectual types especially, tend to live our lives. For some, if a thing can't be explained with the mind (often they even limit it to the brain), then it is a thing that can't be admitted into reality. (And it is possible for the mind to override a lot to limit what we perceive.) I think we will find that there is a lot more in the lower chakras that is vital for understanding who we are as creatures living between the chaos below and the gods above.

Life force processing

The mind chakra contains the most complex information and symbology that we are able to handle. We build up systems that we use for planning our actions and predicting outcomes. While the systems aren't as complex as the ones we can find in the occasional insights of the spirit chakra, we can make them complete and self-consistent if we put enough effort into the process.

We store and analyze patterns. Our consciousness, our thoughts about ourselves, is handled by this chakra. This is where we do what we commonly refer to as thinking and remembering. It is our connection with the physical brain.

In addition, the mind chakra reaches out into the world through the senses to gather information. All chakras store their particular types of memories, but these are the ones we usually mean when we talk about remembering something.

The mind chakra is able to send and receive some energy. We talk about people having a great mental force. When we are speaking about their ability to empower creative insights in others, it is probably a reflection of their ability to transmit life force that contains mind chakra energy. Compared to the lower chakras, this is not a lot of energy, though. The energy that is involved needs to be a small fraction of the amount of energy we use to power the physical brain (about 30 food calories an hour). Let's say that powering the mind takes less than three calories an hour. The mind chakra is much more concerned with information.

Measuring openness

Those who are open on this level are aware of their perceptions, including psychic perceptions, and can interpret them usefully using their intellect. If the chakra is closed down, we may experience troubling dreams or problems with the senses. If the chakra is too open we may experience hallucinations or confusion from too much input. Here's a scale to use for this chakra:

Mark one statement in the outward set point and one statement in the inward set point that comes closest to expressing how you think about your observations of the world. Also mark the external set point and internal set point statements that describe how you think your thoughts should be shared with other people.

Outward Set Point

_____   Very open. My thoughts and understanding of the world is clearer than most and I work to show other people better understandings.

_____   Balanced. I have my understanding of how things work and I share it with some people.

_____   Very Closed. I keep my thoughts to myself.

Inward Set Point

_____ Very open. I'll listen to almost any idea and try it out. I may be sensing things that are not really there.

_____ Balanced. I listen to some people and some ideas, but there are things that I am pretty sure about already, so I don't listen as much to ideas about those topics.

_____ Very Closed. I understand things well, so I don't need to listen to other ideas. Also choose this if you choose to listen only to friends who have the same thoughts as you do.

External Set Point

_____ Building. I want to add to the number of ideas and ways of looking at the world. All viewpoints are valid.

_____ Neutral. Some new ways of looking at the world have worth, some don't. The same goes for old ways of looking at the world.

_____ Destroying. Things would be better if we eliminated all the foolish attempts to understand everything and concentrated on simple facts.

Internal Set Point

_____ Building. I want more thoughts and ideas to think about. I want more mind power to figure things out.

_____ Neutral. I think the number of thoughts and ideas I have is about what it should be.

_____ Destroying. I want fewer thoughts and ideas running around in my head. It hurts when I try to think too much.

Communication Chakra (5)

Traditional observations

Western tradition calls this the throat chakra with a color of blue. All three of the other traditions have two chakras here, talu and vishuddha. Narayana says they have a white center. Waidika and Tantric traditions place the talu in uvular region with 12 petals. The Tantric tradition says the petals are red with the meanings of respect, contentment, offense, self-control, pride, affection, sorrow, depression, purity, dissatisfaction, honor, and anxiety. The vishuddha is in the

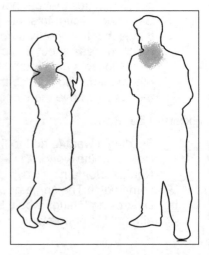

throat region with 16 petals. Tantric tradition says these have a shining smoke color and represent the nine mantras and seven musical tones because this is the chakra of voice. Gods associated with this region are Sadashiwa and Ambara.

My interpretation

The communication chakra region is somewhere near the mouth and throat. Its main responsibilities seem to be communication of all kinds. This probably includes communication between us and other entities in ordinary reality and in non-ordinary reality. This is not the same as experiencing God. That happens through the spirit chakra. So when you pray to God, words are not enough. You also need to reach out to Him and touch Him with the top part of your soul.

Non-Western traditions have two chakras in this region: talu and vishuddha.

The talu chakra is supposed to deal with a set of 12 emotions/feelings: respect, contentment, offense, self-control, pride, affection, sorrow, depression, purity, dissatisfaction, honor, and anxiety. When I first looked at this, I thought it was a curiously mixed set. It didn't make a lot of sense that these emotions would all be grouped together. However, when I read about the work of Paul Ekman,* I noticed that he describes six basic emotions: anger, disgust, fear, happiness, sadness, and surprise. Most of the emotions situated in the chakra can be thought of as combinations of Ekman's emotions. For example dissatisfaction and pride fit in Ekman's disgust category. Purity and honor might fit also, if they are based on avoiding things that disgust us. Sorrow and depression are parts of sadness. Offense is part of anger. Anxiety is part of fear. Contentment and affection might be included in happiness. Respect and self-control involve not showing negative emotions in inappropriate situations. I now believe that this chakra is responsible for communication with other beings through facial expressions of emotions.

The vishuddha chakra is clearly described as being responsible for controlling vocal functions, such as forming the sounds as we speak or musical notes as we sing. I believe it may also hold the template for the basis of our language abilities and work with the manas chakra in the mind region to help us understand language.

Body language is also important in communicating some things, but, according to Ekman,[17] the voice combined with the face is our most accurate way of expressing what we are thinking and feeling.†

So the communication chakra is responsible for communicating to other people what you figure out with your mind or, perhaps, from a blinding flash of inspiration from the angels. I am using this region as best I can to write this book.

---

* Paul Ekman did the research that the television show *Lie to Me* is based on. I found the following two books to be helpful in understanding his work: *Unmasking the Face: A Guide to Recognizing Emotions From Facial Expressions* and *Recognizing Faces and Feelings to Improve Communication and Emotional Life*.

† Another point that can be made here is that the body and soul are not tied together in any absolute way. All parts of the body are available to all parts of the soul. A kiss is more likely to be an expression of the heart chakra than the communication chakra. The hands and arms are tools that all of the chakras use. We will discuss this again when we look at how bodies and souls are tied together.

This chakra is also used to express what happens in the rest of the chakras, including the next one that is related to love and hate. Poets assure us that neither inspiration nor love can be put into words, not until the listener has had similar experiences. However, words can point the way toward an experience. Words and facial expressions can describe how it felt to you. If the people you are talking to have had similar experiences, they will be able to understand. They will be able to translate your words back into feelings they have known.

If they haven't had the experience yet, your words can act as signposts. As they go through life, they will have the experiences and look back on the words you said. Then they might say, "Oh, now I understand" or "Oh, now I know how he felt." If you were telling them something you wanted them to do, they will know that they are on the right track. I have had this experience a lot in my karate practice. Things I was told to look for years ago still show up now and then to let me know I am headed in the right direction (and that I still have a long way to go).

One other striking example of how this chakra region can be used is to express will (situated in the third chakra). Adolph Hitler was an expert at expressing his desire to change German society into his image of what Germany should be. Watching his speeches, you can see how his followers were swayed by his words in ways beyond what the words themselves expressed. He was using words, but he was also communicating to, uniting with, and shaping the will of his followers. Politicians and other leaders, in all times and cultures including our own, use the communication chakra to affect public opinion.

The communication chakra can be used for good or evil, depending on the message that is being conveyed.

Life force processing

This is the chakra of our current age. We have tossed out thinking about political issues, for example, and spend our time throwing words about the issues back and forth. We spend hours texting words to one another, but it is at the cost of taking the time for heartfelt interactions.

Information is sent through this chakra. It can be quite detailed, but it is never as complete as the information in our mind. It is either less complex symbolically, more restricted in time and content, or using fewer spatial and time dimensions. We are working hard to improve the amount of information we can communicate with photographs, movies, holographs, surround sound, and all the rest of our current technology. Even so, the communication through this chakra is always less than what is there in reality or in the mind.*

Similar problems occur when the communication chakra tries to work with heart chakra energy. The communication chakra can't send or receive as much energy as the heart chakra. Relying on communication instead of heart contact leaves us feeling alone and under-energized in our interactions with others. If there is any advocacy for change that comes out of this book, I hope it will be to emphasize the importance of going back to using our minds and hearts instead of relying on just words.

The amount of energy it takes to communicate is very small. If we use the iPhone as an example, we get about four watt-hours for an average day's use. That would be about three food calories. How much time we spend communicating compared with how much of it is done on an iPhone could be used to adjust the energy used, but it's still not very much energy at all.

Measuring openness

Communication involves the exchange of thoughts or experiences. We can be open or closed about our decisions to share. Sometimes we may not be able to find the words to explain our experiences.

Mark one statement in the outward set point and one statement in the inward set point that comes closest to expressing how you communicate. Also mark the external set point and internal set point statements that come closest to describing your thoughts about the purpose of communication.

---

* One of the limits of humans is that most of our representations of the three-dimensional world are done in fewer dimensions. Leaving out 3D movies, pictures have two-dimensions and words are generally one-dimensional. I await the day when researchers put together the songs of whales in a way that shows, for example, they are portraying three-dimensional and, perhaps, multi-sensory representations of their experiences.

Outward Set Point

_____   Very open. I'm talking all the time about anything that comes into my head or heart. Maybe there are more words than substance.
_____   Balanced. I prefer an exchange of thoughts and experiences.
_____   Very Closed. I prefer to keep quiet.

Inward Set Point

_____   Very open. I will listen to everybody even if they aren't making a whole lot of sense.
_____   Balanced. I'm selective about what I listen to.
_____   Very Closed. No one has much that is worthwhile to say.

External Set Point

_____   Building. The world needs more communication between people. Words can change the world.
_____   Neutral. The level of communication is about what it should be right now.
_____   Destroying. We are in an information overload and need to reduce the amount of communication that is available. Other connections need to be used more.

Internal Set Point

_____   Building. I want more communication from others in my life.
_____   Neutral. I think the communication from others is about what it should be.
_____   Destroying. I want less communication from those around me. Sometime I'd prefer that they didn't talk to me at all. (Other types of connection can still be welcome.)

Heart Chakra (4)

Traditional observations

Western tradition calls this the heart chakra with a color of green. Nara-yana says this is anahata with eight petals like the flame of a lamp. Waidika and Tantric traditions place two chakras here in the heart region, anahata and hrit. Both traditions say anahata has 12 petals. The Waidika sees them as still light. The Tantric sees them as deep red, shining red, shining vermillion, yellow, dark blue-yellow, and white with the meanings of lustfulness, fraudulence, indecision, 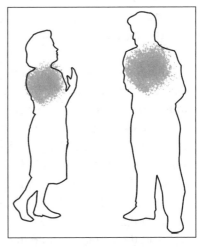 repentance, hope, anxiety, longing, impartiality, arrogance, incompe-tency, discrimination, and defiance. Tantric tradition says that hrit is part of anahata and just below it. Hrit has eight petals (golden, white, red) that represent the eight forms of superpowers as discussed below. Gods asso-ciated with this region are Ishtadevata, Vayu, and Isha.

My interpretation

The fourth chakra region (at the heart) is interconnectedness and affiliation with others, a great mystery and the center of our being. Our feelings for (and our cooperative connections with) other humans and the rest of the entities in the world originate here. Note that we can differentiate the idea of feelings for one another from the interactions through the other chakras. For example, the mind chakra contains our thoughts about one another, but thoughts are not the same as feelings. We will see in the following chakras that the interactions they control are also different from the feeling interactions of the heart chakra. I believe this heart chakra is responsible for both platonic love for your fellow being (agape) and romantic love (eros). (Sexual feelings, on the other hand, are part of the desire chakra.)

The Tantric tradition says there are two chakras in this region: anahata and hrit. Anahata, in Tantric thinking, seems to be responsible for some of the negative things that can go wrong with affiliation like lustfulness and longing. Hope and repentance are found here, too. Jealousy appears in the next chakra, I believe, because it is an emotion that is related more to power than to love.

I think the Tantric tradition (at least the versions I have read) may be missing something here. We experience a great connectedness to one another. It ranges from intensely positive to intensely negative. We may cling so closely that we use the expression "two hearts beating as one." Nothing hurts more than the betrayal of a loved one. We may die for many reasons, but we usually kill ourselves because of something related to love.[18] We may create barriers against the energy of this chakra so strong that, as Debra White Smith[19] says, "...bitterness protected her with a shell so hardened, so thick, that no darts of pain could pierce her heart. But then, neither could love." None of these situations are ideal.

I think affiliation works better when it connects us to other people in positive ways. We keep the idea that we are two separate beings, but we share an understanding of one another that goes beyond words. Love is one of the great positive forces in the universe. It is there for all of us to access through this chakra and to use when we are helping one another through life. All the great healers I have known send their healing energy through this chakra.

We have many sayings about the power of love. For example 1 Corinthians 13:8, "Love never fails. But whether there are prophecies, they will fail; whether there are tongues, they will cease; whether there is knowledge, it will vanish away." That would be chakras 5, 6, and 7 — all gone — but love remains. John Lennon[20] said, "All you need is love." And we all know "love makes the world go round."[21] Or as R. Buckminster Fuller[22] puts it, "Love is metaphysical gravity." If you wonder why sets of souls travel together through lifetime after lifetime, it is love (and its negative counterparts) pulling the souls together.

The other chakra in the heart region contains aspects in some ways even more amazing than love. Here is how Susan Shumsky describes the superpowers that are supposed to be controlled here: [23]

1. The ability to transform your body size to that of an atom.

2. The power to decrease your physical weight or levitate.

3. The power to increase your bodily size or stature or become mighty.

4. The capacity to fulfill desires and go anywhere at will, described by the ancients as "touching the moon with your fingertips."

5. The ability to pass through earth, walk through solid walls, or not be immersed in water, and to assume any desired form.

6. The greatest power and dominion over the five elements…: earth, water, fire, air, and ether, and the subtle sense objects… of which these elements are made, odor, flavor, form, touch, sound. This is also the power to attract and enslave others by enchantment.

7. Mastery over the appearance, disappearance, and aggregation of the five elements and objects in the material world. With this siddhi [accomplishment] you can transcend all human limits.

8. Resolution — the ability to determine the five elements and their nature and to transform them at will. It is also the power to conquer or subordinate others.

I have to say that I have never done any of these things. If you are looking for words from someone who says he has, I suggest reading the collected works of Carlos Castaneda. His experience of these superpowers is the reason many dismiss Castaneda's writings as nonsense, but there is a basis for what he says right here in the Tantric tradition.

Many other traditions have stories of great (and not so great) people who demonstrated some of these powers. Jesus walked on water, changed water into wine, and rose up to heaven. D. D. Home[24] and St. Teresa levitated. In the Zen tradition there is a story of two monks who met one another as they were about to cross a river. After a brief discussion, one monk tossed his hat into the river, stepped on it, and was carried across to the other shore. The other monk said, "If I had known you were that sort of person, I would have killed you on the spot." Apparently in the Zen tradition it's not acceptable to show these superpowers.

We have many stories of vampires and other mythic creatures, Jedi warriors, magicians, and spirits who are all able to perform superpowers. Many wish they had these powers. Conversely, those who believe in only the four physical forces work very hard to stop belief in anything beyond ordinary reality. We see the struggle going on around us now at the beginning of the 21st century, just as it was at the beginning of the 20th century. How it will be resolved this time around is not clear.

As Death says in *Hogfather*,[25] without belief the Sun would not have risen — only a burning ball of gas would have illuminated the sky. It all depends on whether we believe.

For those who believe the world is coming to an end, perhaps this is the end we will see. The heart will reclaim its ability to change the world in ways that seem like superpowers. This time the mind may be able to hold on to the experience so we can share it among all of us — then again, perhaps not.

Life force processing

Of all the chakras, the heart chakra is the most balanced between energy and information. Somehow, that's fitting, since it is the chakra in the center of the soul.

The information that the chakra handles includes relationships between people. In some sense, the information can be represented in simple sentences. Some positive examples include:

- I care for you.
- You are safe with me.
- I am here for you.
- We are together in this.
- God loves you.

The messages include two entities and the relationship between them. One entity or both entities can also be represented by a group, as in "My buddies have my back."

The memories this chakra holds involve the strengths of our connections. We remember in our heart chakra who we are connected to, the strength and reliability of the connection, and the directions of energy flow. We may not remember events or the words that were spoken, but we remember here how we felt when something was happening between us and another person.

The information seems simple, but there are deeper meanings that have to do with the energy flow involved. Where we have problems describing something like love using the communication chakra, it's not a problem of saying "I love you." The problem comes from being unable to describe the energy flow. The energy flow can be extremely powerful, with both positive and negative energy. Words simply can't convey that kind of power to someone who hasn't experienced it. If the same words are heard by someone who has had an experience, they will understand the words as a pale reflection of the energy flow they remember.

The energy from this chakra can be very strong. We have a saying, "When he came into the room, the temperature dropped by 10 degrees." We can calculate the energy required to change the temperature of air by 10 degrees. Changing dry air takes about 140 calories and the water in the air adds another 15 calories. This is significantly more energy than anything the higher chakras handled.

I understand that the temperature of the room does not actually drop by 10 degrees. What we are measuring here is the soul's perception of what is happening. We are translating it to ordinary reality terms just to get a feel for the relative strengths of the phenomena.

One interesting side note to this is that people who are hunting ghosts look for temperature anomalies as one measure of whether a ghost is present. They often carry infrared thermometers that can detect the temperature in a particular direction. When they find an unexplainable (by ordinary reality) cold spot, they often ascribe it to a ghostly presence.

The heart chakra is also the home of the superpowers. One that has been seen is the ability to levitate. One simple way to measure that is to calculate the change in potential energy for a body going up, say, ten feet. The result is about 0.4 calories* for the simple movement up.

---

* 50 kg X 9.81 m/s^2 X 3 m = 1470 joules = 0.35 Calories

Gravity, however, is a constant force so that energy would need to be supplied continuously to keep the person floating

Another example we might look at is the story of two soldiers who were driving down a one-lane road. They ran into enemy fire, got out of their Jeep, picked it up, and turned it around, so they could get out of there. Picking up the Jeep would take about 3.5 calories.* Holding it up and turning it around would take much more energy.

I'm not going to try to calculate the amount of energy it would take to perform some of the other feats the heart chakra is supposed to be able to do, such as transforming elements. Atomic level energies would be involved, and that gets way up there. The interesting point here is that the energy, if someone really can transform elements, has to come up through the bottom chakra. The heart chakra is the one that can handle enough energy and enough information to cause the transformation. The higher chakras would burn out from too much energy.†

Measuring openness

The aspect of the heart chakra that I want to consider here is the part that connects us to other entities. The questions ask how well you share love energies with other people, but the love energy we are talking about can be shared with anything.

Mark one statement in the outward set point and one statement in the inward set point that comes closest to expressing how you share love energy. Also select the external set point and internal set point statements that express your thoughts about the amount of love energy that should be available.

---

* 1000 kg X 9.81 m/s² X 1.5 m = 1470 joules = 3.5 Calories
† Kundalini experts warn about this very problem by saying that the energy from below can travel to the heart, but it should never be forced up into the mind.

Outward Set Point

_____   Very open. I share my love with everybody, even some people who may not have my best interests at heart.

_____   Balanced. I choose to be with people who understand the idea of love energy and we share it to make our lives better.

_____   Very Closed. I've had a rough life and really don't have a lot of love to give or I think that too much love makes the other person soft and unable to deal with the real world.

Inward Set Point

_____   Very open. I really need a lot of love to keep on living. Sometimes I get fooled by something that looks like love, but really isn't.

_____   Balanced. I am happy to accept genuine love when it is offered.

_____   Very Closed. I'm uncomfortable when people say they love me. I don't know if I can trust them and I may be unworthy of love.

External Set Point

_____   Building. We need to increase the loving regard and compassion in interactions between people. The world needs more love.

_____   Neutral. I'm sending the right amount of love into the world right now.

_____   Destroying. People spend too much energy on love and compassion for others. We need to reduce that level of loving regard and interact in other ways.

Internal Set Point

_____   Building. I want more love from others in my life.

_____   Neutral. I think the love I get from others is about what it should be.

_____   Destroying. I want less love from those around me.

Will Chakra (3)

Traditional observations

Western tradition puts this chakra in the lower abdomen with a color of yellow. The Narayana tradition calls this manipura and sees it as five coils of deep red. The Waidika places manipura at the navel with ten petals. The Tantric tradition also places manipura at the naval with ten petals of black, dark-green, or dark blue. The petals stand for spiritual ignorance, thirst, jealousy, treachery, shame, fear, disgust, delusion, foolishness, and sadness. Associated gods are Rudra and Vahni.

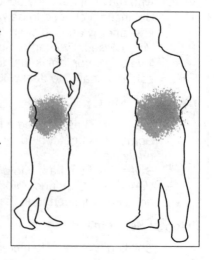

My interpretation

The will chakra is concerned with power. When we seek to dominate another entity, this is where the power comes from. Some believe that when we try to dominate anything in ordinary or non-ordinary reality, we need power from this chakra. In contrast with the heart chakra, which is involved in our cooperative connection with another entity, this chakra is concerned with causing another entity to do what we want, with or without affiliation.

When Jacob wrestled with the angel, I have to believe the power came from here. Those who have encountered a Sasquatch, universally describe having to struggle with an intense fear.* Whatever Sasquatch is, we can be certain that its will chakra is very powerful.

The power from this chakra does not have to be negative in the sense that we are willing another entity to do something harmful. The will chakra is also involved in, for example, health care situations where

---

* See for example, Robert Morgan's (2008) *Bigfoot Observer's Field Manual* or any number of encounters in Janet and Colin Bord's (2005) *Bigfoot Casebook — Updated.*

energy is provided through the will chakra of the health care provider so that the patient will have enough will to get better.

Many traditions consider it to be the center from which all of our power is expressed. Where this power comes from is different in different traditions. When chakras are considered, the chaos chakra is usually named as the source of power. Other traditions, such as the Chinese Qigong, think that this chakra takes sexual energy and converts it into chi that can be used by the rest of the body. Martial artists usually think of this center as the most important for making powerful techniques. The sorcerer's tradition, as described by Castaneda, says that the belly is where the greatest power comes from when the sorcerer is working to affect ordinary or non-ordinary reality.

Even in our Western languages we recognize the importance of the related area of the body when we want to do something difficult. Here are some examples: It takes guts to do the hard stuff. "Guts" is the original x-treme sport. "No guts, no glory." We talk about people as not having a "stomach for it" if they are afraid to do a difficult task. We get butterflies in our stomach when we are afraid. And it takes a strong stomach to watch unpleasant things without getting upset or feeling ill.

When we look at the personality aspects of this chakra, we find spiritual ignorance, thirst, jealousy, treachery, shame, fear, disgust, delusion, foolishness, and sadness. These are dark emotions, indeed. I was having a conversation with a friend* recently in which he asked whether a person can be a genius without having a difficult (I think he used the term horrible) personal life. (One point he cited was the belief that every winner of a scientific Nobel Prize had a spouse who made spending all the winner's time in the lab a relative pleasure.) I couldn't think of a counterexample.

Perhaps it is true that these dark parts of ourselves (and others) are what drive us to do great things. We need to feel a fire in our belly†

---

* Mark Lawrence, who probably qualifies as a genius for his work on neural networks and did, indeed, have a terrible personal life as he was growing up.
† Another example of how important we think this region is in getting things done. Note also that this is the only region that is considered a good place to have a fire.

before we are ready to work on something that is very difficult. I hope that the fire can come from something besides personal suffering, though. Perhaps seeing others in the states that correspond to the emotions of this chakra can fire up the emotions in us and give us the power to accomplish great things.

I know that there are only a few things more dangerous or powerful than a parent whose children are being threatened. For example, there are many stories of mothers who lift cars to save their children.* Of course, when they try to do it again after the danger is past, there is no way they can lift the car. I suggest this is an example of the fire in the will chakra powering the superpowers in the heart chakra. There is also an aspect of the danger shutting down the mind so that there is no rational thought stopping the superpowers from working. It seems that feelings for others can be a powerful force. It would be interesting to know if the Zen monk who objected to the other monk's use of his hat to cross the river would have objected to the mother using the same kind of power to save her child. (Probably not.)

Another aspect of this chakra is the concept of a gut reaction. There is a significant neural network in the stomach region, and apparently we react to many things with our gut as well as our brain. It makes sense that there would be a chakra to correspond to the set of neurons in the abdomen just as there is a chakra that corresponds to the brain.

When we make decisions, most people like to believe that they think through the decision with their minds and make rational decisions. Research shows that we often make decisions in non-rational (emotional) ways and then use our minds to find what appear to be rational reasons for our decisions.[26]

I suggest that the emotions associated with this chakra are the basis for many of our decisions. As I mentioned earlier, some parts of our selves are in the shadow.† This is one of those parts. To be fully human

---

* I found four million references on Google for "mother lifts car off child" (without quotes). If you're skeptical, go take a look.

† One possible definition of "shadow" is that these are the parts of us that process more energy that the communication chakra or mind chakra can handle, and, at the same time, do not have the same level of information content.

we need to be aware of these parts and integrate them with the parts that are in the light. Deborah Bryon,[27] describing her work with the Q'ero shamans, writes extensively about this.

We will see more of the shadow parts in the next two chakras.

Life force processing

The information processed by the will chakra is pretty basic. It usually comes in the form of orders like "Do this!" or "Follow me!" The commands are directed at someone else and there is a verb with an object to describe the action that we want the other person to do. Similarly we react to commands from the will of other people with this chakra. We remember the command and how successful it was, but not the details of what happened.

I'm not sure if our will chakra can be directed at ourselves in the sense that we are giving ourselves orders. I actually try to give myself orders a lot, but I am not consistently successful in getting myself to do what I tell myself to do. I think the will chakra is more effective when it is directed at others while it is in sync with the desire chakra.

The energy handled by the will chakra can be large. One place we find it is in martial arts. So let's use an example from there. It is possible (because I have done it, at least in a practice situation) to stop an attacker by looking at him. What we can calculate is the kinetic energy change for a 200-pound person who is stopped from moving at me at 15 miles per hour. With a little bit of unit conversion we find the answer is about 1 calorie.

If we expand this idea to a battlefield situation, we can look at the power a leader has in controlling the actions of his warriors. The Scotsman William Wallace (Braveheart) led his fighters against the British army. With his personal will he convinced his men to stand against the charge of the British cavalry. Of course, they had a plan, but good plans notoriously get forgotten when there isn't enough will to carry them through.

I don't know how to measure this energy in ordinary-reality equivalents because the calculation ties in with defeating the will of the other group. Tremendous energies may be involved, but they are so evenly balanced that we see only small differences. We might be most accurate in saying that all of the energy that went into the battle was from the will of the participants. Without will on both sides, there would not have been a battle at all.

Measuring openness

The will chakra deals with connections based on willpower. If we are to have people join us in accomplishing a task they are unsure about, we must find some way of making them work with us. Using our will is one of the ways to get work done.

Mark one statement in the outward set point and one statement in the inward set point that comes closest to expressing how you experience will. Also mark a statement in the external set point and internal set point statements that express your thought about how will is used in the world today.

Outward Set Point

_____ Very open. I can get almost anyone to follow my lead. I'm such a natural-born leader that I often don't even have to explain why I want the help.

_____ Balanced. Sometimes I express my will, but I also use other types of connections to get people to work with me.

_____ Very Closed. I have a lot of trouble getting people to do what I want them to do.

Inward Set Point

_____ Very open. I'm the kind of person who volunteers to do things before I'm even asked.

_____ Balanced. I understand that there are times to lead and times to follow someone else.

_____ Very Closed. No one can talk me into doing anything I don't want to do.

External Set Point

_____ Building. The world needs more leaders who can really get things done. — or — I want more influence on what is happening.

_____ Neutral. There are chiefs and there are Indians. We have about the right number of each.

_____ Destroying. I'm tired of all the people who try to boss everyone around and I subvert the process whenever I can get away with it. — or — I want to get rid of some of the power I have so others can take charge.

Internal Set Point

_____ Building. I want the people around me to give me more direction about what I should be doing.

_____ Neutral. My interactions with others in decisions about my life are about what they should be.

_____ Destroying. I'm tired of people telling me what to do and controlling my life.

Desire Chakra (2)

Traditional observations

Western tradition calls this the genital chakra with the color orange. All the other traditions have a six-petaled chakra called svadhisthana. Narayana and Waidika say the petals are the color of a new leaf. The Tantric tradition says the petals are vermillion, deep red, shining red, whitish red, lightning-like, and golden and stand for affection, pitilessness, feeling of all-destructiveness, delusion, disdain, and suspicion. Associated gods are Vishnu and Varuna.

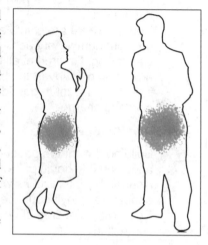

My interpretation

In humans, the positive side of the desire chakra has to do with finding the energy to create things. The negative side has to do with tearing things back down — perhaps to rebuild something new. Traditionally this chakra is considered most for its connection with sexuality, but I believe it is also involved in the creation and destruction of everything else, too.

When we look at the sexual aspects of this chakra we find that we use this chakra to express our desire for another person (or some other object). There are stories about how a man is not able to think with his brain when he sees a beautiful woman. (I've heard women can have the same thing happen to them when they encounter a desirable man.) The common myth is that there is not enough blood to supply the brain and other body parts at the same time. While I completely understand not being able to think, I believe the answer is more likely to be a shift of energy from one chakra to another, rather than a movement of blood. Physical creatures that we are, these lower chakras often take precedence over the higher ones.

I may be biased, but I think sexuality is one of the reasons souls created bodies. Certainly, this chakra provides a very powerful attraction between people. It is difficult to resist and may lead to all sorts of problems when it is expressed too freely. In many discussions about reincarnation, the authors suggest that less spiritually advanced humans may spend lifetime after lifetime returning for sexual pleasure.[28] The implication is that these souls never experience the higher pleasures of moving closer to God. Some disagree with the idea that moving toward God is all that important. As Mark Twain says, go to heaven for the climate, hell for the company.

The Tantric tradition says this chakra is the seat of affection. That tradition also puts affection in the communication chakra. I suspect that two different aspects of affection are being considered. I also note that there is no affection in the heart chakra. All in all, I find that to be strange.

This chakra deals with more than sexuality. That's why I chose to name it the desire chakra. One aspect of desire happens to be sexual, but I think that energy is there for many other purposes, too.

In single-cell creatures, it provides the energy for cell division. Other types of creative forces may also come out of this region, including the drive required to write a book. Freudian and Tantric traditions suggest that we sublimate or transfer sexual energy to form the drive to accomplish other things. It's not that the plan or actions come out of this chakra — those come from other chakras. What comes from the desire chakra is the object of the desire and the energy to create it or tear it down.

As with the will chakra, there are dark aspects to this chakra in the traditional systems including pitilessness, feeling of all-destructiveness, delusion, disdain, suspicion. These are primitive parts of ourselves. In them we see the negative side of generation: destruction. In the Hindu traditions, these forces are represented by Kali, the goddess of annihilation. Some traditions urge moving beyond our destructive parts. Other traditions say we must look at them to bring all of our parts together. My feeling is that we need to recognize that creating something new often requires tearing down something that already exists. Tearing apart something evil can make the world a better place.

In my way of looking at chakras, this is the lowest chakra that is actually in the body. That may mean it was the first chakra souls created as they tried to develop physical life.

Most systems of chakra location have this chakra in the genital area and the chaos chakra (the next chakra down) in the perineal area. I find the idea that two major chakra regions would be within a few inches of one another to be suspicious. This one seems correctly placed. I'll have more to say about the other in the next section.

Life force processing

The information in the desire chakra is very simple. I think desires can usually be expressed in one word, usually as an action. Some examples are reproduce, conquer, destroy, and consume.

We can see the desire chakra at work in many different people. I think artists are the easiest place to look, so let's look at those examples first. Wolfgang Amadeus Mozart seemed to have the desire to amuse and enlighten. One painter, Manet, wished to capture the existence of a person. A very different painter, Picasso, chose to reify by finding the essence of his subject. Various portrait artists have the desire to glorify, capture, and insult, along with many other desires. We can feel it in their work.

The desire chakra works with the other chakras to fulfill the desires. Where the chakras match up, we usually can succeed. It is possible to hold conflicting desires, which is a very painful situation. I believe we remember our desires with this chakra and whether the desires were met, but nothing here remembers what we did.

Freud's work concentrated on desires related to sexuality. It was an important piece of the puzzle, but there is a lot more here.

My desire related to this book may be beyond what I can express in a single word. It is something like "Take the current understanding of what/how we are and shift it to a new understanding that opens up many new pathways for exploring ourselves and connections with others." Perhaps it's "Move human understanding." In one word it might be "Evolve."

The energy the desire chakra handles shows up in many places from tree roots breaking open rocks to the nearly irresistible desire inspired by [insert your favorite movie star here]. However, most of these forces and related energies seem to be composed of energy related to ordinary reality. One (perhaps mythical) example we have is that of Odysseus and the sirens. On his way back from the Trojan Wars, Odysseus' ship went near the island of the sirens. Odysseus had himself bound to the mast with ropes and stuffed wax in the ears of his crew so they couldn't hear the sirens.

Odysseus really, really wanted to go to the sirens, but neither his desire nor the power of the sirens was enough to break the ropes that bound him. Apparently, also, the sirens had to rely on their voices because the desire chakra energy wasn't enough to tempt the men who couldn't hear them. (Or perhaps Homer was writing for an audience that expected a physical world and didn't portray sirens accurately.)

I've put a considerable amount of thought into how to translate what this chakra does into measurable energy. One possibility is that it acts to switch other chakras on or off. In Shakespeare it would turn on the communication chakra at appropriate times. Another possibility is that this chakra represents the power of a muse. If you have read Dan Simmons' *Hyperion*, you will know that he suggests considerable amounts of power are involved. This leads to the third possibility, that the energy to power the other chakras flows through this one. That is my current best guess: Much of the energy our higher chakras use is channeled and directed by our desires.

Measuring openness

The desire chakra is concerned in part with our sexuality. How and where we express our sexuality demonstrates one of the ways we use our energy in this area.

Mark one statement in the outward set point and one statement in the inward set point that comes closest to expressing how you experience sexuality. Also mark the statements in the external set point and internal set point statements that most closely express your views about the place of sexuality in our culture.

Outward Set Point

_____   Very open. I enjoy showing off my body and really appreciate finding a good sexual encounter.

_____   Balanced. There is a place for expressing sexuality, but there are places where I prefer to be restrained.

_____   Very Closed. I really don't have many sexually related feelings.

Inward Set Point

_____   Very open. I'm flattered whenever someone flirts with me and it makes me feel like a whole person when it goes even farther.

_____   Balanced. I love sharing sex with my lover, but it feels weird when someone else comes on to me sexually.

_____   Very Closed. I'd prefer to not be noticed as having a gender.

External Set Point

_____   Building. I want others to be more open about my expressions of sexual behavior. My set of friends and acquaintances are pretty closed to that.

_____   Neutral. The level of sexuality in my relationships seems about right.

_____   Destroying. I want to have others perceive me less sexually than they do now. I'd rather be seen as a person instead of a sex object.

Internal Set Point

_____   Building. I want to be regarded as more sexually desirable.

_____   Neutral. I think my level of sexuality is about what it should be.

_____   Destroying. There's no reason for the amount of sexual content in everything in our culture. I want fewer sexual messages from the culture. I want people to stop coming on to me in a sexual way.

Chaos Chakra (1)

Traditional observations

Western tradition calls this the root chakra with the color red. The other traditions call this chakra muladhara and place it in the perineal region. Narayana tradition says it is a triangle turned round three times. Waidika tradition says it has four red petals. Tantric tradition says there are four petals of blood-red, shining red, yellow, and golden which represent greatest joy, natural pleasure, delight in controlling passion, and blissfulness in concentration. Associated gods are Indra and Brahma.

My interpretation

So far we have seen connections with the realm of gods and demons through the spirit chakra. The next five chakras have been our connections with fellow travelers through the wheel of incarnation. These travelers include people, animals, and spirits with chakras like ours, whether they currently have bodies or not. I'm not sure where plants and all the single-celled creatures fit into this picture. It's something I'm still exploring. I believe it is possible to communicate with plants, but it is not clear exactly which path the communications take.

The bottom chakra is our deep connection to everything else in the universe. And what is that everything else? At the current time, I think of this as chaos, a non-ordered mixture of positive and negative energy available for us to tap into and use to create or destroy our realities. All the people who speak of chakras believe that the energy to power the chakras comes up from what they call the root chakra. This is, in fact, a root in the same sense as a tree root, to bring vital nutrients into our souls. And, like the root of a plant, it sorts through what is there to bring the kind of nutrients we need into our systems.

People usually say this chakra is located at the bottom of the spine, but I believe it's better to say it's in the universe under our feet, just as the top chakra is located above our heads. Perhaps it is even more like the top chakra in that it is a cluster of chakras, some near to our body and some farther away. As with sahasrara in the spirit chakra, we may want to be careful calling it something that belongs to us. The elemental forces are not something mere humans should think they can control.

Susan Shumsky[29] says there are seven chakras below the chaos chakra.* These relate to other life forms (animals, insects, plants, rocks, and minerals). She goes on to say that these chakras do not exist in humans. I disagree with the idea that humans are special to this degree. Later in the book I'll be talking about chakras and kinds of life energy we find in other living creatures and other objects. The bottom line is that I think we are more like everything else than we are different. In the case of the chakras Shumsky is describing, I think they either are the same as some of our higher chakras or are contained as aspects of the chaos chakra.

A possible reason why the chakra traditions placed the chaos chakra at the base of the spine shows up in a quote from the Llewellyn web site's discussion of this chakra,[30] "The first chakra is found at the base of the spine, the point you are sitting on right now." Those who get up and move around as part of their study of energy flow notice that the energy is coming up through the feet from the earth below. Perhaps the people who defined chakras were too concerned with sitting in quiet contemplation and didn't experience the energy flow coming up from below. It's easier to feel this in the middle of a hunt or a battle or while performing healing rites.

A brilliant fellow named Carl Jung talked about the Collective Unconscious.[31] Jung saw it as a place where the archetypes reside and as a place where everything is deeply connected with everything else. (See

---

* The chakras are atala, vitala, sutala, talatala, rasatala, mahatala, and patala. Other references put them in the body and call them the root of our wicked impulses. (Veda, 2011)

the discussion of archetypes below.) When I read his works, I think he is placing the Collective Unconscious here in the lowest chakra. (My interpretation of what he is saying may be wrong.) I think it is more likely that the archetypes, as perfect representations of characteristics, are more properly connected with the spirit chakra. This is the region of possibility, not perfectly realized form.

Shamans, native (as in Native American) healers, Aboriginal hunters, and many others live in this land of energy or visit this land of energy as part of their spirit journeys. In this place they meet other travelers. If the journey takes them down, they are working through the chaos chakra. Note especially that the people on these journeys often speak of creating the landscapes they are traveling through. The raw energy is there, but we need to impose some basic structure on it to be able to process the experience and understand how to gather the energy.

We all draw our energy through this chakra. Some of us are better at it than others. It is something that we can practice and improve on.

Archetypes

Jung considered archetypes to be the psychic templates that life force moves through. The following are archetypes of each person's personality:[32]

- The Self, the regulating center of the psyche and facilitator of individuation
- The Shadow, the opposite of the ego image, often containing qualities with which the ego does not identify, but which it possesses nonetheless
- The Anima, the feminine image
- The Animus, the masculine image
- The Persona, how we present to the world

Of more interest are the various character archetypes. Some of the most interesting ones are the Child, the Hero, the Great Mother, the Wise Old Man, the Wise Old Woman, the Sage, the Trickster or Coyote or Fox, the Devil or Satan, the Scarecrow, the Mentor. Jung believed we build our characters using various parts of the archetypes.

For an excellent explanation of this part of the soul, I recommend Patrick Harpur's book, *The Secret Tradition of the Soul* (known in Great Britain as *A Complete Guide to the Soul*).

Life force processing

I think that the information processed by this chakra is at the level of deciding whether the energy the chakra is connected to will be useful for the soul. Useful energy is gathered in and energy that is not useful is left. If there is a memory it is of the "taste" of the energy and how it affected the rest of the soul system.

As with the spirit chakra, I'm not sure how to measure the energy processed by this chakra. My current belief, which is subject to change, is that the spirit energy of the universe is stored in chaos. Most traditions say that the energy to power the other chakras comes from here.

Perhaps it takes the organizing information of the spirit chakra to sort out the chaos energy (a sort of Maxwell's Demon*) before we can get it. How much energy the chaos chakra processes depends on how the rest of the soul operates. All of this needs to be studied further.

Measuring openness

The chaos chakra is the source of energy for our souls. We gather energy from the aspects of chaos that connect with this chakra.

Mark one statement in the outward set point and one statement in the inward set point that comes closest to expressing how you experience the chaos chakra. Also mark statements in the external set point and internal set point statements that express your view about how chaos should be integrated with ordinary reality.

---

* Maxwell's Demon is a mechanism proposed by the Scottish physicist James Clerk Maxwell to show that the Second Law of Thermodynamics has only a statistical certainty. The demon in his thought experiment could separate air molecules into two chambers by letting hot molecules go into the hot chamber and cold molecules go into the cold chamber. The purpose was to demonstrate hypothetically how to violate the Second Law of Thermodynamics, which states that entropy always increases.

Outward Set Point

_____ Very open. I spend my life in chaos. Ordinary reality is not an attractive place.

_____ Balanced. I'm interested in taking energy from chaos and bringing it back to share with others.

_____ Very Closed. There is no chaos and no soul capable of accessing it.

Inward Set Point

_____ Very open. I'm on fire all the time with energy from chaos.

_____ Balanced. I use the energy I get through this chakra to fill the rest of my chakras full of energy.

_____ Very Closed. My energy comes from food. There is no spiritual energy.

External Set Point

_____ Building. I want to bring more soul energy into the world and reconnect with the mysterious.

_____ Neutral. Some people are able to handle this energy and pass it on to others. Some people are better off leaving it alone. The amount we have in the culture now is about right.

_____ Destroying. I want to stop this non-scientific nonsense by any means at my disposal.

Internal Set Point

_____ Building. I want more connection to the energy in chaos.

_____ Neutral. I think my connections to the mysterious aspects of the world are about what they should be.

_____ Destroying. I want to disconnect from non-ordinary reality; it doesn't really exist, anyway.

Other Traditions with Chakra Equivalents

There are many other traditions that use ideas similar to chakras to explain their views of the world. Let's look at a few of them to study the universality of the idea that the soul is divided into parts that interact with different aspects of ordinary and soul reality.

One of the cultures that describes centers of the body is discussed in Deborah Bryon's *Lessons of the Inca Shamans: Piercing the Veil*, which details the traditions of the Q'ero shamans in the mountains of Peru. The Q'ero shamans describe three centers corresponding with the belly, the heart, and the mind.

The belly area (called *yachai*) is associated with the mythic snake Amaru and the power that comes from the earth. The power used by the belly lets us enter into a state of fluidity where anything is possible. This is where the energy of the spirit can affect physical reality. The belly is the center the Q'ero shamans use to connect with this energy. The snake symbolizes the immediacy of the moment that is felt while we are in this state. Everything is in the now and must be acted on without conscious thought. Note that even though the Q'ero tradition does not speak about a chakra where we have put the desire chakra, the snake traveling about on the earth and the connection it makes with the belly creates a connection that is very similar to the desire chakra-will chakra pair.

The heart of the Q'ero shamans (called *sonqo*) is very similar to the heart chakra described above. It involves a sense of belonging or feeling home that transcends words and experiences. In this center, according to the Q'ero shamans, we experience the universal feeling of love that connects us to the earth and all life on our planet (*munay*). This is where we feel out connection to Pachamama (Mother Earth). The heart is associated with the mythic jaguar, Chocachinchi, who moves through the jungle feeling everything intensely and immediately. The power is used to improve the lives of all the beings in the world.

The third region the Q'ero shamans talk about is the mind. Mind has the ability to exist inside and outside of the framework of sequential time and space. It is used to translate the wordless experiences of the belly and heart into words that can be shared with other people who were not part of the experience. Using the power of the mind with the power of the belly and the heart, we can craft visions of what we want the world to be and move toward them. The mythic creature associated with the mind is the condor, Apucheen. Soaring above the earth, the condor can provide us with a bird's-eye view, allowing us to escape from the details and see the big picture. Because the Q'ero include the idea of communication within their mind, I believe their mind center actually contains both the mind chakra and the communication chakra.

The Q'ero do not talk about a center above the head, but they do have spirits of the mountains that they connect with. It seems like a different way of describing a similar interaction.

Another person who discusses chakra-like centers is Carlos Castaneda. In *Tales of Power*[33] he describes a sorcerer climbing a cliff. He describes light tendrils coming from the solar plexus area to aid in the climb. He also talks about lesser tendrils coming from the chest area and the head area. While the solar plexus is by far the most important center for Castaneda's view of the world, the other centers also play a part.

Martial artists have another tradition that talks about energy centers. Almost every Asian martial art puts the most important energy center in the solar plexus (*tanden* in Japanese). Some traditions look at this as a physical center and others choose to see it as an energy center connected with, but different from, the physical body.

According to Liu Wen Wei, there are three other centers that are important in his view of martial arts.[34] In addition to the solar plexus, Wei describes a center in the upper back (about where the heart chakra is), at the back of the neck (near the communication chakra), and in the same location as the third eye (similar to the sensory part of the mind chakra). While Wei is most concerned with the martial arts aspects of these centers, the functions of his lower area, and the two areas in the neck and head are quite similar to the functions of the will, communication, and mind chakras. Wei does not associate the upper back area with connections between people (unless we are talking about making good striking techniques with the hands and arms), so that is a difference between the traditions.

William C. C. Chen[35] talks about the feet as an important way to get power from a fighting stance with his description of a three-nails connection. He says that, when moving, the feet float easily across the ground, but when it's time to make a technique, it's as if spikes extend from the feet into the ground. He is talking about accessing energy through the feet to power his fighting techniques.

As described by Caylor Adkins,[36] Ida Rolf (the founder of deep therapeutic massage techniques called Structural Integration) identified a set of centers in almost the same locations as Liu Wen Wei. While her approach is based (mostly) in ordinary reality, it is interesting to see that she has also identified the same areas as crucial parts of integrating the body.

All over the world, people have identified centers located near certain parts of the body as important to their traditions. If we are going to understand the soul better, it looks like we better pay attention to the idea that it may be more than a single, uniform blob.

5. Chakra Structure Basics

> If you understand, then things are exactly what
> they are. And, if you do not understand, then
> things are exactly what they are.
>
> — *Gensha, Zen Master*

Each chakra, like the soul, has what might be called an internal structure that describes how it operates. Many people have models of the operations of chakras, but most tend to look at the flow between one or more chakras or between the chakras and other parts of the subtle body.* There are some interesting ideas there, but I think there are even more interesting ideas to pursue in looking at what goes on inside a particular chakra.

In my model, there are three divisions to the functions that a chakra performs: control of internal energy and information, life force moving between the chakra and the rest of the world, and life force moving between chakras within a soul. (The control of the information component of the life force is where my model is most different from other models of chakras.) Each of these divisions is further divided into specific aspects. Table 2 shows the three divisions and the 14 aspects of the soul that are part of this model.

---

* The subtle body is usually described as some variation on an energy field that surrounds the physical body. As long as they don't say it's a "higher part of the electromagnetic spectrum," I can go along with the idea in a general way.

Table 2: Chakra Structure

Internal Energy and Information
    maximum internal, internal set point, internal level, leakage, goal
Outside the soul
    inward ability, inward set point, inward intention, outward ability, outward set point, outward intention, external set point
Inside the soul
    to other chakras, from other chakras

Overview of the Chakra Structure

Let's take a quick look of the various parts of a chakra to see how they all fit together and how they connect with the purpose of a particular chakra. In the chapters that follow, we'll look at each of these components in greater detail.

All of the parts of a chakra are concerned with maintaining a particular life force situation in the chakra. Energy and information (the components of life force) can be stored in a chakra. Life force can come into the chakra from sources outside the soul or from other chakras in the same soul. Life force can go outside the soul or to other chakras inside the soul. How much life force is stored, how and when and where it goes are all determined by aspects of the chakra structure.

This is not a purely mechanical process. There is a strong component of feedback from anything a chakra interacts with. The values for all of the aspects are in a continuous state of flux.

With that background, let's look at the aspects of the chakra.

Life force

The central job of each chakra is to maintain its life force level of both energy and information. Every chakra has a *maximum internal* level. This represents the most energy and information the chakra can possibly store. It is not the level at which we normally operate.

Along with the maximum energy level, the chakra has an *internal set point*. This is where the chakra is most comfortable in the current situation. Different situations have different internal set points and the chakras adjust their preferred level to fit the situation. Information in the form of memories plays a large part in setting the preferred energy level. The Internal Set Point question in the Measuring Openness topic in the previous chapter is a reflection of preferred life force level inside the chakra. Choosing the top item goes along with having an internal set point near the maximum internal level. Choosing the bottom item correlates with having a very low preferred level. The middle answer is, as you might suspect, somewhere in between.

Each chakra has a current *internal level*. If things are going well, this will be the internal set point. For many reasons the stored life force may be quite different from the preferred level. If it is, the chakra will use its ability to move energy to do the best it can to get to the preferred level.

The information of the chakra is probably there for all time. Every moment* the chakra exists it adds to its information, as it interacts with ordinary and non-ordinary reality. The internal level of information is concerned with what the chakra is actually paying attention to in the current moment.

Given the incredible diversity of the world we live in, we need ways to remember how to interact in each known situation and to figure out how to act in situations we haven't experienced yet. Experience helps a chakra try to figure out how to handle situations. We'll talk more about that later, but for now it's important to remember that this memory selection happens in each chakra, not just the mind.

In any energy system, it's a good idea to keep track of *leakage*. I'm using this term to describe energy and information that is lost in ways besides the transfer mechanisms to places inside and outside the soul.

The idea that a chakra has a *goal* may be a puzzling one. I am not sure whether this belongs in the list of aspects of a chakra. I do believe that chakras can make intended changes where the intention to change can be called a goal. What I don't know is whether the goal is a separate thing or made up of internal and external interactions of the chakra.

---

* Some people believe that we don't store all of our memories, only the important ones. There is some evidence in a particular set of near death experiences that may point in that direction. See, for example, Whitfield (1995).

Connections outside the soul

Energy and information can go outside the soul and come from outside the soul. The *inward ability* is the maximum amount of energy and information the soul can take in during a particular length of time. Most of the time the maximum amount is not being brought into the soul.

The preferred amount in the current situation is the *inward set point*. The chakra, based on its current life force level and amount of life force expenditure, would like to receive this amount of energy and information.

How it receives the life force can be very complicated. There are lots of sources of life force in the world. The chakra wants to receive a certain amount of energy and information from each of them. I call this set of values the *inward intention*.

One way to picture this with particular chakras is to look at the Inward Set Point question in the description of each chakra. Choosing the first response means that the inward set point is very high. The chakra will try to gain energy and/or information at near the inward ability. The bottom response means that the chakra does not want any external life force. Little or no energy or information will be coming in, if the chakra chooses what happens. The middle response is in between.

The inward set point is also an important measure of your satisfaction with yourself. When you combine it with your internal set point, it predicts whether you can be successful. For example, if you are wishing for a lot more love in your life, the internal set point will be very high. If your inward ability and your inward set point for love are high, you have a chance to find someone who can give you the love you are looking for. On the other hand, if your inward ability or your inward set point is low, it doesn't matter how much love is coming your way. You will never be able to receive it and will always feel dissatisfied about this kind of interaction with others.

We can consider the outward flow as a mirror image to the inward flow. Life force flowing out of the soul can go to the many possible places in the world. There is a maximum amount of energy and information called the *outward ability*.

The preferred total outward flow is the *outward set point*. This is related to the Outward Set Point question in the last chapter. The top answer corresponds to a very high outward set point. The bottom answer is a very low outward set point.

People have general tendencies related to each of the chakras. They may think of themselves as very smart or very loving or very powerful. Or they may think of themselves as the opposite of those characteristics. (Or anywhere in between.) This is another example of the outward set point. In most of their interactions this will be how they conduct themselves, but there are often particular relationships that bring out the other side of the person's way of being. A person who loves almost everybody may have one or two people that he or she hates. The set point is the normal way a person interacts with others.

Each of the things in the outside world can be sent a certain amount of energy and information. The proportion of the life force for each target is described by the *outward intention*. The differences are part of the set of intentions related to particular types of connections.

In addition to all of this, there is a preferred life force level in the outside world (*external set point*). The soul will do what it can to maintain the level in the outside world at the preferred energy and information level.

In any particular situation you might think there is too much of this chakra's life force in the outer world, too little, or just about the right amount. The statements about the external set point in the previous chapter look at this attitude. The top statement means that the person wants to have a lot more of the energy and/or information associated with the chakra in the external world. The bottom statement means the chakra will try to create a situation where there is a lot less life force in the outside world.

Connections inside the soul

Chakras are powered not only from the outside, and they don't send life force only to the outside. Many descriptions of chakras place great emphasis on the movement of life force between chakras. For example, the kundalini energy flows from the chaos chakra to power all of the rest.

In many of the models there are elaborate descriptions of the paths that energy can take as it moves around the soul. Information flow may be even more complex. Chakras handle different complexities of information, so information transfer may not occur easily to either a higher or a lower chakra.

The model I want to use simplifies the situation somewhat. While detailed analysis of the energy movement may be useful in many situations, when we are looking at connections between souls it seems sufficient to sum each set of pathways into a single value. In this model we need to keep track of pathways *to other chakras* and pathways *from other chakras*. From a chakra's point of view there will be two sets of values: The first set describes the size of the pathways to each of the other chakras. The second set describes the size of the pathways from each of the other chakras. Information is handled differently to account for the translation problems.

When all of these 14 aspects of the structure are put together, we have a representation of a chakra. A chakra is made up of 14 aspects: maximum internal, internal set point, internal level, leakage, goal, inward ability, inward set point, inward intention, outward ability, outward set point, outward intention, external set point, to other chakras, from other chakras.*

In mathematical notation this looks like:

$\text{chakra}_i = \{\text{maximum internal}_i, \text{internal set point}_i, \text{internal level}_i,$
$\text{leakage}_i, \text{goal}_i, \text{inward ability}_i, \text{inward set point}_i, \text{inward intention}_i,$
$\text{outward ability}_i, \text{outward set point}_i, \text{outward intention}_i, \text{external set}$
$\text{point}_i, \text{to other chakras}_i, \text{from other chakras}_i\}$
where i is the chakra number

Mechanisms for Change

Let's start by looking at the general way experience affects a component of the chakra. The basic mechanism is pretty simple. If the chakra considers the experience successful, the component will increase. If the experience is negative (unsuccessful), the component will

---

* Remember that you may skip over the gray sections if you are not interested in the mathematical details.

decrease. Components can have either positive or negative values, so increasing means getting more positive or more negative when an experience is what the chakra wants.

In this simple model, the component of chakra i (ChC$_i$) will change based on the success of an experience (S) in a time interval, as in going from time t to time t+1.*

$$\mathrm{ChC_i}(t+1) = \mathrm{ChC_i}(t) + c_{ic} * S_i(t)$$

where c_{ic} is a constant that represents how much an experience changes a particular component of chakra i.†
c_{ic} has the same sign as ChC. ChC can be positive or negative. Success is positive if the experience is what the chakra wants and negative if it is not what the chakra wants.

Beyond the instantaneous change, there is an integrated aspect to the set of experiences. When we are interacting with a particular close friend, our chakra components will be set with the values we prefer for the connection to that person. We've learned this set of values throughout our experience with this particular person. While there may be momentary, small changes based on the current interaction, the changes will be deviations from the basic set points.

The connection values will be quite different when we are interacting with someone else. Think about dealing with a policeman giving you a traffic ticket. We have (at least, I have) quite different preferences for connecting with friends and connecting with a policeman who has pulled us over.

---

* Definitions of variables and operators for all of the soul equations can be found in Appendix 2.
† As everyone who has worked with ordinary scientific equations knows, all variables are represented by a single letter (sometimes Greek). One of the initiation rites of science is to learn what each of the letters stands for. With a single-letter convention, two letters next to one another imply that the values will be multiplied. We do not have single letter conventions for non-ordinary reality yet, so I will often use multiple-letter variables that come from the variable name. For example, stored life force will be represented by SLF. This convention requires explicitly showing multiplication by using a multiplication sign (*).

The connections with a friend are relatively stable over time. A momentary blip (for example, a misunderstanding) may cause us to change the component values some, but they will generally go back to the usual values pretty quickly. Friendships can change, but this usually happens over a longer interval of time and as the result of many experiences. When our chakra interaction values are being set for this particular interaction, what we use is the summation of all our experiences with this person. We can also choose how to sum up the experiences. Usually we give the most recent experiences more weight, but that is not always the case.

One way to calculate the component value at the current time is to average all the preferred values throughout the experience with this particular person (or type of person in the case of a policeman) and weight them so that the most recent experiences count more than past experiences.

$$ChC(now) = [\text{weighted average}]_{t=0}^{now}(ChC(t))$$

Unfortunately, this is still too simple for real life. There are many more complications to this equation, as we will see.

How much each component will increase or decrease depends on several other factors. We'll look at those factors when we discuss each individual component of the chakra structure in detail in the next four chapters.

6. Chakra Storage

Looking for "a needle in a haystack" requires a
definition of a needle and another definition for
hay.

— *Mounir Ragheb*

The first part of the chakra structure I want to take an in-depth look at is the model for life force stored in a chakra. There are two parts to what is stored in a chakra: chakra energy and chakra information.

One thing that will become clear is that energy and information are qualitatively different. Energy levels are subject to change from moment to moment as energy is taken in or sent out. Information seems to be there all the time, and always more information than we can process, so we need to select how much information and which information we will use at a particular moment. Energy looks at flow while information looks at selection.

Let's start with a discussion of what we mean by energy and information from a chakra's point of view. After that we can divide the discussion into the five internal energy and information parts of the chakra: maximum internal storage, the internal set point, actual internal storage, leakage, and the goal of the chakra.

Chakra Energy

Many people say they have ways to measure the energy in a chakra (for example, by watching the amplitude and direction of a crystal spinning on a chain), but I'm not sure if what they are measuring translates directly to what we usually consider to be energy.

What I would like to propose is that each of us has the capacity to hold a certain amount of energy in a chakra. I believe the capacity can be different in different chakras and that the capacity can change with time. This makes for a potentially confusing situation.

In looking at electromagnetic energy we can say that a battery has a certain amount of energy stored. Different batteries have different capacities. Each battery may be charged to a different fraction of its capacity. Overall, though, we can find a single number that represents the amount of energy each battery contains and, most importantly, we can compare the level of energy in different batteries.

We need similar measures for the energy in a chakra. We need to know the maximum that can be stored and the amount that is currently stored. We have ways to measure the amount of energy that is coming out of a chakra, but I don't know how to measure the amount of energy in the chakra right now. I do know that, unlike batteries, we have to allow for positive and negative chakra energy.

The energy level varies with time, but is relatively constant across situations occurring at about the same time. There are exceptions to the energy level staying constant. We have all had situations where bad news has "totally drained" us. That is another way to say there was a significant drop in energy level. Similarly there are times when we feel "totally charged."

Chakra Information

As we saw in Chapter 5, each chakra processes information at a different level of complexity. The information that is stored in the chakra is at the same degree of complexity.

Usually when we use the term memory, we are referring to what goes on in the mind chakra. We are gathering and storing new information, usually in verbal or other representational form, much of it as directly experienced by the senses. The communication chakra is also involved in this because it would remember the information that it was sending out while other information was coming in.

The other chakras are also able to form memories. I believe they have the same kind of storage mechanisms as the mind chakra, but they store the information that is appropriate for the kinds of experiences they have. That means that they can store experiences that the mind chakra and communication chakra may not be able to grasp.

Let's take a look at the kinds of memories that are associated with each chakra. The list is not intended to be exhaustive. I'm sure you will be able to think of more kinds of memories than I describe here.

The spirit chakra remembers our interactions with gods, devils, demons, and angels. These days most people work pretty hard to not remember or even acknowledge the possibility of this kind of interaction. People who do talk about these conversations are often given strong psychoactive medications. (Luckily there are some exceptions.) In earlier days talking about heaven was less stigmatizing. We have reports of angels singing praises to God, the music of the spheres, and streets of gold. I suggest that heaven is nothing like that, but that this is the best we can do when we try to convert a spirit memory into words that can be spoken in ordinary reality through our communication chakra.

The mind chakra is probably the easiest to describe because it is what we usually mean when we talk about memory. Events are stored in some representational form, something like the information you would find in a movie script that doesn't describe the characters' emotions. Mind can also store memories of what it was searching for in its quest to understand a situation. It probably includes our thoughts about the events, but I wouldn't be surprised if we recreate the thoughts about events each time we remember them.

The communication chakra remembers what was communicated to and received from the outside world in terms of representational signals. It works with the mind chakra to allow us to reconstruct past events. Since the communication chakra is also responsible for communicating emotions, it would also be responsible for remembering the emotional messages it sent out and received.

The heart chakra remembers our connections with other people. It is responsible for the range of feeling that deal with how we are connected to one another. This is the kind of information that actors bring to a movie script when they search in themselves to understand the characters they are playing and how the characters are connected to one another. (Another aspect good actors bring to a script is to understand the power structures and related struggles between characters. That is a subject for the next chakra.) One important observation about this chakra is that it doesn't remember events in the form of "you did this and I did that." It remembers, instead, the type of connection that existed and the energy that was exchanged. The next two chakras probably remember in similar ways.

The will chakra remembers our experiences related to people telling us what to do and our telling other people what they should do. In flocks of chickens (wolf packs, and groups of humans, too) this is the chakra that keeps track of the pecking order (alpha dog, organization chart). The experiences of overcoming obstacles or being defeated by them would be stored here.

The desire chakra remembers our use of energy while creating something new or tearing down something that exists. It also remembers the sexual parts of our sexual encounters. Some people say there are things better than sex.* Many of them, but certainly not all, have to do with creation or destruction. Hunter S. Thompson (1995) in his book about the 1992 presidential campaign suggests politics should be included, too. These are also aspects of the desire chakra. The parts that have to do with positive or negative desires are remembered here.

The chaos chakra remembers its connections to the chaotic source of energy people use to power their lives. Explicit interactions with these energies turn into mythical journeys, battles, and associations as they are translated into words. The chakra remembers the basics of the connections it has made. It remembers successes and failures at tapping into the chaotic energy system that powers our ordinary and soul realities.

Chakras change based on what happens to them. The common term for this is learning. There seem to be two kinds of learning that occur.

---

* Here's one list from TopTenz.net (2011): 10. housework, 9. dating a vampire, 8. weight loss, 7. music, 6. in vitro fertilization, 5. sports, 4. sleep, 3. food, 2. cell phones, and 1. the Internet. The connection of some of these to the desire chakra is tenuous (or non-existent).

The first is memory of events. Each chakra has its own experiences and its memory of them. The second type of learning involves connecting events to preferred set points in the chakra. This is a study of what chakras do with their memories. Experience affects the other aspects of a chakra. The result is that we not only remember what has happened to us, we also learn to deal with it better.

We'll look at both of these aspects of memory in this chapter as we go through the five aspects of what is stored in a chakra.

Maximum Internal

The first aspect of chakra storage looks at the maximum amount we can store, both energy and information.

Maximum Internal Energy

Much as I would like to have it, I don't know of a way to measure maximum internal energy. However, even without having a measure at this time we can propose ways that it might act. When we are born, we have a certain maximum capacity in each chakra. It's not clear how much of this is a result of previous lives or how much the capacity is affected by experiences between lives. My observation is that infants vary greatly in the amount of energy they show. This probably is connected in some way to their maximum capacity.

As we get older, it appears that our energy level increases up to some age between 20 and 60, depending on the chakra involved. The desire chakra seems to peak early. The other chakras have their peak energy at later ages. The spirit chakra may even reach its highest energy level at death.* Again what we can see is the amount of energy expressed. We infer that this is related to the energy capacity.

After the peak age, the energy capacity seems to fall off again. It seems to be related more to health than to years. It's possible that the capacity is there, but the chakra chooses to have a lower set point. It's also possible that the appearance of lower energy is a result of lower capacity or set point for the outward energy flow. I don't think either of

---

* I don't have a clue what happens with the chaos chakra related to age. I'm hoping for more insight into that someday.

these is the case. It looks to me like the energy capacity of a chakra is related to the vitality of the body it is connected to. This sounds like a useful observation. Unfortunately it brings up a similarly difficult question about how to measure the vitality of the body.

Maximum life force energy (MLF_E) capacity is related to the vitality of the body it is in. We may not know the absolute vitality of the body (BV), but we can say that the energy capacity changes as the vitality changes

$$MLF_E(t+1) = MLF_E(t) + a * (BV(t+1) - BV(t))$$

Where a is a constant that relates chakra energy to body vitality.

It is also likely that chakras can increase their ability to hold energy. This is one of the big differences between chakras and batteries. If you overcharge a battery, it burns out. Chakras try very hard to self-regulate their energy level and when they operate near the top of their range, they can increase their capacity. Muscles show characteristics like that, too. It is what you might expect of living, adaptive systems.

Chakras increase their maximum energy (MLF_E) when they are operated at the top of their stored energy (SLF_E) range.

$$MLF_E(t+1) = MLF_E(t) + b * (1 - (MLF_E(t) - SLF_E(t)) / MLF_E(t))$$

Where b is a constant that describes the possible rate of change in MLF_E. It may be different for different chakras and different people.

I believe it is possible to burn out aspects of a chakra. This does not happen often, but it seems to be caused by extremely abusive or traumatic situations. Post-traumatic stress disorder (PTSD) may be related to burning out a chakra's capacity to block negative energy that is coming in.* We will look at this again in the next chapter as it relates to energy flow.

Since the maximum capacity is very difficult to measure, it is lucky that it is not important when we are trying to calculate soul connections. The internal set point and stored energy are much more strongly connected with effects we can observe and more useful in predicting how chakras will act.

---

* PTSD may also be caused by a persistent negative energy state.

Maximum Internal Information

People who work with near death experiences (NDEs) have a class of experiences where the person is led through a set of life memories. The general belief about these life memories is that everything is remembered.[37] The people who report on NDEs do not usually use a chakra model, so it's hard to tell if each chakra holds all of its memories. From the completeness they describe, including remembering how it felt to be in the experience, I think we can assume that their reports include all of the chakras.

Sometimes in NDEs these memories are described as being held in something like little crystal spheres. The spheres are on shelves or racks in very, very large rooms. In the Harry Potter books, J. K. Rowling (2004) describes something similar in the Ministry of Magic.

When we are looking at the maximum amount of information that chakras can store, it looks like we have two choices to meet the requirements of NDEs. One is that the chakras store at least one life's worth of memories. The other is that there is a storage mechanism outside of the chakras that holds the memories and the chakras can access the storage with varying degrees of success. It's hard to see how we can distinguish between the two. I think the answer for maximum internal information is to say "everything" or at least "a lot" without trying to specify the exact place it is stored. While maximum internal energy looks like it can increase (and probably decrease), information only increases.

Internal Set Point

The internal set point is the amount of energy and information the chakra chooses to hold at any given time. Why we don't keep our energy at maximum levels all the time is an interesting question, but it is clear that we don't. It's clearer why we don't try to access all of our information at the same time. There's too much of it, so our set point needs to define how much of our information store we want to use.

Energy Set Point

Some people choose to keep very little energy. Others keep their energy at very high levels. It is possible to hold both positive and negative energy (although not at the same time), so the set point can be either positive or negative. Different chakras can have very different set points.

I believe we change our internal set point based on experiences. Positive experiences will move the set point to be more like the current stored energy.* (We'll talk about stored energy later in this chapter. Simply put, it's the amount of energy currently in the chakra.) Negative experiences will move the set point to be less like the stored energy level.

This can actually be a bit confusing so let's look at the possible situations. We have a certain amount of energy in a chakra. We have a set point. The current amount of energy may be greater or less than the set point. We have success with an experience, which may be positive or negative. Here are the possibilities:

Stored energy compared to set point	Stored Energy	Set point	Success	Change
higher	positive	positive	positive	set point more positive
higher	positive	positive	negative	set point less positive
higher	positive	negative	positive	set point less negative
higher	positive	negative	negative	set point more negative

---

* What makes an experience positive or negative is a fascinating problem all by itself. We all know it's easy to tell when something went well or went badly. And we know how well or how badly with a fair degree of certainty. That's enough of a definition for the purpose of this book. As an added note, we have the ability to adjust our perceptions of an event at any later time and adjust whatever changes in the chakra happened as a result of the earlier perception to be more in line with the later perception.

higher	negative	negative	positive	set point less negative
higher	negative	negative	negative	set point more negative
lower	positive	positive	positive	set point less positive
lower	positive	positive	negative	set point more positive
lower	negative	positive	positive	set point less positive
lower	negative	positive	negative	set point more positive
lower	negative	negative	positive	set point more negative
lower	negative	negative	negative	set point less negative

When the current energy level is the same as the set point, experience doesn't change the set point. For those mathematical purists who want to see 16 cases in a four-item binary situation, here are the four cases that can't happen because the negative and positive in the energy level and set point conflict with the higher and lower in the comparison:

Stored energy compared to set point	Stored Energy	Set point	Success	Change
higher	negative	positive	positive	can't happen
higher	negative	positive	negative	can't happen
lower	positive	negative	positive	can't happen
lower	positive	negative	negative	can't happen

We can write an equation that calculates the change in the energy component of internal set point ($IntSP_E$) as a result of experience. The greater the difference between the stored life force (SLF_E) and the set point, the more change we will see. The greater the absolute value of the success of the experience (S) — more strongly positive or more strongly negative, the greater the change.

$$\text{IntSP}_E(t+1) =$$
$$(\text{IntSP}_E(t) + a * S * (\text{SLF}_E(t) - \text{IntSP}_E(t)))[\text{lim}]\text{MLF}_E(t)$$

where a is a weighting factor describing how quickly we change IntSP

Information Set Point

While near death experiences suggest that at some time (usually after we die) we can access all of our memories, we certainly can't access all of them at the same time while we are alive. Sometimes the chakra is open to many pieces of information, but at other times the amount and kind of information that is considered is very limited.

For example, Paul Ekman's research on anger[38] has shown that we are very selective in the information we access when we are angry. We only remember things and listen to information that supports our current position. After the anger has passed we are able to attend to conflicting evidence and make decisions based on a wider range of evidence.

Exactly how Ekman's research can be represented in a chakra model is an interesting question. Each chakra has a different amount of information it can attend to. Psychological research suggests that the mind chakra can effectively handle about seven things at a time. The desire chakra is probably focused on only one thing. Exactly what constitutes a "thing" is open to discussion, but the significant point is that chakras are capable of setting the amount and kind of information that they want to process.

In this way the information set point is connected to the concept of attention. The information set point can be defined as the sum of the attention the chakra wants to pay to the current situation plus all the attention it is paying to memories of past experiences. We can add up the attention for each of the parts to get the total attention.

The total attention for a single chakra c is the sum of the attentions to each of the parts.

$$A_c = A_c(\text{current}) + \sum_{m=1}^{\text{all memories}} A_{cm}$$

Summing total attention through all the chakras.

$$A_{\text{total}} = \sum_{c=1}^{7} \left(A_c(\text{current}) + \sum_{m=1}^{\text{all memories}} A_{cm} \right)$$

Information and energy set points are tied together with our current actions. Energy moves in the chakra based on the information the chakra has and the information the chakra chooses to pay attention to depends on the type of energy in the chakra. We'll look at this again after we have looked at the other set points information can affect.

Internal Level

Internal level is a measure of the amount of energy currently in the chakra and the set of information that the chakra is currently focusing on. While the set point is where the chakra would like to be, the level is where the chakra actually is. They can be very different.

Internal Energy Level

Maintaining the internal set point is the purpose of the external and internal chakra interactions that we will talk about in the next two chapters. The energy level is the amount of energy that is currently in the chakra. It may be more or less than the energy component of the internal life force set point.

Change in the stored energy comes from energy flowing into or out of the chakra by any of the paths that are available. These include connections to other souls (discussed in Chapter 8), connections within the soul (discussed in Chapter 9), and energy leakage (discussed in this chapter).

The stored energy (SLF_E) of a chakra is based on the previous level of energy, changed by life force leakage of energy (LFL_E), energy moving to and from chakras external to the soul (II_E and OI_E), and energy moving to and from chakras in this soul (LFT_E and LFF_E).

$$SLF_E(t+1) = SLF_E(t) - LFL_E(t) + II_E(t) - OI_E(t) + LFF_E(t) - LFT_E(t)$$

Stored energy is a measure of the current internal state of the chakra, and is based on the effects of all of the other parts of the structure. I'm leaving it as one of the important aspects of the chakra because it ties together all the other aspects. Unfortunately it seems almost impossible to measure accurately, although we have a chance to measure something that may approximate it.

I want to talk about two reasons for this. The first is that measuring the energy in a chakra changes the energy it contains. This should usually be a minor effect, but it definitely depends on who is doing the measuring, as we will see in the second reason.

The most important reason we can't measure the energy in a chakra is that it needs to be measured along a connection.* There is no (healthy) connection that allows unrestricted access to a chakra. All those people who claim to be measuring the amount of energy you have in a chakra are really only measuring the amount of energy you let them see (also limited by the amount they let themselves see). The act of measuring may involve adding energy to the chakra or taking it away, depending on the type of connection you have with the person who is doing the measuring. If the measurement is anything like accurate — not a given — the chakra has at least the energy level that is measured, but it probably has more.

The measurement of stored energy in a chakra represents a minimum value of the stored energy. The measurement is limited by how much life force the chakra being measured allows the measurer to observe (LFO_E) and how much energy the measurer is capable of seeing (LFC_E).

$$SLF_E \geq [min](LFO_E, LFC_E)$$

The change in the stored life force of the chakra caused by the measurement (SLFM) is represented by the equation:

$$SLF_E(t+1) = SLF_E(t) + SLFM$$

Even though we can't measure stored energy accurately on an interval scale,† there are a few things we can say about it. The first is whether there is enough. There are times when we know we don't have enough energy to accomplish what we want to do — not enough mind to solve a problem, not enough will to finish a difficult project, not enough

---

* There's a reason this book is called *Calculating Soul Connections* instead of *Calculating Soul Energy*. Now you know what it is.

† An interval scale defines levels with equal increments between each level. Time, temperature, and distance are examples of interval scales (burlingame and Blaschko, 2010).

love to share with a loved one. This provides us with a nominal scale*
for the amount of energy in the chakra.

We can take that a little bit farther by asking the question: How much
energy do you think you have today [in a particular chakra]? The answers
might be

5 — full of energy
4 — more than enough
3 — barely enough
2 — not enough to do what I need to do
1 — no energy at all

This would be an ordinal scale† where each level represents an
ordered change from the level before. The intervals do not have to be
even and we can't assign an energy quantity to any of the levels. In fact,
if we could find a way to measure the energy as a quantity, we would
probably find a wide range of values for what different people consider
barely enough energy. Among other things, it would depend on how
much each person was trying to do.

One final thought about stored energy is how it compares with the
total amount of energy being expended. Let's look at a very simple
example to explain what I mean.

We'll assume we have a task that requires 100 units of energy. How
much energy do we need to have stored to be able to do the task? We
might have all 100 units available at the beginning of the task. We also
might have almost no energy stored, but we are able to receive energy as
we are doing the task so that we take in and then send out 100 units of
energy while the task is being done. We could also use up some stored
energy and make up for what we don't have stored by taking in more
during the task.

All of these cases happen. I suspect the amount of stored energy
compared to the amount of energy being used varies by task and is
different for each person. I expect we have all started projects where
there was enough energy to get started but then things got tough and we

---

* A nominal scale divides information into categories that are similar in nature.
Gender, state of residence, and "yes or no" are examples of nominal scales.
† It's a particular kind of ordinal scale called a Likert scale.

gave up. What I have noticed is that tasks that are impossible to do alone can be done when other people help. Something about working with other people can provide us with more energy. (And there's the converse where working with other people can drain all our energy and make a normally enjoyable project impossible.)

I think the observation of how quickly we get tired of something points to the idea that the amount of energy we can store is small compared to the amount of energy we use in a day. We need to be replenishing our energy all the time in order to have enough.

Internal Memory Level

One of the great conundrums of modern biology and psychology is how brains store and access memories. In fact, it's been an unsolved problem perhaps since the early 1800s when people first realized that there was a problem. The biggest problem is that no one has found a mechanism in the physical brain capable of handling the enormous amount of material we are able to store.

It is important to note that most people consider two kinds of memory: short-term and long-term.[39] Short-term memory holds about seven items. As a new item comes to the attention of the person, another item drops out of the set. We use the items in our short-term memory to solve problems. I think the structures we see in the physical brain have the capacity to explain short-term memory and at least some of the processes that are used to create solutions to problems.

So for the mind chakra, we can use the models of short-term memory to study the mind chakra's memory level (and perhaps get a clue to how mind and body interact). Other chakras probably have similarities. For example, we talk about a gut feeling. It's simpler than our mind's decision-making process, but that's just what we would expect from a chakra that contains less complex information.

Long-term memory is different. The current ordinary-reality thinking is that a long-term memory is saved when it is important enough to move from short-term memory to long-term memory. I would point out that an awful lot of not very important information is also stuffed into long-term memory.

There have been many suggestions for how the memory process happens. These have included the idea that brain cells each encode a memory, that memories are stored by changes in the connections between neurons, that the brain is a complex hologram, that memories are stored in proteins created by the brain, or that we store memories by having them associated with similar memories. (Of course, this doesn't give a mechanism for how the early memories were stored.)

These days researchers generally say that the memory is saved when it is "rehearsed," that is, when it is considered enough times and is important enough to set up a neural pattern in the brain. The pattern is the memory and can be recalled as a whole when parts of it occur again.

Some try to solve the problem of an ordinary-reality mechanism by stating that different parts of the brain store different types of memories (still leaving out the how).[40] They credit Papez's circuit with the ability to set up a resonance that stores the memories and then suggest that some other structure combines the parts together at a later time to reform the memory. One explanation (which will not be referred to again, so you can skip it if you want to) from Dubuc looks like this:

> The various structures of the limbic system exert their influence on the hippocampus and the temporal lobe via Papez's circuit, also known as the hippocampal/mammillothalamic tract. This circuit is a sub-set of the numerous connections that the limbic structures have with one another. The ... information travels from the hippocampus to the mammillary bodies of the hypothalamus, then on to the anterior thalamic nucleus, the cingulate cortex, and the entorhinal cortex, before finally returning to the hippocampus.
>
> Once the temporary associations of cortical neurons generated by a particular event have made a certain number of such "passes" through Papez's circuit, they will have undergone a physical remodelling that consolidates them. Eventually, these associations will have been strengthened so much that they will stabilize and become independent of the hippocampus. Bilateral lesions of the hippocampus will prevent new long-term

memories from forming, but will not erase those that were encoded before the injury.[41]

Other people put more emphasis on the amygdala as a center of memory processing.* Scans of the brain during recall of traumatic events have shown that the amygdala is involved in the reactions caused by traumatic memories.

Unfortunately, none of these studies have a viable physical mechanism for storing the memory itself or recalling specific memories. The structures of the brain, especially small structures like the amygdala and hippocampus, simply don't have enough storage capacity or processing power to hold and sort through memories.

Perhaps the best summary of the situation is like this, "...the anatomical substrate of working memory is far from being understood in detail. Moreover, the phenomenon of working memory is made all the more complex by the fact that it takes place over time."[42]

This is not to say that the brain isn't involved in processing memories. The involvement of the brain must be included in anything that is proposed as a way memories are stored and accessed.

Let's look at some of the other things that need to go into a theory of memory.

1. Memories have a time structure. We can remember events in approximately the correct time sequence. Mechanisms of association do not account for a time structure.
2. The number of things we remember is very large.
3. Some people with eidetic (photographic) memory can recall the exact wording of many books and reconstruct events as well as a photographic record.
4. The effects memories have on us can change with time. A traumatic event that causes PTSD can be dealt with in ways that allow us to still access the memory but not in a way that causes PTSD.
5. Also dealing with PTSD, sometimes an event is so devastating that we can't even remember what happened. Yet we still act fearfully in

---

* For examples related to storing and modifying fear memories see Dębiec et al (2010) and Newhouse (2008).

similar situations. The associations are very strong, the memory is very significant, yet associations do not bring the memory into consciousness.

6. We need to account for both verbal and non-verbal memories. One place this shows up is in the observation that people don't often have memories from the time before age seven. (The usual explanation is that language hasn't formed well enough to store memories in a way that can be recalled. They are stored as "sensory" memories rather than as verbal descriptions of occurrences. I would modify the statement to say that before age seven the interaction of the chakras is not sufficient to have all the experiences in the lower chakras *also* stored in the mind chakra.*)

7. We store many kinds of memories: facts, words and stories, pictures, tastes and smells, touch, feelings, societal structures, and physical skills.

8. We need to explain how very early memories exist in some people, often all the way back into the womb. Birth memories are actually quite common.† We need to be able to explain how birth memories occur and why some people have them, while most people don't. Here's a quote from a fellow identified only as Mark that provides an example:

> I remember being born. I tried for a moment to tell the people who were around me that WE FORGET! This is because the moment I was born, I watched the memory of where I had been before birth leave me.[43]

---

* The observation that chakras need to integrate before memories from all the chakras are stored leads to an interesting question: Why? If we accept reincarnation, shouldn't this integration continue through the time between incarnations? It doesn't seem to, just as memories of previous lives do not usually persist into the current life. It's evidence for what happens between physical lives, but I don't know what it means yet.

† Most serious health care websites carefully explain that newborns can't form memories yet. (See, for example, Conger, 2011.) Still there are hundreds of other websites devoted to sharing memories of birth (Experience Project, 2011). I suggest that the scientific websites are sacrificing reality to theory. It's not the best way to understand what is going on. Also see Guardian (2011).

9. In a similar vein, a few young children have memories of previous lifetimes. Ian Stevenson[44] spent half his life researching this. We need a mechanism that allows this to happen but prevents it from happening in the majority of cases. Mark's remark in the previous item says he experienced this but didn't explain how it happened.

10. We need a model where damage to the brain (Alzheimer's disease, traumatic brain injury) or inhibition of particular chemical processes (e.g., protein kinase C, zeta) can stop us from storing or accessing memories.

Let's move away from humans to look at memory in other creatures and the kinds of things we need to explain.

Many of the explanations of memory rely on structures in the cortex to do the actual memory storage. However, humans are not the only creatures with memories. Some of the other creatures don't have cortexes and still manage to have memories. We need to account for that.

11. Some migrating birds remember where they made their nests the previous year so they can return to them.

12. Bees remember where flowers are and perform dances to let other bees know how to find the flowers, too. The other bees have to remember the dance as they go to look for the flowers.

13. Bees can do pattern recognition to the level of counting the number of objects in a picture and make a choice later based on the number of objects they saw.[45]

14. In the example earlier in the book where a caterpillar learned to react to an odor and still remembered it when it became a butterfly, we have a case where nerve cells weren't even present. We need to have a model that allows this to happen, too.

There are other requirements of a model for storing and retrieving memories, but let's stop here for now. It's hard to see how a purely physical model can handle all of these conditions, so let's take a look at what happens when we allow memory storage and retrieval in all of the chakras.

We have a better explanation for most of the points about the human mind. The first three points deal with storage mechanisms, which we will talk about later. Points 4 and 5 can be explained if trauma blocks the movement of memories between chakras. Dealing with just the mind is not as effective as some of the energy psychology techniques, which are specifically designed to remove blocks. Points 6 and 7 are more easily explained with a separated set of memories, although the brain model can handle the observation if we allow different functional areas of the brain to store different kinds of memories. Point 8 is not a problem for memory in chakras. Point 9 can't be covered without something outside the physical brain. Points 11, 12, and 13 point out that other creatures store memories, sometimes relatively complicated ones, and they don't have the mechanisms available to humans. Point 14, like point 9, requires something outside a physical nervous system.

And that leaves point 10, which leads to the question, how does the brain interact with the soul? We'll look at that later.

Leakage

The concept of leakage applies well to energy. It looks at energy we have at one time that is somehow gone in the next time without being actively used. There are a couple of ways to account for that. Information leakage does not seem to occur according to near-death experiences and Michael Newton's view[46] of what we are like between lives. What we need to look at is why memories become inaccessible to us.

Energy Leakage

It's all very well and good to talk about energy going out of and energy coming into a chakra. The implication is that we can do some sort of bookkeeping on the energy to know how much energy is in a chakra at a particular time. I believe we can, but there is one more factor that we need to take into account. Energy can leak out of a chakra without being intentionally sent to another location.

There are three ways to look at this:

The first is that chakras are leaky. They need to be trained to hold all the energy they receive so it can be used later. Energy leaks out in proportion to the amount of energy that is in the chakra.

The second is that many disciplines have a concept of "stale" energy. The idea is that when the energy is not flowing through the system, it somehow loses its potency, as a soft drink loses its carbonation in an opened can. I suspect this is just another way to say that chakra energy is lost without using the concept of energy leaking out. In any case, the equation for energy losing potency is probably the same as the equation for energy leakage.

The third is that our intentions are the problem. People intend their energy to be put to particular uses, but we get distracted by events and people. Some energy goes out but it accomplishes no useful purpose. Sometimes a lot of energy is frittered away. Anxiety is a good example of this. I believe the best place to account for this kind of leakage is when we look at connections outside the soul in the next chapter.

Probably the easiest way to understand energy leakage is to say that we can figure out how long it takes for half the energy to go away. This is the same kind of calculation that is used to figure out many other kinds of energy levels, including the amount of energy that will be given off by a radioactive substance.

Different chakras will have different levels of leakage. When we calculate current energy levels, we need to take leakage into account.

Energy leakage (LFL_E) is proportional to the stored energy level (SLF_E). The energy leakage rate (ELR) may be different for each chakra.

$$LFL_E(t) = SLF_E(t) * \left(\frac{1}{2}\right)^{(\Delta t / ELR)}$$

$$SLF_E(t+1) = SLF_E(t) - LFL_E(t)$$

where ELR is the half-life for energy decay in this chakra and Δt is the time between t+1 and t.*

Calculating the change in energy related to leakage is easy. Discovering the value of the half-life (the energy leakage rate), given the amount of energy flowing into and out of a chakra, is much more difficult. The thought that we can isolate a chakra, in the way one can

---

* Yes, I realize that is 1, at least in a sensible unit system where the half-life is measured in the same time units as the change in time.

isolate a radioactive substance to measure its half-life, is foolish at best. I hope that as we become more aware of life energy our tools for measuring it will improve and we'll have a chance to measure something like leakage.*

Information Leakage

When we think about information leakage, the first thing that comes to mind is probably dementia. We lose our ability to access past memories. Interestingly, people talk about a person's spirit being there even if the memories aren't. Apparently chakras besides the mind continue to function even when the mind seems to be failing. I am going to suggest that what we see in dementia is caused by a failure of the physical brain. It suggests that the brains we have evolved really are powerful tools for thinking. Souls alone do not think nearly as well.

Trauma experiences are another place where we can see significant breakdowns in the accessing ability of the information part of the mind chakra. Often people with trauma talk about seeing the experience from outside their bodies. (The technical term is dissociation.) I propose that in extreme situations the mind is unable to store experiences that it can later access. The negative energy associated with the memory is so great experiencing the event again might destroy the chakra.

When the memories resurface later (sometimes years later) as flashbacks, they are the memories from the other chakras making their way into the mind. In some ways this might be better considered as leakage into the mind chakra.

In talking with trauma survivors, I have noticed that some trauma memories come back in parts. In one case the physical pain was remembered first. Later, the hatred that surrounded the event was felt. Still later, the bad feeling about things being done totally against the victim's will emerged. I suggest that each of these was the memory of the experience stored in a different chakra. Having multiple records of the

---

* Note that this kind of measure suffers from something related to the Heisenberg uncertainty principle: The act of measuring the quantity affects the quantity itself.

same experience is one way to explain the fragmented nature of the memory.

We access the memories when they have great meaning for us. Unfortunately the memories that seem to have the greatest meaning are often memories of trauma. They are the ones that jump back to the surface when we have similar experiences and realize that our reactions are not what we think (with our mind) would be optimal. Sam Pappas' flashback is a prime example. Eric Newhouse[47] writes this:

> Sam Pappas was alarmed when he saw the armored deuce-and-a-half truck bristling with Panamanian soldiers parked in front of his house on a quiet suburban street in Great Falls, Montana. It was what he'd been afraid of ever since he returned from combat in Panama in 1989 with a mission to topple dictator Manuel Noriega and protect the Panama Canal. Since then, Pappas said he had spent most of his nights patrolling the perimeter of his home to make sure that the bad guys didn't sneak in and kidnap his children. During the day, he'd catnap a bit. And now, he'd let his guard down and they were about to attack in broad daylight.
>
> "I ran to the basement to the gun locker, but I couldn't find the key and I was beating on it to get it open," he said. "My daughter was home at the time and called 9-1-1. The cops came and I was in attack mode, but they talked me down and got me to an ambulance and restrained me. Thank God the gun locker was locked or I would have opened up on the ice cream man."
>
> That's called a flashback. The deuce-and-a-half truck that Pappas thought he saw was actually a Schwan's ice cream delivery truck, but the post-traumatic stress in his mind turned it into a kind of a living nightmare. Flashbacks have been described as a video that plays in your mind — you see it, hear it, feel it, smell it — but you can't turn it off.

We have another example at the end of Part III on page 248 of this book. Grant Leland was driving in his hometown and suddenly all he could see was a road he had patrolled in Iraq. Attention can focus on the memory while what is happening in the present is lost.

Flashbacks do not heal themselves. The person who is experiencing the flashback is so immersed in the experience that all the bad effects are there again. (Success is negative.) So, in fact, the flashbacks will keep getting worse without intervention.

We only see a change when the mind chakra and the chakra with the memory work together to heal the damage. Strong positive energy needs to come from somewhere to counteract the negative energy of the chakra. There are many possible sources of the energy. The most effective seems to come through the heart chakra. It can come in the form of good intentions or friendship or love.

Often a counselor is involved in the healing process and he or she will be communicating with words. The best counselors are the ones who understand that more than the brain and verbal representations are involved. They also send their caring and good intentions along with the message to the mind.

The chakra that is holding the traumatic experience has to have success (a positive situation) while focusing on the experience of the trauma. When that happens, the equations we talked about in the previous section can change the effect the traumatic experience has on us now. The memory of the trauma will always be there, but it will now be connected to situations besides the initial damage.

The appropriate time for the counseling process is also clear from this model. The bottom line is don't try to counsel a person while the problem is still going on. For example, counseling people about trauma while they are still in a shelter after a flood (fire, earthquake) has destroyed their home is a *bad* idea. There is nothing positive to work with. It's better to concentrate on getting back to normal life first: fixing the home, replacing furniture, returning to school or work. When there are positives, when the immediate problems of life are under control, that's the time to work through the trauma.[48]

Finding the right balance of current and past and putting the attention on the chakra that is holding the traumatic experience are the keys. Drugs miss on all counts. Talk therapy is often focused too much on the communication chakra. That's why a large variety of other techniques from logotherapy that uses faith to neurotherapy and EMDR (Eye-

Movement Desensitization and Reprocessing) seem to be more effective.[49]

Goal

The goal of a chakra reflects what the chakra would choose to be, if it could. It is not the same as a desire for the desire chakra, and it is different from the internal set point. What I am proposing is that a chakra has the ability to look at itself and have a goal for a new structure.

The new structure would include 13 of the elements that are part of a chakra, all except the goal element. While the goal is held by a chakra, there is a good chance that it comes from outside the chakra, most likely from another soul.

This is the kind of goal we see in counseling, where a therapist suggests another way of reacting to situations or a better way to interact with others. Some of the instruction is on individual actions, but I think the majority is suggesting a change in the structure of the chakras. If the chakra accepts the suggestion, it becomes a goal.

Gender Differences

Let's finish the chapter with something that shows the benefits of a theory that has energy and information stored in each chakra. It allows us to get a better handle on one of the great mysteries: Why is there a difference between Martians and Venusians?*

A friend, who shall remain nameless, suggested to me that women remember the emotional content of an interaction while men remember the words and actions of an interaction. He suggested that when women are remembering a past event, they create word content that goes along with the emotions they felt rather than remembering the actual words that were spoken. This leads to situations where a woman will say, "You called me a stupid bitch," when, in fact, the man said, "I think you might be wrong about that."

---

* Apologies to John Gray and his book, *Men are from Mars, Women Are from Venus.*

My friend's implication was that the male's ability to remember the exact words of a conversation is superior to remembering the emotions of the conversation.* Allow me to disagree.

From what we have discussed before it should be clear that my friend believes males remember this kind of conversation with their mind chakra and communication chakra. Women remember with their heart chakras. I think both types of memory have advantages and disadvantages.

In my friend's view, a male's mind chakra and communication chakra are able to remember exact events, as they would appear in a movie script. If required, males may fill in pieces they don't remember exactly so that the situation makes sense to them. Very little filling in is required in my friend's model. What males don't get out of these memories is how they felt when they were in the earlier situation. So the hypothetical males are required to reconstruct the emotions they felt from their memory of the conversation.

When my friend says that females remember the emotions, he grants them the ability to remember the emotions accurately. What he also says is that the females don't accurately remember the words that got them to the emotions, so they need to make up many of them.

In the example above, a real possibility is that the words were exactly as reported by the man. However, what the man doesn't remember (and might not have even been aware of at the time) is that, while he was speaking the non-confrontational words, his heart chakra was sending out, "God, what a stupid bitch!" The woman's memory of what was going on emotionally could be accurate, too.

The problem is that memories from different chakras, especially as remembered by different people, will often not agree. Both of the people will feel wronged because their memories are not being honored. No one wants to look at these details during an argument — sadly. During a calmer discussion, perhaps both people can look at where the other person's memory is coming from before they decide it is wrong. It's

---

* It turns out that this friend is actually not all that good at remembering the actual words of a conversation. Well, at least his memory of some of the conversations we have had is different from mine.

good for us to know what kinds of memories we recall accurately and what kinds we don't remember well.

7. External Chakra Connections

A man should look for what is, and not for what he thinks should be.

— *Albert Einstein*

At a given instant in our existence, our soul is in a particular state. Each chakra has a certain amount of life force, a certain ability to send out and receive life force, and a certain desired level of life force in the world around us and in the chakra itself. If the chakra or the outside world are not in the desired states, the chakra will try to adjust them.

We are able to calculate the interactions between the chakra and the outside world with the information about structure that we have already. The energy and information components of life force exist in both places and can flow in either direction, either moving out of the chakra into the outside world or moving from the outside world into the chakra.

Outward Flow

The outward flow of life force will depend on four things: the amount of life force available to the chakra, the ability of the chakra to send life force into the outside world, the chakra's feeling for how much of this particular kind of life force should be in the outside world, and the intention of the chakra to send out life force.

The more life force the chakra has available, the more it will be able to affect the outside world. Life force may be available in the chakra itself, or the chakra may have the ability to pull life force from outside sources and channel it in a particular direction. The higher its ability to transfer life force, the faster the life force will flow. The greater the difference between what the chakra sees as the ideal state on the outside and the current state, the longer it will take to change the outside. In cases where the potential life force flow seems like it is more than is required, chakras can limit the amount of life force sent out so it is what the situation requires.

How that works should be fairly obvious. A chakra can transfer life force to something outside itself. What is outside can be another person, an animal, a plant, or something inanimate like a work of art. The particular kind of information that can be transferred as part of the life force transfer will depend on which chakra is sending the information out and the capabilities of the receiver. The act of writing this book involves a transfer of life force* from inside me to the keyboard, then into the document, and finally out to you as you read it. Once I put the life force in the book, I believe my part of the task is finished. At that time the life force is in the book and it's your responsibility to take as much as you want.

It is not necessary for a chakra to have more life force than the outside world for it to transfer life force from the chakra to the outside. We are capable of draining our life force down to nothing when we are committed to getting something accomplished. Doing that is probably not the wisest decision we can make. *Amadeus*, the movie (or play) about Mozart's life and death, delivers a powerful message about completely draining one's life force to accomplish a goal. Mozart died before he could finish his Requiem.

When we look at the speed life force can be transferred, we are concerned with the outward ability aspect of a chakra, its ability to transfer life force out. Some people wish very badly to do something in

---

* Hopefully some life force from the mind and some from the heart. I wouldn't feel badly if the gods were inspiring me through the spirit chakra or if energy from chaos came through, too.

the world, but they feel blocked in some way. They may not have the energy to fight the status quo. They may not know how to show their love effectively. They may have brilliant thoughts but not be able to find the words to express them. In all those cases some chakra (lower abdomen, heart, throat, in that order) is not able to transfer life force out.

Other times the life force is transferred faster than it can be absorbed. From the middle of the 20th century, we have been hearing that people (society) can't keep up with the rapid pace of innovation. That might be one example of more coming out of the mind chakras of our inventive folks than the rest of the population can absorb. Another example that is going on as I write this book is the manic life force coming out of Charlie Sheen.* It's a case of intention gone wild.

The ability to transfer life force is something like the ability of water to flow through a hose. The larger the hose, the more water can flow through. When we are effectively in control of our chakras, we can control the flow so that we don't overwhelm the person we are sending the life force to. It's something like the spigot on a hose.

Sometimes it's necessary to apply your full power. Professional athletes are usually going all out through the will chakra because everybody performs at such a high level of skill. On the other hand, when you are playing checkers with a five-year-old, it's probably a good idea to hold back on the amount of mental energy you send out of the mind chakra so the kid doesn't get too discouraged to continue. The decision to limit the amount of life force coming out of a chakra is called its intention.

The ability of a chakra to transfer life force out is relatively constant. The chakra starts with a certain amount of ability, probably something that it carries over from previous lives. We learn to transfer more life

---

* Charlie Sheen is/was a well-known actor whose apparent bipolar disorder caused him and those around him a great deal of trouble in 2011. He took his problems on the road and did shows to demonstrate the level of his comic genius. His audiences didn't always agree. I suggest that too much life force came through the chaos chakra into the mind chakra, which overloaded the throat and heart to the extent that he lost the ability to communicate effectively and to understand the feelings of others. Everything was going out and nothing was coming in.

force as we have experiences with sending it out. In some complicated way sending life force increases the ability to send life force. We learn to make better connections, which means life force can flow faster as the connections get stronger.

We also have experience where we send life force out and something bad happens because of it. The flow can be damaged in ways that do not recover easily. If we continue with the hose analogy, it's like getting a kink in the hose.

I want to make it clear before we go on that I don't really think life force transfer out of a chakra is like water flowing through a hose. There is no physical or spiritual object associated with a chakra to contain the flow. With a hose, it doesn't matter where the water is flowing. The flow depends on the qualities of the hose. With a chakra the flow depends on the connection between the sending chakra and the chakra receiving the energy. For an example let's take a look at our ability to love. We don't change in our intrinsic ability to love, but there are some people we find it easy to care about and other people we don't find at all lovable.

The third aspect of outward flow is the difference between what we want and what is actually in the world. If there is only a little bit of difference between what we see as the ideal state and our perception of how things are now, it doesn't take long to send that life force into the system and cause a change. If there is a big difference, it can take a lot of life force from our chakra to make a change. In the most difficult kinds of cases, we can be trying to change a whole culture. The life force required to do something like that can seem beyond the life force available to any single person. However, we know that cultures do change in ways that seem impossible, simply through the ongoing, long-term work of one person.

If the change is successful, one person recruits a second person, then a third, until there is enough life force in the system to support the new viewpoint. Founders of the world's religions (Jesus, Buddha, and Mohamed, for example) are obvious examples, but we can also look at Galileo's revolutionary view of the solar system to see how changes happen. The computer revolution that is happening during our lives started with an idea that spread from a small group of people to billions. A huge social revolution is also taking place at the beginning of the 21st

century. Woman's rights are spreading throughout the world and gay rights are spreading throughout the US. There has been tremendous resistance from entrenched culture to both of these movements. The final outcome is still uncertain, but studying the life force from supporters of change and defenders of the status quo provides valuable lessons in the use of the heart chakra to change the social structure.

There are two aspects of the gay rights situation that demonstrate some interesting points about chakras, in general, and the heart chakra, in particular. The first is the question of whether we can know if the life force in a chakra is positive or negative. The second is whether negative life force in a chakra can be used to make the situation in the world more positive (or whether positive life force can make the world more negative).

In the gay rights situation I see two clearly divided groups. One is strongly anti-gay and the other accepts the lifestyle.

The radical version of the anti-gay faction says that the gay lifestyle is an abomination and gays should be removed from the face of the earth. A milder version allows a person to be gay, but the lifestyle should never be practiced. The follow-on to that is that God will take care of punishing the person when He makes His judgment after the gay person dies.

The other side either is gay or sees being gay as just another sexual state of being. The desire chakra, for whatever reason, is wired differently. The attraction is to a person of the same sex instead of a person of the opposite sex. This side accepts the idea of being gay.

It is clear that a gay person will feel different aspects of the life force from the two groups, just as a person fighting the gay movement will also feel different aspects of the life force. We can say for sure that the life force from one group is negative relative to the life force from the other group, but can we find an absolute scale of positive and negative?

Let's take a closer look at the situation. A gay couple is using the heart chakra to form a bond, presumably for the benefit of both of the people.* Those who accept the gay lifestyle will, in general, support the

---

* If this is one of those desire chakra things, just for the sex, we might feel the same way about the situation as we would when a heterosexual couple has an affair — disapproving because of the harm the affair is causing to others.

relationship and help it succeed. Generally they will be providing the support through their heart chakras. (There are many little details about what might be going on that would affect the support. I'm going to stay with the overall situation.) The argument here is that as long as it's doing no harm, the behavior should be allowed.

Those who do not accept the gay lifestyle will be using life force from the will chakra to try to prevent the actions of the heart chakra in the gay couple. Sometimes they do actual harm to the couple to make sure their will is followed. The usual reason given for this is that God has said He doesn't approve of this lifestyle. (This information would be available by connecting with God through the spirit chakra and then relaying the information to the will chakra for implementation.) The argument is that God needs humans to enforce His laws on earth.

I think the two crucial differences in the situation are the parts where humans are acting in God's name and the effect of using one chakra to affect something that is based in another chakra. I'm going to leave the question until we look at the interactions of two entities and the differences between connections that use the same chakra and connections that use different chakras.

This still leaves the question of whether it's possible to use positive life force to make an external situation more negative or vice versa. I believe the answer for a particular chakra is no. In the gay lifestyle question this would mean that approval (from the heart chakra) of a gay relationship would not be able to make the love in the relationship less. It would also mean that hate (from the heart chakra) of a gay relationship would not make the love greater. When the point is raised (correctly) that opposition to a relationship will often make the relationship stronger, I reply: It's the will chakra that is providing the opposition. It's the will chakra of the people in the relationship that is making the relationship stronger. The heart chakra doesn't need to change.*

---

* This is famous parenting advice, "If your daughter is going out with a total jerk, don't try to break up the relationship. It will just make her more likely to stay with the guy. Just fill up her heart with your love and her heart will have the energy to figure out on its own."

So here's the bottom line for me. If a chakra is in a negative state, it can only make the outside world more negative. If the chakra has positive life force, it can only make the world more positive.

There are several things that we might want to calculate regarding the outward flow of life force from a chakra. They include the maximum amount of life force that can come out of the chakra and the amount of life force actually coming out of the chakra, the amount of change in the life force of the chakra, the amount of change in the life force in the world, and the time it will take to bring about a certain amount of change.

The maximum amount of life force that can come out of the chakra is the available life force (LFA) — from either the stored life force or through channeling — limited by the outward ability (OA)

$$LF_{max} = LFA[lim]OA$$

The amount of life force actually coming out of the chakra toward each of the targets of the life force (LF_i) can be calculated by looking at the total amount of life force the chakra intends to send out (OI_{total}) and reducing it so that the total life force going out is limited by the maximum life force (LF_{max})

$$OI_{total} = \sum_{i=1}^{intended\ targets} OI_i$$

if $LF_{max} < OI_{total}$ then

$$LF_i = LF_{max} * \frac{OI_i}{OI_{total}}$$

else

$$LF_i = OI_i$$

endif

The amount of change in the life force of the chakra because of life force going out is calculated by subtracting the life force going out from the life force in the chakra. (Life force may also be flowing in, but we'll talk about that later.)

$$SLF(t+1) = SLF(t) - \sum_{i=1}^{\text{intended targets}} (LF_i)$$

The amount of change in the life force in the world (WLF) is the energy flowing into the world reduced by the connection strength (CS), which we will specify in Part III.

$$WLF(t+1) = WLF(t) + \sum_{i=1}^{\text{intended targets}} (LF_i * CS_i)$$

The time (CT) it will take to bring about a certain amount of life force change (ΔLF) in a particular target is found by figuring out how many time intervals it will take to get that much life force out into the world given the current flow rate (LF).

$$CT_i = \frac{\Delta LF_i}{LF_i}$$

Outward Ability

Outward ability (OA) is made up of two aspects. The first (outward ability to send, OAS) is the maximum amount of life force the chakra is able to send out. The second (outward ability to block, OAB) is the chakra's ability to stop life force from being taken. Let's take a look at how these work.

Outward ability to send is the simplest. It doesn't depend on the situation or the person we are interacting with. It is a basic measure of the maximum ability we have to send life force out through a chakra.

We can compare it to our physical strength. There are some problems with this comparison because there are times when we show exceptional strength in emergency conditions. Think about physical strength in "ordinary" circumstances and you will have a better idea what I am describing. (What is "ordinary," you might ask? That's an excellent question that I'm going to ignore.)

At any given moment we have a certain amount of physical strength. We can lift one pound or 1000 pounds, depending on how strong we are.[50] In the same way we can send life force out from a chakra. We don't always send out the maximum amount, just as we don't always exert our maximum strength, but this is the ability we have.

Just as we can increase our physical strength, we can increase our ability to send out more life force from a chakra. Athletic trainers have a pretty good idea how to increase an athlete's abilities. At some basic level, we improve by repeating an activity many times with increasing levels of effort. We build up our physical muscles so they can do more.

In the same way we can increase the ability of our chakras to make them "stronger." (This is especially apt for the will chakra. A better term for most of the chakras would probably be "more effective." In the communication chakra we learn to express ourselves better. In the heart chakra we learn to show our caring more effectively.) We do it by having the intention to use the chakra more effectively and by acting on that intention.* I believe improvement in our ability happens faster when we are working in the upper range of our current maximum ability. This is similar to how we increase physical strength.

The change in ability in any given time interval is a function of how much we are trying to increase our ability. Increases happen more quickly when we are trying to send out energy at a rate closer to our current maximum ability. If we are not trying to increase the ability, there will be no change.

$$OAS(t+1) = OAS(t) + a * \left(1 - \left(\left(OAS(t) - |LF_o(t)|\right) / OAS(t)\right)\right)$$

where LF_o is the outward flow and a is a constant that describes how fast the outward ability changes.

The maximum outward ability for a chakra depends on how much we have "exercised" the chakra throughout all of our incarnations. Exercised is defined as getting close to the maximum outward ability. We are summing up all of the changes described in the previous equation. Note that outward ability is constantly increasing with this model.

$$OAS_{now} = \sum_{t=0}^{now} a * \left(1 - \left(\left(OAS(t) - |LF_o(t)|\right) / OAS(t)\right)\right)$$

---

* I'm leaving out the complication that would arise if we consider the possibility of different abilities to send out negative and positive life force. Outward ability in the definition I'm using is the maximum of the absolute value of outward negative ability and the absolute value of the outward positive ability.

The analogy of outward ability to physical strength leads to the interesting question of whether we can "pull a chakra" the same way we pull a muscle by trying to do too much. I don't think chakras can be damaged by our own efforts. (I may be wrong about that.) I do know that trying to increase outward abilities can sometimes lead to aches and pains similar to a heavy workout. I am leaving open the question of whether outward ability can decrease. Our outward intention and outward set point can both decrease. Because of those effects it's hard to see if there is a change in outward ability.

The second aspect of outward ability is the ability to block something outside us from taking life force that we don't want to give. I think most of us have experienced the type of person who tries to "suck the energy out of us." It's a great expression because I think the person really is trying to suck a particular type of chakra life force out of us. Another term for this type of person is energy vampire.

I believe the concept of boundaries can be explained by combining the outward ability to block discussed here and the inward ability to block, described later in this chapter. Boundaries are usually defined as conscious and healthy mechanisms we develop to make sure that other people do not cause us emotional harm. We sense when someone has "stepped over the line" because it feels like the other person is trying to do something that would be unhealthy for us. A sense of boundaries let's us know that we need to stop the interaction to protect ourselves. In chakra terms, this would be sensing that someone is trying to take life force from us or use life force to make us do something that wouldn't be healthy for us. When our inward and outward ability to block is in place, we can adequately protect our boundaries.

Each chakra has a certain amount of ability to stop someone or something else from taking life force that we don't want to give. As with the ability to send life force, I think the ability to block life force from escaping increases as we exercise the ability. Each time we successfully recognize and restrict the energy draw we get better at deciding the life force that goes out from us.

The change in ability in any given time interval is a function of how strong the outward draw (LF_D) is. Increases happen more quickly when we block a force at a strength closer to our current maximum ability. If we are not in a situation where something is trying to draw energy from us, there will be no change.

$$OAB(t+1) = OAB(t) + a * \left(1 - \left(\left(OAB(t) - \left|LF_D(t)\right|\right)/OAB(t)\right)\right)$$

$$OAB(t) \geq \left|LF_D(t)\right|$$

where a is a constant that describes how fast the outward ability can change.

Unlike the outward ability to send, I believe the outward ability to block can be broken. We can lose our ability to block the flow of life force to another person or in a particular situation. If we can leave the situation that is harming our ability, there is a chance that the chakra's ability to block escaping life force can recover. If we can't leave the situation, healing probably can't occur.

The change in ability in any given time interval is a function of how strong the sucking force is. Decreases happen more quickly when the force we are trying to block is much stronger than our current maximum ability. If we are not in a situation where something is trying to draw energy from us, there will be no change.

$$OAB(t+1) = OAB(t) + a * \left(\left(OAB(t) - \left|LF_D(t)\right|\right)/OAB(t)\right),$$

$$OAB(t) < \left|LF_D(t)\right|$$

where a is a constant that describes how fast the outward ability can change.

Our ability to stop energy from being stolen from us depends on all that has happened to us in the past. The maximum blocking ability for a chakra depends on how much we have "exercised" the chakra and how much it has been damaged throughout all of our incarnations.

We are summing up all of the changes described in the previous two equations.

$$OAB_{now} = \sum_{t=0}^{now} \Delta OAB(t)$$

with $\Delta OAB(t)$ as described in the previous two equations.

If we are in situations where the drawing force is so strong that the ability to block goes negative, that chakra will be throwing life force away. Death is the most likely result. The more typical case is the one where someone can steal life force from us at will, but we can block the outward life force flow to other people. In that situation the best option seems to be avoiding the person who drains our life force until we rebuild our ability to block the outward flow of life force so that it is strong enough to block the flow to the person who has been stealing it.

Another aspect of the outward ability that is similar to physical strength is that it varies from day to day. Some days we feel really strong; some days our thinking (mind chakra) is crystal clear. Other days we might be sick, sleepy, hung over, or hungry. On those days we don't feel as strong and we don't have as much ability to send life force out from a chakra. So our apparent ability at any given time may be less than our maximum ability.

The apparent outward ability is a function of our outward ability modified by our current state of being (CSB). The current state of physical being probably affects each chakra in a similar way.

$$OA_{apparent} = CSB * OA$$

Emotions (happy, angry, sad, horny) can make a difference, too, but I think they are how one chakra affects another chakra, which is something we will look at in the next chapter.

Physical strength increases up to about age 28 and decreases as we age more. This is certainly a part of having a physical body. I don't believe there is a similar decline in the outward ability of the chakras themselves, but it seems like a good reason to get a new body when the warranty on the current one expires. I think the outward ability stays about the same from one life to the next, but measuring the change across lifetimes is beyond anything we can do now.

Outward Set Point

The outward ability, described above, is what you can do. The outward set point is what you want to do. There needs to be a balance between the outward set point and the inward set point so that the life force level in the chakra is maintained somewhere near the internal set point. While outward ability is changed slowly over time, the outward set point is changed more quickly based on success in day-to-day interactions. Some examples may help to explain this.

When some people walk into a room, they take it over. Everyone feels the life force and starts to pay attention. The way people take over a group varies a lot. Some come into the room with bubbling joy and instantly everyone feels happy. Bill Cosby comes to mind as someone with this kind of life force. Others come in and people get nervous. ("Oh crap, it's my mother-in-law/ex-wife/boss*!") They seem to radiate evil intent, especially toward the people in the room and the people in the room react to that. In other situations the person who comes in offers brilliant insights or clever ideas that everyone wants to try to understand. Richard Feynman was like that. So was George Carlin.

Each of these people has a very high outward set point for at least one of their chakras. We feel the life force coming out of the person — sometimes positive, sometimes negative — always powerful.

Contrast that with the people who hardly seem to be there. If we notice them at all, it's fleeting and we never have a sense that we know anything about the person. We may use words like shy, timid, quiet, and withdrawn to describe them. Their outward set point is low. Very little life force goes from them to us.

It is not clear whether the lack of life force flow is caused by a lack of energy or a severely low outward set point. When people are depressed, they may have very little life force. Even if they have a high outward set point, they don't have any life force in them to flow out.

Other people may have life force, but they don't choose to share it. Perhaps they have been hurt by "giving too much," so they shut down the flow. Perhaps their general experience is that letting people know that they exist leads to bad consequences. Children of abusers often have this reaction. People with eating disorders, especially anorexia, are said to have "small emotions." The life force inside isn't necessarily small, but what gets to the surface for the world to see is consistently restricted. For whatever reason, these people have very low outward set points most of the time.

---

* Not Bruce Springsteen.

Where each of us puts his or her outward set point is based on several factors. The primary one is how successful we have been when we sent out life force in the past. It doesn't matter if the life force we sent was positive or negative. It doesn't matter how we define success. (Getting people to laugh at our jokes and getting a new friend are successes. Getting our way by being a jerk and making everyone as miserable as we are can be successes, too.). What matters is that showing emotions had the effect we wanted. There are four cases:

- When we get the desired effect by sending out more life force than normal, the outward set point will go up.
- When we don't get the desired effect by sending out more life force, the outward set point will go down.
- When we get the desired effect by sending out less life force than we usually do, the outward set point will go down.
- When we don't get the desired effect by sending out less life force, the outward set point will go up.

Outward set point changes based on the success we have when we send out life force. Success (S) can be positive or negative. LF_S is the energy actually sent.

$$OSP(t+1) = (OSP(t) + a * S(t) * (LF_s(t) - OSP(t)))[lim]OA(t)$$

where a is a weighting factor describing how quickly we change OSP.

The outward set point (OSP) is, of course, limited by our outward ability. We can't choose to do more than we actually can do.

Another factor is how much life force we have. Sometimes our positive life force level is so high that we can't help bubbling over with energy. "Bubbling over" is a great term for the experience, because it implies that no matter what our usual outward set point is, we exceed that with life force that goes over the top.* (Extra life force means that our life force level is above our internal set point.) This is the case when we get a lot of positive life force and we have a positive OSP. There are three other cases.

---

* You can think of a dam with a normal water flow through the sluice gates and water going over the spillway because there has been a lot of rain upstream.

The second case is when we have an excess of negative life force and a negative OSP. We need to dump the excess, so we make everyone else even more miserable than usual.

The third case is having a lot of negative life force when we have a positive OSP. It's possible that we will shift to a negative OSP and dump the excess negative life force on others to make them miserable, too, but that isn't going to be the usual case. Normally the fact that we have no positive life force means that we won't send out any life force at all. The negative life force is all we have available and we block it with our outward intention, which we will discuss next, so that we don't send negative life force out. Friends will notice and, hopefully, send positive life force to take care of the negative life force we have.

The fourth case is when we have a negative OSP. (We like to make people miserable.) Then something makes us happy. This is like the third case in reverse. Rather than giving out our positive life force to our friends, we stuff it with our outward intention and immediately try to find something that will make our life force negative again.

Some call this self-sabotage and have difficulty understanding why the person would act that way. It's actually pretty clear that it's hard to act differently. Only in extraordinary circumstances will a person have so much excess positive life force that it bubbles over enough to make the actual life force flow be positive. Then the person has to achieve success when giving out the positive life force. Then it has to last long enough for the OSP to move from negative to positive, because it doesn't move instantly. And all the while, the person is fighting to gather in negative life force to get back to his or her usual set point. The end result is that people who sabotage themselves are very likely to continue with that behavior regardless of what anyone tries to do to help.

The base OSP probably doesn't actually change much, but we can find an excess outward life force that is a temporary change in the OSP caused by the excess life force in the chakra.

The excess OSP is the difference in stored life force level and the internal set point of the chakra.

$$OSP_{excess} = SLF - IntSP$$

The set point for the outward life force flow at the current time is the OSP at the current time plus the excess OSP.

$$OSP = \left(OSP_{base} + OSP_{excess}\right)[lim]OA$$

It is possible for this set point to be higher than the outward ability. In that case the energy going out will be limited by the outward ability.

Outward Intention

Outward intention describes the amount of life force we choose to give at any given instant. It can change during our interaction with one person and it certainly changes as we focus our attention on different people in the group we are with or different tasks we are performing. The outward intention usually averages out to be our outward set point. Each of us chooses how much we will let the outward flow vary in relation to the set point. Some people vary a lot between situations; others seem to be the same all the time.

Two things related to outward intention are very important. One is that outward intention changes the fastest of all the outward aspects. It's like the signal on the carrier wave. The second is that it's an array of values rather than a single value like the outward set point. We have an outward intention toward everything our chakra is connected to, regardless of whether it is physically present or not.

Outward intention is an array with one element for every connection the chakra currently holds. It's a lot of elements. Some are active and some are not part of the current situation. Each connection that is active has an outward intention value that modifies the outward set point relative to the particular connection.

$$OI = \left\{OI_1, OI_2, \ldots\right\}$$

where OI_c is the outward intention to a particular connection

Again it might be helpful to look at an example.

If we are in a situation where we are spending the evening with good friends, we should expect a lot of activity in the heart chakra. Basically we will be giving a lot of heart life force (love) and getting a lot of heart life force back. The outward set point will be open most of the time, as will the inward set point, so the life force can flow. The best part of this kind of situation is that at the end of the evening there is usually more heart life force than there was at the beginning of the evening. We either generate the life force as we interact or it flows to us from some reservoir in the universe.

Most people seem to prefer having high life force flows in the heart chakra. (It's not necessarily true for every chakra and it's not true for everybody in the heart chakra.) There is something about sharing love that feels right to most people. So when the situation is appropriate, we usually open up the flow.

If a friend who is usually there is missing, some of the life force will be flowing that direction, even though the person isn't there. If there is concern about the person, a lot of life force can be flowing.

Now let's add a friend to the mix who needs exceptional amounts of love energy. Maybe they are just breaking up with a partner or they have suffered some other kind of loss. In the group setting they will usually need more love energy than they have to give back. Friends are good sources of this kind of life force, so each will share more with the friend than they get back, but no one will be especially drained. Given that the situation usually generates life force, there may still be enough heart energy to increase it for everyone, but probably not as much as it would have been if everyone was happy.

It's a different situation if this friend always needs love energy. Then the friend is just a sink for the life force of the group. At some point people in the group may get tired of the support they are giving and lower their outward intention relative to that person. Less life force flows in the direction of the person who is seen as too needy. Life force can still flow to other members of the group because outward intention changes depending on who is the target of the energy. If you pay attention to your feelings in this kind of situation, you will probably feel yourself shut down relative to a life-force-draining person who comes into the room.

The exception to shutting down when you are around a life-force-draining person occurs when that person is able to overcome your ability to block your outward life force flow. In that case your life force flows out whether you want it to or not.

Another thing to notice is that we connect differently with different members of a group. With one there might be an intense physical attraction. With another we enjoy good conversation. Some are good friends and others are not.

The point to get from the example is that we switch our outward life force flow as we interact with each of the people. We have a normal way of interacting, but around that average we may vary a great deal depending on the exact situation we are in. That rapid change is reflected in the outward intention.

One of the characteristics of outward intention is how quickly it changes. For some people the change takes place in an instant. Other people take a long time to change. Paul Ekman[51] has done research in the field of emotional response related to anger. He found that people vary along a continuum in how quickly they get angry. Some go off like a stick of dynamite while others do a slow boil. Similarly people take different amounts of time to get over anger. For some it happens quickly while others stay angry for a long time. Ekman found three other characteristics of anger: the intensity of the anger, how quickly it went away once it started to subside, and the frequency of angry episodes. He found that there was no strong correlation between any of the characteristics. For example, a person who got angry quickly was equally likely to stay angry a long time or get over it quickly.

From Ekman's work we can guess that outward intention has similar characteristics. To understand the details of how a person's outward intention functions, we probably need to look at how quickly it starts up, how long it lasts, how quickly it falls off when the situation changes, and how intense the reaction is. For this book it is enough to note that the characteristics exist. If you are using the ideas in this book to understand people better, looking at these factors in outward intention will help clarify some of the ways people differ in their interactions with people and situations.

If we are going to calculate outward intention, we need to understand what causes it to change. I believe it is based on the previous history with the person (or situation*). We move toward the level of outward life force flow that we normally have with the person. It changes because of what happened. For each event we increase or decrease the outward intention for this connection as a result of what happened. As always, positive results will cause us to do more of what we are doing. Negative results will cause us to do less. During an event, we increase, stay at a level, and decrease in ways that are related to the work Ekman did on people's experience of anger.

Outward intention to a particular connection changes based on what has happened in the relationship.

$$OI(t_2) = \left(OI(t_1) + \int_{t=t_1}^{t_2} a * S(t) * (LF_s(t) - OI(t)) \right) [\lim] OA(t_2)$$

where a is how quickly the outward intention can change.

When considering how the changes will occur during an event, each person has a characteristic time signature for ramping up, duration, and ramping down. For any particular event there will be a curve represented by the amplitude as a function of time, Amp(t).

$$OI(t) = OI_0 * Amp(t)$$

To determine where the life force of a particular chakra is flowing, we need to divide up the life force that is available (generally the outward set point) in proportion to the outward intention for each of the connections. Two considerations are important here.

- Current focus. As we shift our attention from one thing to another, we send a larger portion of the life force to what we are focusing on.
- The surroundings. We seldom lose contact with what is around us even when we are concentrating intently on one person. Usually the surroundings have a significant effect on our life force flow, since life force can flow to many places all at the same time.

---

* "Situation" refers to a very specific set of circumstances. In Paris or with Ilsa is not specific enough. It probably needs to be in Paris with Ilsa at the foot of the Eiffel Tower just as the sun is setting. The farther the current situation is from the last time, the less similar our outward intention will be.

The simple case would be that the life force is divided proportionally. I don't see any reason at this time to look for something more complicated. This is complicated enough.

Outward intention for a particular connection helps to set the amount of life force that flows into that connection. Our outward set point (OSP) is how much total life force we want to send out. When the total of our outward intentions (OI) is greater than our outward set point, the life force for each connection is reduced so that the life force to each is in the same ratio as our original outward intentions, but the total is reduced to our outward set point.

$$\text{if } OSP < \sum_{c=1}^{allconnections} OI_c \text{ then}$$

$$LF_c = OSP * \frac{OI_c}{\sum_{c=1}^{allconnections} OI_c}$$

else

$$LF_c = OI_c$$

endif

where c is a particular connection

The fact that we are sending life force out does not mean that it is received. We will look at the factors of connection that come into play in Part III. Lost life force is still flowing out, it just doesn't reach its target.

Inward Flow

In the same way as the outward flow of life force, the inward flow of life force depends on four things: the amount of life force in the chakra relative to the maximum amount it can store, the ability of the chakra to bring in life force from the outside world, the chakra's feeling for how much life force it should have, and the intention of the chakra to bring in life force.

The more life force capacity the chakra has (and the lower its current life force stores), the more it will be able to bring in from the outside world. The higher its ability to transfer life force, the faster the life force will flow. The greater the difference between what the chakra sees as its ideal life force state and its current life force state, the longer it will take to change the life force state of the chakra. In cases where the potential life force flow seems like it is more than is required, chakras try to limit the amount of life force brought in to keep it at a comfortable level.

The way life force comes into a chakra is similar to the way life force is sent out of a chakra. The chakra has a connection to something in the outside world. It can be a person, animal, creative work like music or a book, or any other thing that can contain a particular kind of life force. Through the connection a chakra is able to absorb life force up to its maximum capacity.

Life force of a chakra can be either positive or negative, so it is possible for a chakra to absorb the kind of life force in the thing it is connected to. The idea of ending up in a bummer from absorbing bad vibes is explained by this aspect of chakra functioning.* If a chakra is bringing in life force from a negative influence, the life force in the chakra will get more negative, even moving from positive to negative. Bringing in life force from a positive source can reduce negative life force in a chakra and increase positive life force. The folk wisdom that we should surround ourselves with positive people to make our lives better (or to give us strength and support) is in agreement with this model of chakra function.

The absorption of life force has two limits. The first is the maximum capacity of the chakra. While the maximum capacity can change over a person's lifetime, it is relatively constant over a small experience set.† So there is a maximum amount of life force that can be absorbed.

The other limit is the amount of life force in the outside source. A person's chakra can't absorb more life force from the outside world than is there to absorb. It's an interesting question whether a person can absorb positive life force, get the source down to zero, and then absorb more life force in a way that turns the source negative. The other

---

* Explaining "bummer" and "bad vibes" involves having grown up during the sixties, watching stoner movies from that era, or reading the era's great literature, such as Tom Wolfe's (1982) *Electric Kool-Aid Acid Test,* which is about Ken Kesey and the Merry Pranksters. Basically the idea is that you can get into a bad state of mind from being in a place where negative influences prevail.
† Some might say period of time, but time doesn't exist the same way in all the chakras.

possibility is that when the source hits zero that's all that can be absorbed. I think both situations can occur, but moving from positive to negative only happens in entities capable of self-reflection.

There are two aspects to how quickly a chakra can absorb life force. One is the inward ability and the other is the inward intention. Inward ability describes the maximum inward flow rate. It is a function of experience in the same way as outward ability. Inward intention describes how the chakra chooses to limit the amount of life force that is flowing in. In a healthy situation, a chakra can choose to accept positive life force and reject negative life force (unless the person likes chakras full of negative energy and then it works the other way around).

The final aspect of getting life force from outside involves the chakra's preferred life force level. Chakras do not necessarily prefer to be as full of life force as they can. There are times when a chakra will be below the desired life force level, but there are also times when the chakra will have more life force than it is comfortable with. Decisions will be made about what to do with available outside life force based on the current life force in the chakra and its preferred life force level.

Generally when we think of life force, we are considering the energy component rather than the information component. However, the information component is also important. One example here is the concept of "too much information." We sometimes prefer to limit the amount of information we are receiving. On the outward flow side we have the similar situation of "I've just got to tell you this" as a way of releasing too much information.

The maximum amount of life force coming into the chakra is the life force in the outside world limited by the inward ability (IA)

$$LF_{max} = LF_{world} \left[\text{lim} \right] IA$$

The amount of life force coming into the chakra from each of the sources of life force (LF_i) can be calculated by looking at the total amount of life force the chakra intends to bring in (II) and reducing it so that the total life force coming in ($LF_{intended}$) is limited by the maximum amount of life force in the outside world (LF_{max}).

$$\text{II}_{\text{total}} = \sum_{i=1}^{\text{intended targets}} \text{II}_i$$

$$\text{if } \text{LF}_{\text{max}} < \text{II}_{\text{total}} \text{ then}$$

$$\text{LF}_i = \text{LF}_{\text{max}} * \frac{\text{II}_i}{\text{II}_{\text{total}}}$$

else

$$\text{LF}_i = \text{II}_i \qquad .$$

endif

The amount of change in the life force of the chakra from life force coming in is calculated from the life force that actually comes into the chakra. (Life force may also be flowing out, but that is not shown in this calculation.)

$$\text{SLF}(t+1) = \text{SLF}(t) + \sum_{i=1}^{\text{all intended sources}} \text{LF}_i$$

The amount of change in the life force in the world (WLF) is the life force flowing in reduced by the connection strength (CS), which we will specify in Part III.

$$\text{WLF}(t+1) = \text{WLF}(t) - \sum_{i=1}^{\text{all intended sources}} (\text{LF}_i * \text{CS}_i)$$

The time (CT) it will take to bring about a certain amount of change in a particular target is calculated by seeing how many time intervals the current flow will take to make the desired change.

$$\text{CT}_i = \frac{\Delta \text{LF}_i}{\text{LF}_i}$$

Any time we talk about world life force, we need to realize that the world is a big place with lots of life force moving around. It's not clear that life force we take from the world affects the world as a whole very much. It may have a significant effect on a particular source. This is different from the case where life force is going out of a chakra into the world. In that case the life force can be focused on particular targets in ways that help even more life force flow toward the target. The net result is that long-term concentration on a task can accomplish a major change and that there will almost always be enough life force to get it done. The most limiting factor is likely to be the inward and outward ability of the chakra.

Inward Ability

There seem to be two aspects to the inward ability of a chakra. The first is the ability of the chakra to accept life force from outside sources. It is similar to outward ability in that it represents a maximum capacity. This can change with time. The second is the ability to block life force aimed at the chakra. As we grow up, we experience other people sending life force to us or using their life force on us to try to make us do something. The second aspect of inward ability measures how well we can limit the life force coming in and stop forces outside us from affecting us. It is the mirror image of the aspect of the outward ability that lets us block someone from taking life force from us and is the second aspect of having psychological boundaries.

Let's call the first aspect the inward ability to accept life force (IAA). The best case seems to be that we can accept as much life force as possible. There are advantages to being able to accept a lot of life force, so increasing our capacity seems to be the goal. We still have the ability to limit the life force coming in when that is appropriate with the inward set point and inward intention (depending on our ability to block inward life force flow).

As with outward ability the change in inward ability to accept life force in any given time interval is a function of how much we are trying to increase our ability. Increases happen more quickly when we are trying to pull in life force at a rate closer to our current maximum ability. If we are not trying to increase the ability, there will be no change.

$$IAA(t+1) = IAA(t) + a * \left(1 - \left(\left(IAA(t) - \left|LF_i(t)\right|\right) / IAA(t)\right)\right)$$

where a is a constant that describes how fast the inward ability to accept life force changes.

The ability to block inward life force flow is an important part of differentiating ourselves from other people. We describe situations where we are "forced to do something against our will" and when we are "smothered with love." I suggest that both of these describe a situation where a chakra's ability to block life force was overwhelmed by the force coming in from the outside.*

One situation where we need to learn to block life force coming in is where there is a lot of negative life force coming our way as we are growing up. Perhaps all we hear is criticism. Maybe our parents were always telling us what to do, so we didn't learn to make decisions for ourselves. As we got older, the preferred situation was that it was possible to block more and more from the outside.

When we successfully block inward life force flow, our ability to block the flow in the future increases. The closer we are to our limits, the more we increase our ability.

The change in inward ability to block life force is a function of how close we are to our maximum ability. The closer we are, the faster our ability increases

$$IAB(t+1) = IAB(t) + a * \left(1 - \left(\left(IAB(t) - |LF_i(t)|\right)/IAB(t)\right)\right),$$

as long as $IAB(t) \geq |LF_i(t)|$

where a is a constant that describes how fast the inward ability to accept energy changes.

If the situation is overwhelming and we are unable to block the inward life force flow, our ability to block the flow in the future decreases. The more we are overwhelmed, the greater the damage to our ability to block inward flow in the future. In a sense we are burning out the chakra's ability to block life force coming in.

The inward ability to block life force may eventually be completely broken. In this case the person has not been able to separate from others (or a particular other). There are no limits on the inward flow. The person is controlled by outside forces. One variation on this is when a child is never allowed to separate from a parent. The parent rules the child's life. If there are limits on how much influence others outside the dyad can exert on the child, the limits come from the parent, not the child.

---

* We also talk about being "blinded by his brilliance," "taken in by a silver tongue," and "enchanted by her siren call." The use of glamour by the Good People probably is also an aspect of overwhelming the inward blocking ability of a chakra.

People who are in a hostage situation or who are being tortured are exposed to this level of trauma. When we talk about breaking someone's will, we are referring to a broken inward ability of the will chakra. We also talk about sexual addiction for the desire chakra and being smothered by love for the heart chakra.

The change in inward ability to block life force is a function of how much we are overwhelmed. The more we are overwhelmed, the faster our ability decreases

$$IAB(t+1) = IAB(t) + a * \left(\left((IAB(t) - |LF_i(t)|) / IAB(t) \right) \right),$$

as long as $IAB(t) < |LF_i(t)|$

where a is a constant that describes how fast the inward ability to accept life force changes.

As with the outward ability, the inward ability is affected by our current physical and emotional condition.

The apparent inward ability is a function of our inward ability modified by our current state of being. The current state of physical being (CSB) probably affects each chakra in a similar way.

$$IA_{apparent} = CSB * IA$$

Inward Set Point

The inward set point is how much life force a chakra wants to bring in. There needs to be a balance between the outward set point and the inward set point so that the life force level in the chakra is maintained somewhere near the internal set point. As with the outward components of the soul, the inward ability changes slowly over time and the inward set point changes more quickly based on success in day-to-day interactions.

Every chakra needs life force to function. That life force can come from outside or from one of the other chakras. The inward set point is related to the life force coming from outside the soul.

Where each chakra puts its inward set point is based on several factors. The primary one is how successful the chakra has been at gathering life force in the past. That is a function of the places we have tried to get life force from. If we are looking for positive support in getting a project finished and receive it, it's a success. If there is a lack of support or active antagonism to the project, the search for life force is a failure.

We can also try to get negative life force as a way to maintain a negative image of ourselves. If we get the negative life force we are looking for, that is also a success. Perhaps it's not a healthy success, but it will lead us to do more of what we are doing and to increase our inward set point to receive more of the negative life force.

We learn from what has happened to us whether it is a good idea for us to seek life force from outside sources. There are four cases:

- When we get the desired effect by taking in more life force, the inward set point will go up.
- When we don't get the desired effect by taking in more life force, the inward set point will go down.
- When we get the desired effect by accepting less life force, the inward set point will go down.
- When we don't get the desired effect by accepting less life force, the inward set point will go up.

Inward set point changes based on the success we have when we take life force from outside sources. Success (S) can be positive or negative. $(LF_i(t) - InwSP(t))$ is a calculation of how far above or below the current inward set point this interaction was.

$$InwSP(t+1) = (InwSP(t) + a * S(t) * (LF_i(t) - InwSP(t)))[lim]IA(t)$$

where a is a weighting factor describing how quickly we change InwSP.

The inward set point is, of course, limited by our inward ability. We can't choose to pull more life force in than our maximum capacity. If life force is coming toward us, we can't block more than our inward ability to block life force lets us.

Another factor for how much life force we try to bring in is how much life force we have relative to our internal set point. This is a factor in addition to the inward set point when we calculate the amount of life force that we are trying to pull in.

Sometimes our life force level is so high that we really don't need any extra life force. We don't try to pull any in. In fact, we will be sending the extra life force out. Other times our life force level is lower than our internal set point. In that case we try to pull extra life force in. Note that the life force and internal set point can be positive or negative.

There are two more cases that we can look at. The third is where we have a positive inward set point and currently have a negative life force level. Something hasn't been working as it should. Positive inward set points should bring in positive life force. Either the chakra may adjust to a negative inward set point based on its failure or it may look to bring in even more positive life force, hopefully from other sources.

The fourth case is the inverse of the third case, positive life force and a negative inward set point. Again searching for more life force (negative this time) or setting the inward set point to a positive valence are possible results.

The base inward set point probably doesn't actually change much, but we can find an excess inward life force that is a temporary change in the inward set point caused by life force levels in the chakra that are different from the internal set point.

The excess inward set point (InwSP) is the difference in current energy level and the internal set point of the chakra.

$$InwSP_{excess} = IntSP - SLF$$

The set point for the inward life force flow at the current time is the InwSP at the current time plus the excess InwSP.

$$InwSP = (InwSP_{base} + InwSP_{excess})[\lim]A$$

The interactions of the outward set point, inward set point, and internal set point are quite complicated.* Their dance through the life force of the world could lead to almost any result, depending on the initial conditions and ongoing input. Some interesting observations come out of unusual configurations of the set points and actual life force levels. Let's look at one.

Folk wisdom suggests that people who appear to be the most generous with their life force are often the worst at handling negative

---

* In fact they are a good example of a chaotic system. For more on chaos, you might take a look at James Gleick's (1987), *Chaos: Making a New Science.*

situations. (They become the neediest.) Usually this is ascribed to the idea that they were just pretending to be happy. The equations for outward and inward set point actually predict the reaction we see. The person's internal set point is highly positive. The outward set point is also highly positive. When the life force level of a chakra goes negative, there is a great need to gain positive life force, so the life force required to get back to normal is very high. If the life force isn't there, it can lead to a total collapse much faster than in someone whose outward set point is set to send out much less life force.

Inward Intention

Inward intention is the mirror image of outward intention. Inward intention describes the amount of life force we choose to accept at any given instant. It changes as we interact with one person and it changes even more as we pay attention to different people or different tasks. The inward set point is the most important part of setting the inward intention, but the current life force level and the type of life force that is available also have effects on the inward intention. We choose how much we will let the inward flow vary in relation to the set point so that the stored life force is kept at our preferred level. Unlike the outward intention, which we control pretty much by ourselves, the inward intention can't pull life force out of nothing. If it isn't there, we can't get it, even if we need it badly.

Again, like outward intention, inward intention changes the fastest of all the inward aspects. It is also an array of values rather than a single value like the inward set point. We have an inward intention toward everything our chakra is connected to, regardless of whether it is physically present or not. It is possible to get life force from far away, if we have the connection. Think of the soldier receiving a care package from home. We know that life force to keep on fighting comes with the physical objects in the package. Good wishes and reminders of connection with a person far away come with the package, too.

We will see in Part III that long-distance (soul) connections are not very good at sending life force. So much is lost because the connection is inefficient. When a real thing, such as a care package, arrives, it means that the connection has moved into a closer distance. The contents are things that can be touched. The more personal the things are, the more efficiently they will transfer life force from the sender to the receiver.

Inward intention is an array with one element for every connection the chakra currently holds. It's a lot of elements. Some are active and some are not, based on the current situation. Each connection that is active has an inward intention value that modifies the inward set point relative to the particular connection.

$$II = \{II_c\}$$

where II_c is the inward intention to a particular connection.

Let's take another look at the example we used for outward intention: spending the evening with a group of friends.

We can expect to be receiving a lot of heart life force, but it will not be the same from each person. Some friends are powerful sources of life force. We can soak up the life force from them (have a high inward intention in relation to them) and get as much as we need.

Other friends might be more reserved. Less life force is available, so we can take less in. Usually there is a higher than normal life force flow in a situation with close friends, so it is likely that inward and outward set points will both be high. Inward intentions will also be high for the same reason.

This time let's look at the friend who is in a bad situation as it affects your inward intention. The friend may be radiating negative life force, and you want none of it. In that case you would be setting your inward intention to block the life force coming from the friend. If things work well, the friend will receive enough positive life force from the others in the group to balance out the negative life force. If things work out badly, the friend's negative life force will bring the whole group's life force down. It all depends on the ability of members of the group to block negative life force coming toward them relative to the strength of the friend's negative life force.

Again like outward intention, we connect differently with different members of a group. From one we accept the sexual life force that goes with flirting. From another we reject that kind of life force, but we are happy to have a good conversation.

The point to get from the example is that we switch our inward life force flow as we interact with each of the people. We have a normal way of interacting, but around that average we may vary a great deal depending on the exact situation we are in. That rapid change is reflected in the inward intention, both in accepting life force we want and in blocking life force we don't want.

The time it takes to change inward intention is a characteristic of each person. In Ekman's research,[52] which we looked at with outward intention, he also discovered that people who are angry filter the information they take in. All they hear are statements that support their anger. In my terms, this seems to be equivalent to blocking some types of inward life force (especially the information component). I don't know if Ekman's discovery about anger generalizes to all the other emotions. It seems like it probably does in the case of love.

Inward intention changes in ways similar to how outward intention changes. It is also based on the previous history with the person or situation. We change the intention based on what is happening. As always, positive results will cause us to do more of what we are doing. Negative results will cause us to do less.

Inward intention to a particular connection changes based on what has happened in the relationship.

$$II(t_2) = \left(II(t_1) + \int_{t=t_1}^{t_2} a * S(t) * (LF_S(t) - II(t))\right)[\lim]A(t_2)$$

where a is how quickly the outward intention can change.

When considering how the changes will occur during an event, each person has a characteristic time signature for ramping up, duration, and ramping down. For any particular event there will be a curve represented by the amplitude as a function of time, Amp(t).

$$II(t) = II_0 * Amp(t)$$

To determine where the life force of a particular chakra is coming from, we need to divide up the life force coming in (either the inward set point or the maximum amount of life force available in the situation) in proportion to the inward intention for each of the connections. Two considerations are important here.

- Current focus. As we shift our attention from one thing to another, we receive more life force from what we are focusing on.
- The surroundings. We receive life force from the rest of what is around us even when we are concentrating intently on one person. Usually the surroundings have a significant effect on our life force flow, since life force can flow from many places all at the same time.

The simple case would be that the life force is received proportionally. I don't see any reason at this time to look for something more complicated. This is complicated enough.

Inward intention for a particular connection helps to set the amount of life force that flows from that connection. A certain amount of life force is available in the environment, we have an inward set point, and we have a certain amount of ability to block life force coming in. These three factors combine with our intention to determine how much life force we receive from each source.

If life force available is greater than the inward set point and ability to block is high enough to block excess life force, then we have a simple proportion from each of the available sources.

if $\left(\sum_{c=1}^{\text{all connections}} LF_c \geq \text{InwSP} \right)$ and $\left(\text{IAB} \geq [\text{max}]_c LF \right)$ then

$$LF_c = \text{ISP} * II_c / \sum_{c=1}^{\text{all connections}} II_c$$

where IAB is the inward ability to block and c is a particular connection.

If the energy available is not sufficient, then we draw all the energy available.

elseif $\sum_{c=1}^{\text{all connections}} LF_c < \text{ILFSP}$ then

$$LF = \sum_{c=1}^{\text{all connections}} LF_c$$

If some life force (either positive or negative) is able to overcome the blocking ability, all of that excess life force goes in as inward life force. The rest of the environment contributes what it can to set the inward life force to the inward set point.

$$\text{elseif } IAB < \lfloor max \rfloor_c LF \text{ then}$$

$$IE_c = \sum_{c=1}^{\overset{\text{all connections}}{\text{where } LF_c > IAB}} (LF_c - IAB) + \sum_{c=1}^{\overset{\text{all connections}}{\text{where } \lfloor sign \rfloor IAB = \lfloor sign \rfloor LF_c}} LF_c$$

endif

What is being left out here is that it takes life force in the chakra to block unwanted life force from connections.

Assume you are trying to solve a problem. (I'm thinking of a *New York Times* Thursday or Friday crossword puzzle, as I write this.*) When I'm well rested, I can solve the puzzle fairly easily even when I'm also sort of paying attention to the baseball game on the radio.† I seem to be putting about 70% of my mind life force on the puzzle, 20% on the radio, and about 10% for everything else. (I'd love to have a way to measure that.) When I'm tired, presumably with less life force available for thought, and working on a puzzle of about the same difficulty, I need all the attention I can summon to solve the puzzle. Sometimes even that isn't enough. I may not have enough life force to block out other things, so I can't focus on the puzzle. That's what the blocking part of inward intention is all about.

Interactions between Information and Energy

In most of the discussions in this chapter and the previous one, we have talked more about the life force's energy aspects than about the information aspects. It is important see how information affects the parts of the chakra.

---

* The connection here is an interesting one we will discuss in Part III. Am I connected to a puzzle that has its particular kind of thought energy or in some indirect way to the creator of the puzzle? And, if it's a connection to the creator, what happens after the creator dies? I'm hoping that the connection is to the puzzle itself. I'd hate to think that I'd be stuck with a connection to you, the reader, for the whole existence of this book.

† When he was President, Bill Clinton was reputed to be able to solve a *New York Times* Sunday puzzle during staff meetings and still pay attention to what was being discussed. (I can do that, too, but I can't do it with the Saturday puzzle, which is generally much harder.)

Each chakra has its own way to store experiences, so we can look at how the experiences affect the chakra when they are recalled or when we are in a similar situation.

I believe that each experience carries with it values for some aspects of the chakra. The six chakra aspects that are affected most by information are the internal set point, inward set point, inward intention, outward set point, outward intention, and external set point. Let's call the group of six aspects "set points."

When a chakra recalls an experience, the set points are reset closer to what they were when the experience occurred. Similarly, when we are in a situation that is like a previous experience, the chakra's set points are reset so they are near to where they were during the previous experience.

We have already proposed equations that calculate how the set points change based on the current situation. Now let's look at how a change in the situation can move the set points.

Let's look at a few examples of the kinds of situations that can change energy set points drastically:

- A plane flies into the World Trade Center.
- A President is shot.
- An Afghan IED explodes and blows the truck ahead of you off the road.
- In the middle of an argument with one person, a good friend calls.
- While you're peacefully driving down the road, a police car in back of you turns on its emergency lights and siren.
- An argument gets settled (you think), but the next day the person you were arguing with brings up the topic again.
- Your boss catches you surfing the web again (and that's not your job).

Whatever your feelings were the moment before, events like this cause an instant transformation. In the first two cases, the reaction is usually shock. We've never experienced this before and we have nothing that tells us how to react. In the third case, the soldiers involved will probably be bounced right back into how they felt the last time an IED exploded.

For the rest, we move toward how we felt the last time we were in the situation. We might cheerfully talk with the friend and go right back to the anger of the argument when we hang up. We remember the last time the cops pulled us over. We're heading right back into the worst of the argument from the day before. We remember what happened the last time we were caught.

Even if an event doesn't reoccur, remembering the event can move our set points toward where they were when we experienced the event. Sam Pappas' flashback (described on page 96) is a prime example of a flashback that totally wipes out his current reality and resets the set points to where they were in the traumatic situation.

The point for us is that extreme experiences can take us back to places we have been before and bring back the same set points we had at the time. More than the brain, and more than the mind, is involved. Let's look at how set points change based on remembered or re-experienced situations.

The simplest way to look at the question is to assume that we can measure the amount of attention we are paying to the current situation relative to the amount of attention we are paying to remembered experiences. The current situation has its own set points. Each remembered situation has different set points. The current set points are the average of the current situation and all of the memories weighted by the amount of attention each is receiving.

For each aspect we average the aspect in the current situation (current) with all values of the aspect in all of the currently active memories (m), weighting the ones that are receiving more attention (A) as being more significant. For the internal set point (IntSP) the equation would look like this.

$$\text{IntSP}_{total} = \frac{\text{IntSP}_{current} * A_{current} + \sum_{m=1}^{all\ memories} (\text{IntSP}_m * A_m)}{A_{total}}$$

Similar calculations work for the other five set points.

We already looked at how these six aspects are affected by what is currently happening, but we need to refine that equation to take into account the effect of memories. Again looking at the internal set point situation, we need to adjust the values associated with the current situation, but we need to lower the amount of change based on how much attention is being paid to the current situation, as opposed to how much is being paid to memories.

The internal set point equation we had before needs to be modified for the attention it is receiving in the current situation ($A_{current} / A_{total}$).

$$IntSP_{current}(t+1)$$

$$= \left(IntSP_{current}(t) + \frac{A_{current}}{A_{total}} * a * S * (SLF_E(t) - IntSP_{current}(t)) \right)$$

$$[lim] MLF_E(t)$$

where a is a weighting factor describing how quickly we change IntSP. Similar calculations work for the other five set points.

At the same time we are changing the set points for the current situation, we also affect the set points for all the memories in the same way. We can change how past experiences affect us in the present. The memory remains but how it affects us (how it changes our set points and our connections to everything else in the world) can change. Each memory is changed by the amount of attention it is receiving.

The IntSP equation can also be used to calculate how the set points of remembered experiences change. It depends on the amount of attention (A_i / A_{total}) currently being given to the memory (i).

$$IntSP_i(t+1) =$$

$$\left(IntSP_i(t) + \frac{A_i}{A_{total}} * a * S * (SLF_E(t) - IntSP_i(t)) \right) [lim] IA(t)$$

where a is a weighting factor describing how quickly we change IntSP. Similar calculations work for each active memory in resetting each of the six set points.

Emotional Freedom Techniques (EFT)[53] talks a great deal about the idea of resetting the level we have on things that have happened to us in the past. Two important aspects of EFT are making sure the current situation is positive (through the affirmations while rubbing the "sore point") and clearly focusing on each aspect of the traumatic event while tapping on points that seem to be fairly well related to chakra connection locations. The result is that the success level of the current situation is high and maximum attention is being put on the memory. Both of these are important in quickly changing the set points associated with the experience.

8. Internal Chakra Connections

When you are in rhythm with the symphonic pulse of the universe, you can feel the electrifying current of the life force, a hundred thousand gigawatts of light bursting out of each and every cell.
— *Christine Pechera (in* Writing for Wellness*)*

The connections between chakras within a soul appear to be remarkably complex. Each tradition has different ways of looking at these connections and there are many traditions that consider them.

The yoga traditions speak of kundalini and how it follows a path up through each of the chakras. Some New Age practices see the auras as important in the energy flow between parts of the soul/body.

Chinese martial arts look at the energy flow from the floor through the striking point. Liang and Yang say this about the understanding of the Hsing Yi Chuan style:[54]

In your body there are twelve Chi channels which function like rivers and distribute Chi throughout your body. There are also eight "extraordinary Chi vessels" which function like reservoirs, storing and regulating Chi in your body.

139

They go on to describe the locations, connections, and paths of each of these channels and vessels.

Qigong discusses what I call the flow between chakras this way:[55]

> All qigong forms aim, in some way or another, to open, balance and clarify the flow of qi through the meridians. In the course of our lives, when we have experiences that we're not able, in the moment, fully to digest, the energy of those experiences — like undigested food in our intestines — creates blockages in the meridians. The particular patterns created in our bodymind by these energetic blockages define what in Buddhism is called "ego" — our own unique way of being unconscious, which we mistakenly believe to be who we are, fundamentally.*

> Qigong practice helps us to untie these energetic knots, allowing energy/awareness to once again flow freely in and as the Present Moment: a luminous emptiness in which the play of our bodily elements continuously unfolds.

Reninger defines the meridians this way:[56]

> The subtle channels through which qi travels, within the energetic anatomy of the human body. The twelve main meridians/mai and the eight extra meridians/mai define the territory of acupuncture and qigong practice.

I don't want to suggest that the great amount of work others have put into understanding this part of the question is not worthwhile. Sources that go beyond the basics of the chakras tend to spend a lot of time discussing the other aspects of the soul that are involved in the connections between the chakras. For questions of using life energy and healing, these studies are vitally important. Each of the many paths may be a relevant piece of the puzzle. However, the goal of this book seems to be better served by looking at the similarities of the paths rather than the different variations that appear in each particular discipline.

---

* I have a problem with the concept of "who we are" described here. I would say that the blockages are, in fact, *exactly* who we are right now. We are our current soul structure. The good news is that who we are now is not who we have to be in the future.

An additional consideration is that other disciplines seem to be missing what I think is a vital part of the model: the transfer of information between chakras. In this book I want to include the idea that energy and information are both transferred between chakras. My model of the mechanisms of energy transfer inside a soul is, perhaps, simpler than it might be. This is because the more important question of energy transfer and communication of information between souls does not appear to be greatly affected by the exact mechanisms of the internal transfer.*

Life Force Conversions

Two kinds of conversions are required when we are making transfers between chakras. The energy needs to be converted and so does the information. The lower chakras seem to be able to handle more energy, but not nearly as much information. When we move life force between chakras, both types of conversions need to be taken into account.

Energy Conversion

When chakras share energy with another chakra, there is some kind of conversion factor. Energy from one chakra is not worth as much to another chakra.† For example, mind energy may not convert well to heart energy. In that case transferring energy from heart to mind and then back to heart would leave the soul with less energy than it started with. We'll put the conversion factors in the equation, even though we don't know what they are. It's one of the things that experiments can try to discover.

---

* This is one of several statements that might come back to haunt me if it turns out to be just plain wrong. The good news is that the energy transfer we calculate using a single value for the pathway can be expanded to a more complex calculation if required.

† Conversion of energy between chakras is not the same question as the relative power of chakras that we looked at in Chapter 7. For example, the energy of water going through a dam is much greater than the energy it takes to read a book at night, but a light is far more useful for that purpose than a river. What we are talking about here is the efficiency of the conversion from the kinetic energy of the water to the electrical energy of the light. (It's about 90%. U.S. Department of the Interior, 2005)

The conversion of energy between chakras (CEC_{nm}) accounts for inefficiencies of energy conversion when energy (LF_E) moves between chakras.

$$LF_{En} = CEC_{nm} * LF_{Em}$$

where n and m are two different chakras.

One of the joys of using mathematical notation is that we can put a whole lot of information in a compact form. The table below represents all of the conversion values between pairs of chakras. For the moment* we can hope that the conversion values are the same for all souls.

When the Qigong practices, as described above, talk about blockages in meridians, they are probably talking about reductions in the amount of energy flow between chakras. However, there may be some part of what they call blockage that is better thought of as energy loss.

We can create a seven-by-seven matrix that represents the complete set of conversion values.

CEC =

1	CEC_{12}	CEC_{13}	CEC_{14}	CEC_{15}	CEC_{16}	CEC_{17}
CEC_{21}	1	CEC_{23}	CEC_{24}	CEC_{25}	CEC_{26}	CEC_{27}
CEC_{31}	CEC_{32}	1	CEC_{34}	CEC_{35}	CEC_{36}	CEC_{37}
CEC_{41}	CEC_{42}	CEC_{43}	1	CEC_{45}	CEC_{46}	CEC_{47}
CEC_{51}	CEC_{52}	CEC_{53}	CEC_{54}	1	CEC_{56}	CEC_{57}
CEC_{61}	CEC_{62}	CEC_{63}	CEC_{64}	CEC_{65}	1	CEC_{67}
CEC_{71}	CEC_{72}	CEC_{73}	CEC_{74}	CEC_{75}	CEC_{76}	1

We expect that $0 <= CEC_{nm} <= 1$.

Information Conversion

As we discussed in the description of the chakras, each chakra can handle a particular complexity of information. When information is passed between chakras, it needs to be significantly modified to match the receiving chakra's capacity. For example, a troubadour can sing a love song and his ladylove can listen to it using the communication

---

* Until we can figure out how to conduct the relevant experiments.

chakra. However, when the message gets to her heart chakra, it is simplified to something like, "He loves me."

When information moves from a higher chakra to a lower chakra, it needs to be simplified. That can be done fairly easily. Details and subtleties are lost, but the basic message is usually clear. The real problems occur when information moves from a lower chakra to a higher chakra.

One way to think about the situation is to consider what you need to do when you have a cranky baby. The baby knows it wants something. It might be food or a clean diaper or a nap or the shiny toy over there. As a caretaker, it's your job to figure out what the desire is. The time-tested method is to go through the usual list of desires until you find the solution that satisfies the baby. Problems occur when you need to figure out an issue that is not on the usual list. You have to keep on looking for other possibilities. It can be a real challenge.

The desire chakra in our soul is like the cranky baby. It knows it wants something. It may have the energy to act, but finding a set of actions that fulfills the desire may be beyond its capacity. Let's look at what happens between the desire chakra and the mind chakra when the desire chakra wants something.

To get what it wants, the desire chakra sends a message to mind chakra. Unfortunately the information sent is very simple and does not necessarily lead to a clear set of actions. The information might be so primitive that mind chakra struggles to find a path that will lead to what is desired.* A negotiation needs to take place.

Doing the best it can, the mind chakra sends a proposed set of actions and results to the desire chakra in terms it understands. The desire chakra compares the results with its desire and decides whether they are sufficient. The negotiation, which includes the translation of information during every interchange, continues until the desire is resolved.

Other chakras also take part in this negotiation. They have their preferred life force states and want a solution that moves them toward

---

* Consider the case of a young adolescent and the sexual desires related to other young adolescents. Often the mind chakra is way beyond its capacity when it tries to solve this one.

their goal. The heart chakra, for example, might be looking for a loving relationship with another person. The troubadour and his ladylove find one way to establish that connection through a song.

Sometimes the situation is not resolved. This is especially likely when several chakras are involved in the interaction and they have a mix of positive and negative energy, leading to incompatible preferred life force states. There may not be a solution that satisfies all of the chakras at the same time. It can lead to barely perceived dissatisfaction or great unhappiness, depending on the situation. Resolving these incompatibilities can happen, but it usually requires life force (both information and energy) from outside the individual's soul. Counseling is one way we receive this outside life force.

I'm not going to claim that I have a good mathematical model for information conversion. Information density decreases as we move to lower chakras. It increases as we move to higher chakras, but I believe the higher chakras are supplying the additional information to fill in what is passed to them from the lower chakras.

The conversion of information between chakras (CIC_{nm}) accounts for different capacities of the chakras as information (LF_i) moves between them.

$$LF_{ln} = CIC_{nm} * LF_{lm}$$

where n and m are two different chakras.

We can create a seven-by-seven matrix that represents the complete set of conversion values.

CIC =

1	CIC_{12}	CIC_{13}	CIC_{14}	CIC_{15}	CIC_{16}	CIC_{17}
CIC_{21}	1	CIC_{23}	CIC_{24}	CIC_{25}	CIC_{26}	CIC_{27}
CIC_{31}	CIC_{32}	1	CIC_{34}	CIC_{35}	CIC_{36}	CIC_{37}
CIC_{41}	CIC_{42}	CIC_{43}	1	CIC_{45}	CIC_{46}	CIC_{47}
CIC_{51}	CIC_{52}	CIC_{53}	CIC_{54}	1	CIC_{56}	CIC_{57}
CIC_{61}	CIC_{62}	CIC_{63}	CIC_{64}	CIC_{65}	1	CIC_{67}
CIC_{71}	CIC_{72}	CIC_{73}	CIC_{74}	CIC_{75}	CIC_{76}	1

This view of information conversion explains the observation that decision making often involves making a decision and then rationalizing why we made it. It isn't quite that simple because there is a negotiation, but the observation that we don't make decisions rationally (with the mind chakra) holds true.

The chakra model makes it clear how this happens. One of the lower chakras with its powerful energy drives the process. The rest of the chakras, including the mind chakra that does the rationalizing, fall into line with the decision. When we try to figure ourselves out, we need to understand that decisions can come from different chakras and the process they use to work together.

Total Conversion

Converting both aspects of life force is done by converting energy with the energy conversion and information with the information conversion.

The conversion of life force between chakras ($CLFC_{nm}$) accounts for different capacities of the chakras as life force moves between them.

$$LF_n = CLFC_{nm} * LF_m$$

where n and m are two different chakras.
CLFC is the combination of the conversion factors for each aspect of life force.

$$CLFC = CEC[and]CIC$$

Life Force Pathways

There are one or more life force pathways between each pair of chakras. Since we are not looking at the details here, we can assign a single value to the amount of life force that can be transferred in each direction between the pair. The value is, of course, the sum of the size of all the pathways.

The size of the life force pathway from chakra n to chakra m ($LFPF_{nm}$) is the sum of each of the pathways ($PF_{nm\,i}$) in that direction between the pair.

$$LFPF_{nm} = \sum_{i=1}^{all\,pathways} PF_{nm\,i}$$

where i is a pathway for energy transfer.

Similarly, the size of the energy pathway to chakra $_n$ from chakra $_m$ ($LFPT_{nm}$) is the sum of each of the pathways ($PT_{nm\,i}$) in that direction between the pair.

$$LFPT_{nm} = \sum_{i=1}^{all\,pathways} PT_{nm\,i}$$

where i is a pathway for energy transfer.

Similar to the conversion values above, we can create a matrix that represents all of the pathway sizes between pairs of chakras. I do not expect the size of the pathway in one direction to be the same as the size of the pathway in the other direction. For example, just because the heart chakra is able to supply a lot of life force to the communication chakra for a particular person does not mean that the communication chakra can supply a lot of life force to the heart chakra.

The size of life force pathways between chakras in the soul (LFP) can be represented by a seven-by-seven matrix. We will use the convention that a chakra can't transfer energy to or from itself.

$$LFP = \begin{matrix} 0 & LFP_{12} & LFP_{13} & LFP_{14} & LFP_{15} & LFP_{16} & LFP_{17} \\ LFP_{21} & 0 & LFP_{23} & LFP_{24} & LFP_{25} & LFP_{26} & LFP_{27} \\ LFP_{31} & LFP_{32} & 0 & LFP_{34} & LFP_{35} & LFP_{36} & LFP_{37} \\ LFP_{41} & LFP_{42} & LFP_{43} & 0 & LFP_{45} & LFP_{46} & LFP_{47} \\ LFP_{51} & LFP_{52} & LFP_{53} & LFP_{54} & 0 & LFP_{56} & LFP_{57} \\ LFP_{61} & LFP_{62} & LFP_{63} & LFP_{64} & LFP_{65} & 0 & LFP_{67} \\ LFP_{71} & LFP_{72} & LFP_{73} & LFP_{74} & LFP_{75} & LFP_{76} & 0 \end{matrix}$$

Note that in making this matrix we are shifting from the chakra's perspective to the soul's perspective. Chakra $_1$, for example would have a pathway from it to chakra $_2$ ($LFPT_{12}$). Chakra $_2$ sees a pathway to it from chakra $_1$ ($LFPF_{21}$). From the soul's perspective, these paths are the same so that $LFP_{21} = LFPF_{21} = LFPT_{12}$. The chakra numbers in the subscript describe the direction the energy is flowing.

The size of the life force pathways can change with time. In fact changing the size of the internal life force pathways is one of the major goals of many of the disciplines that deal with chakras and/or life force.*

I expect that the changes in the size of the pathways will be similar to the changes we saw earlier when we discussed the ability for the external pathways. When the flow is toward the top of the available size and the situation is positive, the size will increase. When the flow is high and the situation is negative, the size of the pathway will decrease.† The energy will change along each of the pathways independently of the other pathways.

The size of the life force pathway from chakra n to chakra m (LFP_{nm}) will change based on the success we have when we take life force from other chakras. Success (S) can be positive or negative. LFF_{nm} is the energy that is actually flowing. ($LFP_{nm} - LFF_{nm}$) is a calculation of how far above or below the current capacity of the connection between chakras this interaction was.

$$LFP_{nm}(t+1) = LFP_{nm}(t) + a*S$$
$$*(1-((LFP_{nm}(t)-|LFF_{nm}(t)|)/LFP_{nm}(t))$$

where a is a weighting factor describing how quickly we change LFP.

Life Force Transfer

Each chakra, as we have discussed, has a preferred life force level (the internal set point). It can get life force from external sources, and it can also get life force from internal sources (the other chakras in the soul). When one chakra is low on life force, it will ask other chakras to share their life force.

At any given time we have a set of seven values that represents the life force stored in each of the chakras (stored life force, SLF). We have another set of values for the set point for each chakra (internal set point,

---

* Qigong's goal of removing blockages is one of the ways the size of the pathway can change.

† The ability to increase the flow of either part of life force needs to take into account the relative capacities of the individual chakras to handle information and energy.

IntSP). To find out how far each chakra is from its preferred life force value we can subtract the two sets of values.

At this point the chakras will try to move their life force levels closer to their set points by taking life force from or giving life force to other chakras. The amount of life force that can be transferred is based on the size of the pathways. The amount of life force that leaves one chakra and enters the other chakra is adjusted based on the conversion factors discussed earlier.

The transfer is different for energy and information, so we will look at each separately.

Energy Transfer

Energy transfer can be a complicated calculation, but the process really isn't all that hard to understand. Imagine an ice cube tray with seven spaces for cubes (representing each of the chakras). When we fill the tray with water, one source of water for each chakra, any extra water will run out of the full chakra into an empty chakra. It's a little harder to picture the life force pathways, but you can think of tubes of different sizes connecting each of the spaces for cubes.*

The final result is that the chakras do the best they can to distribute energy part of the life force among themselves. Chakras that have life force levels above their set points send life force out. Chakras with life force levels below their set points take life force in. No chakra can take in life force above its maximum level. There are some interesting complications that we will look at after the mathematical details.

To calculate energy shifts in the life force we can start by looking at the amount of energy the chakra has available to send out (LFA_E). The energy available is the difference between the stored energy (SLF_E) in the chakra and the internal set point of the chakra ($IntSP_E$). Chakras can have either positive or negative values for the stored energy and set points. The same equations work with any of the combination of conditions.

---

* It turns out that the fluid dynamics equations for the water example are pretty horrible in their own right, especially if the flows are fast enough to have one flow interfering with another flow.

$$LFA_{Ei} = SLF_{Ei} - IntSP_{Ei}$$

Next we look at the interaction of each chakra with one other chakra. The chakras will try to balance the energy between them so that both are the same distance from their set point. The amount that the chakra we are calculating (i) tries to send to the other chakra (j) is half of the difference between the energy available values of the two chakras.

$$LF_{Egoal} = LFA_{Ei} - \frac{LFA_{Ei} + LFA_{Ej}}{2} = \frac{LFA_{Ei}}{2} - \frac{LFA_{Ej}}{2}$$

The chakras can only send the type (positive or negative) of energy they have and only as much as they have. The limited amount of energy is

$$LF_{Elimit\ i} = LF_{Egoal}[lim]SLF_{Ei}$$

where the [lim] operator is defined as

if $LF_{Egoal} > 0$ and $SLF_{Ei} > 0$ then

$$LF_{Elimit\ i} = [min](LF_{Egoal}, SLF_{Ei})$$

elseif $LF_{goal} < 0$ and $SLF_i < 0$ then

$$LF_{Elimit\ i} = [max](LF_{Egoal}, SLF_{Ei})$$

else

$$LF_{Elimit\ i} = 0$$

endif

The energy transfer (LFT_E) also depends on the capacity of the link between them (LFP_E).

$$LFT_{Eij} = LF_{Elimit}[abslim]LFP_{Eij}$$

where the [abslim] operator is defined as

if $LF_{Elimit} > 0$ then

$$LFT_{Eij} = [min](LF_{Elimit\ i}, LFP_{Eij})$$

else

$$LFT_{Eij} = [max](LF_{Elimit\ i}, LFP_{Eij})$$

endif

Putting all these together gives the equation.*

$$LFT_{Eij} = \left(\left(\frac{LFA_{Ei}}{2} - \frac{LFA_{Ej}}{2}\right)[lim]SLF_{Ei}\right)[abslim]LFP_{Eij}$$

Putting this back into terms that are direct properties of the soul by changing energy available back to stored life force and life force set points gives

$$LFT_{Eij} = \left(\left(\frac{SLF_{Ei} - IntSP_{Ei}}{2} - \frac{SLF_{Ej} - IntSP_{Ej}}{2}\right)[lim]SLF_{Ei}\right)$$
$$[abslim]LFP_{Eij}$$

This is the amount of energy that gets transferred from chakra i. The amount that is received by chakra j depends on the energy conversion factors (CEC). The change in energy from this one transfer is

$$SLF_{Ei}(t+1) = SLF_{Ei}(t) - LFT_{Eij}$$
$$SLF_{Ej}(t+1) = SLF_{Ej}(t) + LFT_{Eij} * CEC_{ij}$$

One important point to remember is that we are dealing with positive and negative energy, which I believe act in some ways like two separate things. For example, a chakra can send out negative energy, if it has some; or it can send out positive energy, if it has some. What it can't do is send out negative energy if it has no energy or only positive energy and vice versa.

A chakra that has negative energy can get positive energy from other chakras. The two types of energy cancel each other out to reduce the energy in the chakra. I don't believe that a chakra can hold both types of energy, at least not for very long, so the simple assumption here is that we can cancel them.

The equations handle all of these conditions.

There is an interesting situation that is predicted by these equations. (You don't have to read the equations to understand this point.) Usually energy travels in only one direction between a pair of chakras. However,

---

* If you care, [lim] and [abslim] are commutative but not associative.

there is one set of cases where energy is predicted to travel in both directions. One chakra in the pair needs to have positive stored energy and the other chakra needs to have negative stored energy. Reaching the balance point between the chakras must involve moving the type of energy that each chakra has available. For example, reaching the balance point might be best achieved by having the positive chakra send positive energy and the negative chakra send negative energy. In that case, they both send their energy. This is especially interesting since the energy movement can cause the chakras to get twice as much change as they really want.

In the most exciting (not in a pleasant way) situation the chakras have exactly the same set point and the positive stored energy in one is exactly balanced by the negative stored energy in the other. As long as there are no restrictions on the amount of energy flow between the chakras (and no outside influences), the energy will bounce back and forth forever with the chakras bouncing from positive to negative with every cycle. (This sounds intensely uncomfortable, even paralyzing, to me.) If the set point or the energy levels differ by a little bit, the movement back and forth will damp out. The greater the differences, the sooner the system quiets down to no energy movement.

Now the question is, does this really mean anything or is it just a strange effect of the equations? Let's take a look at a couple of scenarios.

One scenario we spoke of in the discussion of inward set point in Chapter 8 was that a strongly positive person may be more devastated by something bad happening. That's what this result predicts. If the negative balances the positive, the chakras may never settle down without outside influences. Someone who is more negative is actually able to absorb the added negative experience much more easily.

The other scenario is "good cop, bad cop." Haven't you always wondered how that could possibly work? Here's what these equations predict. The good cop sends positive energy to the heart chakra of the interviewee. The bad cop sends negative energy to the will chakra. The chakras, as they are trying to balance the energy, get into this feedback loop that never resolves itself. Cops know that they have to keep up a careful interaction with the person they are interviewing to keep him or her off balance. This theory provides an explanation of what that balance is all about.

It turns out that even if the chakras involved decide to shut down and hold no energy (the internal set point goes to zero), it doesn't help. The prediction is that the energy will still bounce between them.

Information Transfer

The internal transfer of information is more severely restricted than the internal transfer of energy because different chakras have vastly different capacities for holding information. Information is generally not intrinsically positive or negative. The complications we found with positive and negative energy are not found in information transfer. The other difference is that information is not lost to one chakra when it is given to another chakra.

We still need to take into account the different internal set points and internal levels of each pair of chakras to figure out when information will be transferred from one chakra to another. I have experienced times in relations with others where either the head or the heart had more understanding of what was going on. Occasionally I feel the information moving from one to the other as I try to act appropriately. When one chakra needs more information than it has, it will accept information from the other chakras.

The concept of too much information can be seen in chakras. If a chakra feels like it has more information than it can handle, it will try to send the information to other chakras for processing. This will usually be the lower chakras sending information to the higher chakras. It could be in the form of a warning that something is wrong, but it can also be a feeling that something needs to be done to make things better.

Information is transferred to chakras that need it and from chakras that have too much.

$$LFT_{lij} = \left(\left(\frac{SLF_{li} - IntSP_{li}}{2} - \frac{SLF_{j} - IntSP_{lj}}{2} \right) [lim]SLF_{li} \right)$$

$$[abslim]LFP_{lij}$$

All we need to do is figure out how much information the second chakra receives.

The only equation we need to have for the transfer of information is the calculation of the amount of information received.

$$SLF_{ii}(t+1) = SLF_{ii}(t)$$
$$SLF_{ij}(t+1) = SLF_{ij}(t) + LFT_{ij} * CEC_{ij}$$

Life Force Transfer

The calculations described above cover one pair of chakras as they transfer life force in one direction. The same calculation is then used for all of the chakra pairs. There will be 42 of them.*

We can use the following vector equation to describe the calculations of all of the chakra pairs.

$$\mathbf{LFT} = \left(\left(\frac{\mathbf{SLF} - \mathbf{IntSP}}{2} [\text{pair dif}] \frac{\mathbf{SLF} - \mathbf{IntSP}}{2} \right) [\text{lim}] \mathbf{SLF} \right)$$
$$[\text{abs lim}] \mathbf{LFP}$$
$$\mathbf{SLF}(t+1) = \mathbf{SLF}(t) - [\textit{from}] \mathbf{LFT}(t) + [\textit{to}] \mathbf{LFT}(t) * \mathbf{CEC}$$

Additional Observations

There are some other interesting observations that we need to look at to understand the internal transfer of life force between chakras.

Changing Focus

We can quickly change which chakra has the focus of our interactions (and gets the most life force). This happens with a change in the set points of the set of chakras. Most people are unaware of this change, since it happens below the level of thought.

Paul Ekman describes the phenomenon when he looks at the rise of emotional intensity.[57] We have to translate a little bit from his discussions of the strength of emotions to life force in particular chakras, but the

---

* Douglas Adams also discusses the number 42 in a remarkable similar context. Context similarity being very much in the eye of the beholder, of course.

concept that there are changes we are unaware of as we change focus comes through clearly.

We can easily see the effect as we move through a crowd of people. Let's suppose we're heading down the stairs of a busy New York subway. The predominant life force when I do that is in the mind chakra and the will chakra. I'm watching for and avoiding danger while trying to keep from being jostled too much by the crowds of people. If someone approaches me asking for money, I turn on more negative will and shut down my heart chakra. (Others may be more generous — more heart — or, perhaps, more intimidated — less will.) However, if I see a friend in the crowd, life force zips over to my heart chakra as we talk.*

How life force shifts is based on our past experiences. We'll have more to say about that in the next chapter.

Blocked and Inadequate Pathways

It is possible for pathways to become "blocked." Trauma of one kind or another is usually at the root of these blockages.

The people who study energy psychology techniques, such as EFT†, work on these blockages and other problems in the flow of life force between chakras. (Most have a different model that includes energy flow but not the separation of functions that is provided by chakras.)

When paths are blocked, life force can't flow along them. Some pairs of chakras may not be able to share life force directly. This would be reflected in the life force pathway matrix.

Sometimes there are less direct pathways for sharing life force. For example, there may be a block between chakras three and four. However, there might be an available path from chakra three to chakra five and from chakra five to chakra four. In that case the life force might be able to move from chakra three to five and then to four. It would be a less efficient path, subject to all the restrictions regarding life force available,

---

* Spotting a beautiful woman/handsome man moves the life force to another chakra.

† EFT is Emotional Freedom Techniques. Someone interested in energy healing can pick up this set of techniques easily and at minimal cost. See the EFT website, http://www.eftuniverse.com/, for more information.

positive and negative values, path capacity, and conversion factors. Clearing out the blockages makes souls better at sharing life force effectively.

Even when there isn't a complete blockage, there may be restrictions on the flow of life force. When there are restrictions, the life force just takes longer to move between chakras and may also move by less direct paths.

Lack of Life Force

It's possible that none of the chakras has extra life force. In that case the soul will proceed as best it can in a low life force state. Like a flashlight with a dying battery, the soul will glow dimly.

Life force the soul needs may not be available from outside the soul, or the soul may be in a state that cannot accept outside life force because of problems with one or more of the three inward components. I think clinical depression may have this kind of life force pattern and a lack of ability to accept life force from outside. Others will need to do more work to see if this is a useful model for treatment.

Inconsistent Set Points

Some chakras may have negative set points while other chakras have positive set points. There are lots of examples. One is in the person who is actually loving (heart chakra) but everything that comes out of his or her mouth is negative (communication chakra).

Situations like this cause confusion in the people who interact with the person. Some get a positive message and others get a negative message but most get the well-known mixed message. The person is probably also confused by what is happening.

Again, I hope this model will help clarify the situation for all concerned and provide some direction for making things better. In this case, the person with the inconsistent set points might look at using the mind chakra to go through what is happening in the communication chakra. If the communications become positive and the feedback is positive, then the set point will move to positive. As we've discussed earlier, it's a lot of work to change set points from negative to positive, but it is doable. Cognitive Behavioral Therapy (CBT) focuses on using the mind in this way.

Memories and Internal Life Force Flow

Memories can change set points of the chakras moment by moment. Changes in set points affect the internal life force flow. We'll be discussing this in the next chapter.

It's also possible that information affects the size of the energy pathways between chakras. However, I believe that the change in the energy component of the set points is sufficient for explaining what we have observed so far (which is almost nothing). More detailed observations may require revisiting this assumption.

9. Soul Integration

Love is at the heart of every incarnation as that which brings and holds the diverse elements together so that the alloy of individuality can emerge.

— *David Spangler*

When chakras are studied separately, they are like pieces of the puzzle. It takes combining all of the chakras together to see the complete picture of a soul that integrates with the spirit world at the top, the body through the middle five chakras, and the chaos at the bottom. In this chapter we will start by looking at how chakras are connected together.

Turning Chakras into Soul

The basic configuration of the soul contains the seven chakras. A fascinating question is just how closely are these chakras integrated? Do they all hum along in harmony? Are they all well coordinated to reach the goals of the soul? And just who or what is in charge, anyway?

Aristotle said this about human nature:[58]

Man is a conjugal animal, meaning an animal which is born to couple when an adult, thus building a household (oikos) and in more successful cases, a clan or small village still run upon patriarchal lines.[59]

Man is a political animal, meaning an animal with an innate propensity to develop more complex communities the size of a city or town, with a division of labor and law-making. This type of community is different in kind from a large family, and requires the special use of human reason.[60]

Man is a mimetic animal. Man loves to use his imagination (and not only to make laws and run town councils). He says, "we enjoy looking at accurate likenesses of things which are themselves painful to see, obscene beasts, for instance, and corpses." And the "reason why we enjoy seeing likenesses is that, as we look, we learn and infer what each is, for instance, 'that is so and so.' "[61]

For Aristotle, reason is not only what is most special about humanity compared to other animals, but it is also what we were meant to achieve at our best.

Sigmund Freud divided personality into three parts:

- id: the primitive urges
- ego: the part of us that acts
- superego: the controlling part that keeps the id and ego in line with society's demands

Some parts of modern psychology have made different observations relative to these questions. One division, proposed by John D. Mayer,[62] looks like the following:

> The System Set employs several distinctions: Those between the inner personality and its plans for outward expression, that between consciousness and non-conscious systems, and that between cognition, on the one hand, and motivation and emotion on the other. Applying these time-honored distinctions to a comprehensive collection of functions, one possible solution to the division issue is to identify four more-or-less discrete groups of function (Mayer, 2001).
>
> 1. The energy lattice. This functional group provides direction to the person, drawing on subsystems that both motivate the individual and qualify those motives with emotions that guide the individual's social behavior.

2. The knowledge works. This functional group involves the individual's models of the self and the world, along with the intelligences that operate to construct those models and to think with them.
3. The social actor. This functional group involves the individual's characteristic or preferred styles of social expression, including attachment patterns, as well as the person's social skills.
4. The conscious executive. This functional group involves the capacity to self-reflect and self-govern, as well as the conscious experience of those portions of personality to which the individual has access. (Most personality processes are regarded as non-conscious; that is, unconnected or disconnected from consciousness)

The exact details of any particular system are not the main point. Whether the systems are compatible really isn't all that important either. The point is that throughout history people who have asked the question about what we are have often come up with the answer that we are not unified, single-purpose beings. We have parts and the parts don't always get along.

Table 3 shows the seven parts in the chakra model. While it seems clear that it would be best if all our parts worked together for a common goal, it's also clear that most of us just don't work that way. We fight battles between being in a loving family (chakra 4) and soaking up the chaotic energy of gambling or drugs (chakra 1). Teenagers and parents

Table 3: The Chakras in a Soul

Spirit Chakra (7)
Mind Chakra (6)
Communication Chakra (5)
Heart Chakra (4)
Will Chakra (3)
Desire Chakra (2)
Chaos Chakra (1)

struggle with will and heart until the teenagers can strike a new balance when they become adults. Spirit and mind may pull us toward different solutions as we face problems in our lives. Sexual exploitation in the workplace tangles the will chakra and desire chakra and then they battle with society's feelings about appropriate interconnectedness. I'm not sure where maintaining a healthy weight fits in, but it certainly demonstrates another place where many of us are not single-intentioned in our lives. Here's one more example taken from Jon Ronson's *The Men Who Stare at Goats*:

> And then a sniper fired a single shot from somewhere into Jim's platoon.
>
> Everyone just stood there. The sniper fired again, and the Americans started running toward the one and only palm tree in sight. Jim was running so fast that he skidded face first into it. He heard someone behind him shout, "VC in black pajamas, one hundred meters."
>
> About twenty seconds later, Jim thought, Why is nobody shooting? What are they waiting for? They can't be waiting for me to instruct them to shoot, can they?
>
> "TAKE HIM OUT!" screamed Jim.
>
> And so the soldiers started shooting, and when it was over a small team walked forward to find the body. But, for all the gunfire, they had failed to hit the sniper.
>
> How had that happened?
>
> ...
>
> Jim had yelled for his soldiers to kill the sniper, and they had all, as one, and with every shot, fired high.
>
> "This came to be understood as a common reaction when fresh soldiers fire on humans," Jim said. "It is not a natural thing to shoot people."
>
> (What Jim had seen tallied with studies conducted after the Second World War by military historian General S. L. A. Marshall. He interviewed thousands of American infantrymen and concluded that only 15 to 20 percent of them had actually

shot to kill. The rest had fired high or not fired at all, busying themselves however else they could.

And 98 percent of the soldiers who did shoot to kill were later found to have been deeply traumatized by their actions. The other 2 percent were diagnosed as "aggressive psychopathic personalities," who basically didn't mind killing people under any circumstances, at home or abroad....)

In this case will (in the form of wanting to stay alive) loses out to heart (in the form of not wanting to hurt a fellow human being).

Somehow, though, all these chakras fit together and make up a soul, which, for the most part, lets us act in our world.

The soul is made up of the set of chakras.

soul = {chakra}

One aspect of the integration process involves the relative importance of each chakra. Do we first search for love or security? Is our desire to be an artist so overwhelming that we throw away everything else to pursue our muse? Is our relationship with our God the prime motivator in our life? It's hard to conceive of an absolute measure of importance, but we can use an importance scale to get a subjective measure. For each chakra in the box below, rate it in the range from very important to not important at all.

The ratings you assign will give you some information about which chakras you think are most important and which you rely on the most

---

Take the seven chakras and rate each one on a scale of 5 for very important to 1 for not important at all.

_____ Spirit Chakra — Connection with God or the gods
_____ Mind Chakra — Senses and thoughts
_____ Communication Chakra — Passing information between entities
_____ Heart Chakra — Connection to other entities
_____ Will Chakra — Personal power
_____ Desire Chakra — Creative and destructive impulses
_____ Chaos Chakra — Connection with chaos and primal energy

when you make choices. Comparing your ratings and the ratings of others may help you understand your connections better.

Interactions between Chakras

The question now is how do chakras work together to decide what to do. We already talked a little about how chakras interact when we looked at the way chakras share life force with other chakras. If we combine that with what we said about experience, we should have enough to explain most of the decision-making process without adding any additional mechanisms. I especially want to avoid the idea that there is some controlling part of our selves that mediates between the chakras.

So here's how I think it works. In any particular situation each chakra has information about what it did in the past and what it intends to do in the present situation. The past situation may or may not be directly related to the current situation, but there will usually be enough similarity for the chakra to have an indication of what it did before and the level of success the soul, as a whole, obtained. The intended solutions are shared among the chakras. The experience also sets the desired life force levels in each of the chakras. Chakras that have found a good solution in the past will have high life force set points. They will be asking the other chakras to help with the proposed solution and contribute their kind of life force.

Once the desired life force levels are set, the chakras share their life force, as best they can, so that they achieve the kind of balance we talked about in Chapter 9. The chakra (or chakras) with the highest life force level take control of the situation. If the solutions the various chakras come up with are in agreement, all of the chakras will work together. If different chakras have incompatible preferred actions, we will see a less effective response. The common phrase, "being of two minds," gets translated in a chakra model to "having a divided soul."

Interestingly, this model clearly predicts that we act more quickly and more decisively when all aspects of a situation point to a particular solution. It also predicts that people who focus on a particular type of interaction (say through heart or through will) will also be far more decisive than people who consider many aspects of a situation before deciding.* It has the capability of distinguishing between types of indecision and inability to act. Measures of the life force in chakras as actions are being taken would provide good evidence for the motivations of the person being studied.

Self-Aware Souls

One of the biggest differences between the energy in life force and the kinds of energy we deal with in ordinary reality is that souls are aware of themselves and the energy states of their chakras. Information is part of the life force. Souls can do things to change their energy and information levels.

I am not suggesting anything like total awareness or the ability to make changes easily, accurately, or in any situation. We all know better than that. But we also know that we usually have some sense when something is wrong in our lives. We try to fix what makes us uncomfortable as best we can. Although it's not the only way to look at what is going on, one way to think about how we try to make changes is to look at how we are changing the life force states in our set of chakras.

The life force level in a chakra is affected by life force going out to others, life force coming in from others, life force from spirit (chakra 7), life force from chaos (chakra 1), and life force from other chakras. Internal change to the chakra states involves moving the life force between chakras.

Self-awareness comes in because we realize that we will be in the position to make decisions in the future. Most entities on the earth do not appear to have that capacity. We are able to watch ourselves in the present. At the same time we realize that we may be facing similar situations in the future and know how to study what has happened in the past to make better choices the next time.

I believe this ability to study the past and predict the future is partly because of our mind chakra. But even more than that, I think it's because of our physical brain. We spent a lot of evolutionary energy to develop a

---

* It does not say that decisiveness is necessarily a good thing. Deciding to use a hammer when you are being screwed will probably make things worse.

brain, so I have to believe it serves some useful purpose. Thinking certainly seems like a strong possibility.

What I believe the brain allows us to do that we can't do any other way is to imagine future scenarios. The imagination produced by the brain is powerful enough to allow the chakras to react to it. When the chakras react, they store the thought experiences, reset their life force levels, and prepare to deal differently with events in the future.

We know this works. Athletes and performers improve their abilities by imagining themselves making exact movements. Most of us rehearse what we are going to say in difficult situations (or what we should have said). We relive our bad experiences until we can detach from them by having better ways to cope with what happened.

Also coming out of this model is an explanation for some of the things that happen during dreams. Most of our waking thought processes use mind chakra and communication chakra memories. In dreams the mind seems to be able to access and process memories from the other chakras. Dream images are interpretations the mind chakra makes of those memories. All the chakras are freer in a dream state to react to the situation the brain presents, so this can be a more effective way of planning future actions, especially actions that are not directly related to the mind.

Many animals also dream, so we can guess that they are also adjusting reactions to past events. To the extent that they are making plans for the future they are also self-aware.

The purpose of sleep and dreaming becomes clearer. In a relatively safe environment, with the body shut down, the soul has time to integrate all of its parts in a mostly unified way of interacting with the world. Self-awareness and the ability of the soul to adjust the responses of all of its parts is how we appear as integrated as we do.

III. Simple Soul Connections

...we know that we do not know all the laws *as yet*.

— *Richard Feynman*

In this part of the book I want to take what we discussed about individual souls and look at how two souls connect to one another. In Part II we looked at how individual chakras can move life force in and out. Now we are going to look in greater detail at how two souls in an interaction relate to one another.

We'll look at the details about how we are connected and the consequences of being connected in non-ordinary reality. For the most part this section will look at the simplest kinds of soul connections — the connections between the same chakra in two different souls. In Part IV we will look at the more complex interactions that happen when each of the chakras in one soul interacts with each of the chakras in a second soul.

10. Ordinary and Non-Ordinary Connections

It is common for measurement development to operate as the foundation and driving force behind the increased understanding and universal acceptance of concepts.

— *Mounir Ragheb*

One of the most important aspects of connections between souls in non-ordinary reality is that they are not like physical connections in ordinary reality. Ordinary reality is concerned with space and time. Soul reality is not. When we are talking about souls, I think size in the sense of tall or wide or long does not apply. Time doesn't tick the same way for souls as it does for physical objects.

I want to compare a two-soul case with the case of two physical bodies to highlight the differences between the two types of reality. The two-body problem (at least for gravitation and electromagnetism) is quite familiar to anyone who has studied physics. If we were talking about physical forces, such as electricity or gravitation, we could write down all the relevant equations and have a full understanding of the system.

Most people, even without studying physics, have a pretty good understanding of what is going on, even if they can't figure out all of the details. Gravity pulls us down; and the more mass we have, the harder it pulls. Static electricity makes our hair stand on end because those extra electrons on our body push each other apart. Compasses line up along the magnetic field of the earth. Things like that. With a few more years of study, people might also be able to understand the corrections that relativity requires.

The two-soul problem has some added complications. Let's start by looking at the simplest case. We imagine a universe with nothing in it except two entities capable of sending, receiving, and storing life force. I ask you to imagine that these are souls with no bodies. Having only souls avoids complications from physical reactions. To further simplify this case, let's assume that the souls are interacting only through their heart chakras.

Connections

For physical bodies, connections are pretty simple. The non-relativistic solution for gravity includes mass and distance. For electromagnetism, mass, distance, and velocity are required to calculate the resulting forces and fields. For souls… well, let's take a look at some of the complications.

At any given time, each of these souls has a certain amount of stored life force, which we will call SLF_1 and SLF_2. This is roughly equivalent to mass in a two-body gravitational system or charge in a two-body electromagnetic system. The more you have of it (life energy, mass, or charge), the more effect you can have on the other body or soul.

In simple two-body problems we always need to know about distance. For physical objects the force between them gets stronger as the physical distance gets closer. Guess what? I don't think physical distance means much to souls. I suggest that what matters instead is the connection between the two souls.

Our colloquial use of the words connection and interaction suggests that we think of connection using distance terms. We say things like, "I feel closer to him than ever." or "We have just been drifting apart." I think the connection between two souls is specific to that pair of souls and can be measured, but it's not the same as pulling out a tape measure to find the distance between two bodies.

For the two-soul problem the connection is the amount of life force that is sent between the two souls. As we described in Chapter 8, the sending soul has a particular amount of life force it wants to send called the outward intention (OI_1). Souls choose to send all or only part of their stored life force. The amount actually sent is limited by the outward ability (OA_1) and the amount of stored life force the soul has available (SLF_1).

Souls also have the ability to accept or block life force coming toward them. The receiving soul receives the life force sent, limited by its inward ability (IA_2) and its inward intention (II_2).

To a certain extent, the more life force we have, the better we are able to sense other life force, but several other factors are involved. We'll go into those in the rest of Part III. What we want to remember now is that energy available, energy sent, and energy received are not necessarily the same. We will say the energies received are the connections called C_{12} and C_{21}.*

Velocity and Momentum

In a two-body problem, velocity is how far a body is moving in a particular direction in a given amount of time. Gravity doesn't care about velocity; it only cares about distance. Electromagnetism does care because some of its force depends on the movement of the bodies. For a physical body momentum is mass times velocity. Momentum, like energy, is conserved in physical interactions.

Souls start to look very non-physical when we look for something like "soul velocity" or "soul momentum." With souls we are trying to work without having a concept of physical distance, as described above. (As we will see in a moment, we also are missing a consistent physical time.) However, we can choose to say the change in connection as a function of something that kind of looks like time is the rough equivalent of velocity.

I am proposing that momentum is conserved in soul interactions as it is conserved in physical interactions. The rough equivalent of momentum

---

* The numbers 12 and 21 refer to the direction of the connection. C_{12} is the energy moving from soul 1 to soul 2. C_{21} is the energy from soul 2 to soul 1.

for souls might be the stored life force multiplied by the change in the connection between the souls.

One of the possible uses of momentum is in describing changes to the interaction the two souls have. Just as the force of gravity can pull objects toward one another, life force can move souls closer together or farther apart.

As with the connection, the rate of change in the connection, which we are calling velocity, is specific to each pair of souls. Let's call it V_{12}. (And there probably is a V_{21} for the velocity as sensed by the other soul.) Momentum is similar with the added factor that the amount of stored life force can also change as the result of interactions. We have an M_{12} and an M_{21}.

Time

In a two-body problem, calculations are done based on current conditions to predict what the system will look like at some time in the future. We have had relatively accurate clocks for over 300 years, so we are pretty used to the idea of intervals of time. (Galileo did not have a clock, so he used his pulse or the beat from music to measure intervals when he was doing his experiments. The concept of a consistent time interval was a novel idea back when Galileo realized he needed to have one for the work he was doing, but in the modern world we would find it hard to live without the idea of time intervals.*)

I'm not sure we can talk about time in a two-soul universe the same way we talk about time in a two-body universe. We have too many examples of time slowing down or speeding up to think that time flows in uniform intervals for things that are alive. Here are some examples: When you are in a hospital emergency room worried about a loved one who was just in an accident, the clock seems to forget about moving. The same thing happens at the end of the workday for many people. "Time sure flies when you're having fun." The years seem to get shorter as we get older. People who have had near death experiences sometimes report that their whole life flashed by in seconds.

---

* For example, how could we know that a great split end runs a 4.33-second 40-yard dash, but that guy who runs a 4.62 doesn't have a chance of turning pro.

These examples are usually ascribed to quirks of human psychology rather than expected consequences of the life force. Well, what would you expect? The people doing the ascribing don't believe in a life force, so they have to give some reason for the observed phenomena. (Saying it's human psychology doesn't do much for predicting when and where the events will happen, so it's really just more words.)

I do have an example of an event where there is a quantifiable difference in performance: an athlete who is in "the zone." When an athlete is in the zone, time moves slower, a baseball is easier to hit, the basketball always goes into the basket, the tiniest openings look big enough for a running back to drive a truck through. Athletes can feel when they are in the zone and their performance provides a measure that they are right. When this has happened to me in karate, I felt like I had all the time in the world to figure out what my opponent was doing and to decide the best technique to counter his move. Feeling this is life-changing and time never seems the same again.

So I don't think we can talk about the same kind of time in a two-soul problem that we would use for a two-body problem. However, I believe we can talk about a series of events that has some time-like quality. Events between two souls have some duration, which might not be the same for each soul. We can measure the duration at least subjectively. Without going into any details, let's call the duration of the series of events T_1 for soul 1 and T_2 for soul 2. In most instances, T_1 is the same as T_2 and probably the same as the time from the clock on the wall.

We also have some examples of souls being able to sense the future. There was the certain knowledge that I needed to move from the dating site at Yahoo.com to Match.com if I wanted to meet the right person, and there was also the insistent insight about exactly the right message to write at exactly the right time. Many of us have run into people who will be important in our lives in the strangest of places under the most unusual of circumstances. And we know that we were supposed to meet.

We are in contact with many people a day. Most don't get noticed at all. But we know in that instant, and this is the point, that this meeting is different. We are seeing the future possibilities in a way that is not allowed by physical forces. Perhaps we can conclude that time does not affect souls in the same way as it affects physical objects.

If time is not a barrier, we hope the calculations we will be developing predict that we pay more attention to (have a stronger connection with) someone we will be spending more time with in the future. Since "soul momentum" is a function of the change in connection strength, it means that life force from souls can work consistently throughout a whole life to bring a pair of souls together even if they started far apart.

Calculations

We have five aspects in the soul system: the life force of each soul (SLF), the connections between the souls (C), the velocity of the souls relative to one another (V), the momentum of the souls (M), and the duration of a series of events (T). The problem with these aspects is that describing any of them can be tricky. It's a lot easier in the physical world.

If we are talking about gravity, we know that the gravitational force from an object (the equivalent of SLF) depends on the mass of the object. The transmission (what would be C for souls) depends on the distance between the objects. Time would be measured in a standard physical unit such as seconds. That's about as simple as it gets. (Corrections for relativity add some complexity.) We would see the effect of the interaction by measuring how the objects moved relative to one another.

If we are talking about transmitting electricity down a wire, we can talk about the number of watts that travel through the wire in a given amount of time. The main factors for transmission are the voltage difference between the two ends of the wire (SLF) and the resistance of the wire (C). Resistance is not quite as simple as distance, but it has the same feel. For any given wire, the resistance goes up linearly as a function of the length. That means there is twice as much resistance when the wire is twice as long. Higher resistances mean that less electricity can go down the wire. The meter that measures the current is tracking energy being sent, but that is something outside the system we are proposing. Perhaps we can look at the device at the end of the wire that is holding the charge. The charge it holds is a way of talking about the energy received. Longer transmission times (T) mean that more charge will be transmitted.

Moving back to the realm of souls, we have to be careful to not get confused by expecting soul transmission of life force to be more than somewhat analogous to the transmission of physical forces. The strength of the signal seems most similar. The ability to choose the strength of a connection and limit the amount of energy received seems the most dissimilar. Souls can choose to connect with a signal or ignore it. Physical objects do not have choices.

We also can't assume that souls know anything about time as we measure it in the physical world. We will assume, instead, that they understand a series of events. The number (and intensity) of events is probably more important than the physical time the events take to happen.

Two-Soul Solution

With that background, let's take a look at solving the two-soul problem. In the following we can see the story in pictures and text.*

1. In the beginning we have two souls. They are both sitting there, minding their own business.	**1** **2**

* Please reset the genders to match your personal preferences.

2. Now let's say that soul 1 is surveying his surroundings and notices soul 2. He sends a little pulse of life force in her direction, asking her to make a closer connection with him.	
3. At this point, soul 2 has a choice. (Bodies in a two-body problem do not have choices about gravity or electromagnetic force.) She can accept the life force from soul 1 or she can reject it. If she rejects it, we go back to state 1. If she accepts it, there is now a closer connection between the two souls.	
3a. Some cultures believe there are little spirits with arrows who are responsible for this kind of interaction. Could be. In that case Cupid decides whether the connection becomes closer regardless of what soul 1 and soul 2 think.	

4. Let's take Cupid back out of the problem and look at what happens to the souls regardless of how the decision to bring about a closer connection is made. Since soul 1 and soul 2 agreed on an attracting force, the two souls will start to move together.

5. If nothing restricts the connection, the two souls will pull themselves right into one another. It could be two souls forming one for a lifelong unity of soul bliss. On the other hand, it could be a real mess. That's what I would expect.

6. If no further changes take place, the souls will connect for eternity. They may throw out additional bits of life force to bring themselves closer or reduce the life force sent between them and move farther apart.

7. Maybe they decide to turn off the life force between them. Then they just drift apart.

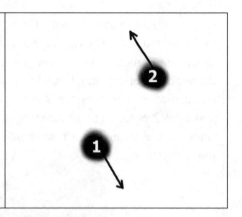

I'd like to make a few observations on this simple problem to show that these ideas actually offer some understanding about the human condition.

- A relationship that starts with an intense attraction between two almost unconnected souls happens very quickly. The souls come very close together briefly. If no further life force is applied to hold the souls close together (and it can be hard to find additional life force when the initial attraction used so much of it), they will fly rapidly apart, back to the original, almost nonexistent connection. What we have here is a one-night stand.
- A relationship that starts with some connections already in place, say family and friends, does not require as much life force to bring the two souls together. They also won't fly as far apart after they move closer. If the closer connection is enjoyed, either soul can add to the force pulling them together. They get closer. Over time (experiences) the souls can decide how close they want to be and establish a stable relationship with a reasonably consistent amount of connection between them. What we have here is the picture of a long-term relationship.

Other Considerations

Most of the examples in this chapter are positive interactions of the heart chakra between two souls. Let's take a brief look at other possibilities for the connections.

Different Chakras

Each chakra has its particular mix of information and energy, which affects the exact set of interactions we see. However, the contrasts between soul connections and physical connections would still be as sharply defined. Any of the five middle chakras would give similar examples.

We can connect based on aspects of the mind chakra, up to and including a Vulcan mind meld. Information transfer would dominate the interaction, but the concepts of connection, velocity, momentum, and time would be as different from physical bodies as anything associated with the heart chakra.

Desire may be more of a factor than heart in a one-night stand. Energy would dominate, but the contrasts between physical bodies and souls are still sharply drawn.

Positive and Negative

Gravity always pulls things together, but electromagnetism has the ability to attract or repel. In that way calculations for what happens to souls are more like calculations for electromagnetism.

We can choose to receive either positive or negative life force. When we receive the kind of life force we want, we move closer to the sender. When we receive the negative life force when we want positive (or positive when we want negative) we move farther away. We can also change whether we want positive or negative energy. Physical objects don't have the same kind of choices that souls have.

Multiple Souls

There are several aspects of the problem that come up when we move from a two-soul problem to a multiple-soul situation. The most obvious is how do we add up the life force contributions from different souls? It is probably enough, in general, to use the simple addition of forces we see with gravity.

A second question is how do the added souls (and, of course, other things in the universe) affect the communication between soul 1 and soul 2? Sometimes they may make the connection better, even without affecting the strength of the signal or the receptivity of the receiver. Other times they may make the connection worse. It's probably a complicated process of interactions, although I think it can be calculated. This effect will interact with how we add up life forces.

It is interesting that we can gain some insight into the nature of souls while looking at them as discreet things. We might think that the huge number of souls in the world would make the situation one where our only hope would be to use something like the movement of water in the ocean (fluid dynamics) as the basis for figuring out what is going on. However, I think souls are not like that because we can choose who we send our life force to and we usually don't send it to very many people at all. We make only a few connections and most of them are made in pairs.

In the following chapters we'll take a more detailed look at the aspects that govern the transmission of energy between souls: sensitivity of the receiver, strength of the sender, the connection between the souls, what happens when a message is sent, possible blocks and enhancements, and the effects of the duration of the interaction.

11. Sending and Sensing

Physical sense has four fundamental limitations,
namely, size, obscurity, distance, and time.
— *Shyam Sundar Goswami*

When people talk about the life force moving between souls, they usually are looking at the information passed between two people. We have ESP experiments and knowledge of something that has happened to a loved one and the occasional message from creatures on Alpha-Centauri.* These connections are through the mind and communication chakras.

There are other kinds of connections, too. We have the healing force of Reiki and forces in martial arts through the heart chakra and will chakra. The wants we feel in the desire chakra are also powerful forces that we are sensitive to.

When we use information to talk about the life force from a sender or the sensitivity of a receiver, it is relatively easy to measure. There are many kinds of information: pictures, sounds, emotions, thoughts, interactional patterns, spiritual inspiration, and more. My daughter, for example, sometimes hears me when I think something very loudly. Counting how much information a person is capable of transmitting through non-physical communication is something we know how to do.

The energy part of life force is more difficult to quantify. We saw some examples when we talked about the life force in the individual chakras, but there were many times when I said I really didn't know how

---

* I tend to be dubious about this, but see Akemi (2009) for more details.

to measure the energy being handled. That lack will continue to be evident in this chapter. To the best of my ability we will look at both information and energy, but the information part will be discussed more.

Measuring Life Force

To measure the information part of a connection we need a way to count what is transmitted. One way is by counting the number of bits of information a person can send or receive in a second.

In the physical world we are sensory creatures and our senses rely on nerve firings to gather information. We might think about using the number of times our nerves fire as the measure of the information we are taking in. There are a couple of problems with this approach. One is that information is not the same as stimulus, so we would be measuring the wrong thing. The other is that the measure is not sensitive to changes in interest and attention, which are important aspects of the amount of information we are receiving.

I suggest we look, instead, at another measure of information. One idea is to use the concept that information can be transmitted, either by our mind or by some sort of physical transmitting device. It's hard to measure what is sent by the mind, but it's easier to measure the information sent to a computer or as a television signal. A short, low-resolution movie (YouTube style) requires about 200,000 bits* per second for the picture and sound.

We usually pay attention to more than one thing. Seven is usually considered the magic number for things we can attend to at one time so that gets us to 1.4 million bits per second. Our sensory information is much better than YouTube quality, so let's multiply that number by about ten. We're also paying attention to our surroundings, which adds more. Some of us can attend to more information than others. Allow me to wave my hands and suggest that a range from 10 million to 100 million bits per second is something we can consider as a possibility. It turns out that our capabilities are not really all that important. As long as we

---

* Note that this is bits, not bytes. Resolutions and compressions vary widely. I'm only looking to get this value within a couple of orders of magnitude.

measure all of the information in the same way, using this method to measure information will be effective.

To measure energy transfer we need a way to measure energy lost by the sender or given to the receiver. If this shows up in the physical world, such as in research that shows people can do more work in a supportive setting, we can measure the change in work accomplished. Usually, though, accurate measures of energy transfer are much more difficult than measures of information transfer. When we try to measure the energy component of life force, I will continue to use food calories, as we did in the discussion of the chakras.

Different chakras process different mixes of information and energy. In this chapter there is more about the mind chakra and communication chakra because those are the ones primarily responsible for processing the kind of information we are measuring.

Ability to Sense

First let's look at the chakra component we called the inward ability to accept. It is a measure of how well a soul can sense signals coming in. There are many things that determine how well a particular person can sense life force communications.

The first is the basic set of abilities that we are born with. When we use the reincarnation model, the simplest idea is that we are born with abilities similar to what we had in our previous life. There might well be some changes from the time between lives, too. These abilities can change as a result of life experiences. We don't start each life the same way. If we are not using the reincarnation model, we can still assume that people are born with a particular set of abilities. We expect it will be something like a normal bell curve.

Our families make a huge difference in how well we can use life force. Diane Steinbach talks about how her abilities were encouraged by her family.

> As a child I was brought up to question perceived reality and to try to reach out to the other side. My mother was a believer in the paranormal and spoke openly about her mother's own eerie ability to know when someone was in trouble or had passed

away. My mom believed in following your instincts and felt that spirit guides or Angels were watching over us. She encouraged my own fascination with the paranormal by monitoring Ouija board sessions, and trying to validate findings, as well as continuing to share stories of her own communications with the other side.

Although I wasn't actively doing readings until I was in my thirties, she encouraged the belief in the spirit world and shared books on paranormal topics, which led me to know that there is a big universe out there full of unknowns. This type of upbringing helped me to accept my own ability to communicate with those on the other side and to trust in my own instincts and perceptions no matter how unlikely they may seem.[63]

We can see that Diane was encouraged to develop her abilities in an atmosphere of acceptance (and that she did develop them). Similar suggestions of positive family involvement show up in Ian Stevenson's work[64] on previous lives.

Other families strongly discourage any kind of non-ordinary communication. It's not clear that the abilities go away, but we learn to ignore the signals when they aren't acknowledged or when they are actively discouraged.

I suspect that ability is actually lost when it isn't used. We can see similar effects in ordinary communication. A normal baby is born with the ability to speak all of the phonemes of any language on earth. As the baby and its caretakers interact, the baby learns to use the sounds its caretakers use. It loses the ability to make sounds that are not part of the native language. Even more significantly, it loses the ability to hear the sounds it doesn't use. Japanese, for example, don't distinguish between the English 'r' and 'l' sounds. They have trouble when the meaning of a sentence is changed by the tone of the speaker's voice, for example, a statement that is made sarcastically. English speakers have difficulty making the double 'r' sound in Spanish and the click languages are beyond the ability of most of them. They have similar amounts of trouble using the tonal aspect of Chinese, where words that have the same phonetic sounds are differentiated by the differences in the starting, middle, and end tones of the word.

The implication is that we lose abilities we don't use. Beyond that, we need to practice to move from a potential ability to skillful use of a talent. Families that don't believe in psychic ability never give their children a chance to develop the skill.

The society that we are raised in has a strong effect on our abilities. There is a strong interaction between family and society, of course. Most families try to fit in with the people they live with. (This can be a matter of survival.) A family may allow non-ordinary communication within the family, but discourage it outside the family group.

Some societies encourage life force training for people who show strong natural abilities. The Native Americans understand the need for a medicine man who can help the tribe with spiritual matters. Some Native American cultures expect all of their people to go through a ceremony or a quest as a rite of passage into adulthood. These almost always have non-ordinary aspects. Similar rites are found throughout the world, especially in Africa (before AIDS), native parts of South America, and Australia. Cultures that have these rites also have extensive training for people who are especially adept in using the life force. These people become the medicine women or men, shamans, kahunas, curanderos, altomesayoqs, or whatever other name they use. They are given a special place in the society and are expected to perform an exceptionally difficult role.

There are other life experiences that change our abilities to use life force. These exist even in societies that don't have non-ordinary traditions. I've already talked about my karate experiences. My karate practice was a vital factor in my development. Other people find similar groups where they can train their abilities. Martial arts groups, meditation practices, Wicca, Reiki, and dozens of other traditions help enhance our abilities to sense the life force. As we will see in the next section, there are even more places where we learn to send life force, even though that's not what we call it.

To summarize, the ability to practice communication skills is an important factor in improving them. In that, skills related to communication between souls are like any other skill. We have a level of ability we are born with and positive or negative experiences that make us better or worse at life force communication. We can add them all up to find our current sensing ability.

Let's use the following variables:
IAA is inward ability to sense
IntA is intrinsic ability
LA is learning ability
PosI is positive interactions
NegI is negative interactions
i is the counter for the number of incidents in the person's life
The equation we can use to determine a person's current ability looks like this:

$$IAA(t) = IntA + \sum_{i=1}^{life}(LA_i * PosI_i) + \sum_{i=1}^{life}(LA_i * NegI_i)$$

where learning ability and intrinsic ability may or may not be related. NegI has a negative sign so that negative incidents reduce the sensing ability. Learning ability may be different for different incidents.

It's not a particularly useful equation, though, because searching for all the positive and negative effects is not a practical exercise. "If I have to go through all of the bad things that happened to me, it will take the rest of this life and probably one more to resolve them" [Anonymous]. Better ways to figure out our current skill level are discussed later in this chapter.

There is another curious aspect of some people who can sense soul communication. Especially in Western culture, where the life force is not generally accepted, often people who develop the ability to sense soul communication have had some kind of brain injury just before they found they can sense spirits, ghosts, or whatever. Some of the better-known names are John Edward, James Van Praagh, and George Anderson.[65] I suggest that what may have happened is the brain has lost some of its ability to ignore the soul.

I think this is related to what I call the Tiger in the Jungle situation. When we are in a dangerous situation in the physical world, such as walking through a jungle where there are tigers, it is best to pay attention to the physical world rather than the spirit world. If we are so busy paying attention to the dead spirits around us that we don't pay attention to the tiger, the tiger will find it much easier to pay special attention to us. In the Western world, the dangers are less, but our brains still ignore the soul most of the time.

We need to ask how the newfound ability to sense soul communication interacts with the ability to sense other forms of life force. I think it probably reduces the ability of the mind-brain system. We see a similar situation in ordinary communication. People who have injuries to their brains often have less ability to understand conversation in a noisy place. The sounds are all there, but their brains can't sort out the sounds they want to hear from the sounds they want to ignore.[66]

I think a similar problem may occur with non-ordinary communication. The "sounds" are all there in the mind chakra or communication chakra, but it is hard for the person's brain to separate out the part it wants to consider. Besides, imagine you are a dead spirit who wants to communicate with a living person. Wouldn't you hang around a person who could hear you? You might have a chance of getting a message through. With thousands of these spirits drawn toward the person who has lost the ability to block them out, it's hard to believe anything else in the soul realm could be heard over all of that noise.

Another observation about people who have become more sensitive to communications from other entities because of injuries is that they do not seem to be any better at sending life force. They don't suddenly become master Reiki practitioners or genius martial artists, which use different chakras. In fact, the opposite may be true. They may lose some of their abilities to use (rather than sense) the life force. How damaging even a small head injury can be for many aspects of life is well documented.[67] It would not be surprising if the ability to use the life force is one of the abilities that also suffers.

Surprisingly (okay, not very surprisingly), there aren't any studies measuring loss or gain of a person's ability to use the life force related to brain injuries. I have friends who became less able to do martial arts after a brain injury. However, no life force explanations are required for that. Everything gets harder after a brain injury.

Looking at brain injuries is useful in thinking about the way we all sense life force from a particular source. We have the signal we want to receive and a lot of noise from other sources of life force. What we need are some accurate measures of a person's ability to sense life force. There are some standard equations in signal processing that answer the questions in ordinary reality. I think we can use the ideas in soul communication, too, if we substitute soul variables for ordinary variables appropriately.

Most equations dealing with the ability to receive a signal are based on the original signal strength, the distance between the sender and the receiver, the amount of noise, and the efficiency of the filter being used. Signal strength, noise, and filter sensitivity are all pretty much the same. We do need to use connection instead of distance. When we find a way to create standard signals and ambient noise, we will be able to measure the sensing and filtering ability of people who are receiving non-ordinary communication. This will be far more practical than trying to add up a whole life's worth of experiences.

To express this as an equation, we need to reduce our current ability to sense non-ordinary communication to take account of the amount of noise we are also experiencing and our ability to filter the noise. Replacing channel capacity with sensing ability in the Shannon–Hartley theorem[68] gives us this equation:

$$IAA = B * \log_2\left(1 + \frac{S}{N}\right)$$

where
IAA is the inward ability to accept
B is the bandwidth of the channel
S is the average received signal power over the bandwidth
N is the average noise or interference power over the bandwidth
S/N is the signal-to-noise ratio
Bandwidth is an electronics term, which is probably related to inward ability.

Another vital aspect of the sensitivity to receive a signal is the ability to amplify the signal into something that can be sensed. The whole point of an ordinary receiver (for example, radios and televisions) is to detect and filter a small signal, then increase its power to turn it into light and sound. In the same way, a non-ordinary receiver (for example, a soul) needs to increase focus on the signal it receives so that it is powerful enough for the mind/brain of the person to detect.

The most important effect comes from the ability to change our inward intention of what is being attended to. Lower chakras can sense and take in energy which is then used by the higher chakras to increase their ability to attend to information being sent to them. Out of the many connections that are trying to get our attention, we have the ability to focus on a particular one by resetting our inward intentions through the interactions of the chakras. The ability to focus greatly increases the sensitivity to receive a particular signal.

Outward Ability to Send

We measure the sending strength a soul is capable of with the outward ability to send. Different people have different abilities to send a life force signal. It is a situation similar to the ability to sense a signal, but there are some striking differences that are important to consider.

I don't think that the outward ability to send and inward ability to accept are necessarily tied to one another. One person may be able to sense life force well, but not be especially good at sending a signal. Another person may be a strong sender without being able to sense the life force signals being returned. A lot more research needs to be done before we will be able to define the connection, if any, between the abilities of sending and receiving.

The most important difference between sending and sensing is that a person can sense what other people are thinking and/or feeling without anyone else knowing it — as long as the person keeps quiet about it. If a person sends out strong life force signals, the situation is very different. Other people can sense that something is going on. They may not know exactly what they are feeling, especially in Western culture where we are not trained to work with the life force, but they do sense something.

I say that we are not trained to use life force in Western culture, but that really isn't true. We are not often trained to use life force as life force, but there are many instances where our training seems to clearly enhance our ability to use life force on others. Where we are not trained well is in sensing when life force is being sent towards us. It might help to look at some examples of how we are trained to use life force without acknowledging it as life force. Note how many of these involve using life force sent from the heart chakra, will chakra, and desire chakra to reinforce a message sent in ordinary reality.

Performers have many ways to use life force as part of their profession. Singers and wind instrument players are consistently taught to use the diaphragm for breathing and even to use areas below the diaphragm. There are no lung areas below the diaphragm, but using the area all the way from the pubic bone on up significantly increases the ability of the performer. There are physiological reasons why this happens, but the breath is also closely tied to the life force. When we watch a performer, one of the ways we judge the performance is by how powerful, sensual, or emotional it is. All of those attributes are connected to the chakras in the extended range of breathing.

Actors and actresses learn to create a character. They connect on many levels. One of the most important is the performer's ability to project the life energy of the character they are portraying. It hasn't always been that way. When I watch movies from the 1930s, it seems to me like the performers were much less likely to get deep into the psyche of their characters. They projected less life force. Each era has its own preferences for the amount of life force it wants from its performers.

We can see one more example in the movies. Audrey Hepburn and Julie Ormand are both beautiful women. Both played the title role in the movie *Sabrina*. Almost without exception, people prefer the Hepburn version. When critics comment on the differences, they talk about how much more lively, dynamic, and connected-to-the-audience the Hepburn character is. In Western terms, this is described as personality. I think we can also look at it from the perspective of sending life force.

In the world of business we see leaders and followers. We talk about powerful people rising to the top of their profession. So what is this power thing we are talking about? I suggest it is life force from the will chakra. One person can use this personal power to convince others to follow him or her. Everyone is born with some of it. Some are born with a lot and, if business training programs are to be believed, it can be learned. Dale Carnegie talks about winning friends and influencing people — using positive energy from the heart chakra to change people's minds. It is one technique, but other equally successful businessmen are as friendly as a shark and still have people following them. They are more likely to be using the will chakra.

A businessman such as Warren Buffet appears to care for the companies he controls, the people in them, and his investors. He seems to be using this power to help others (as well as himself). On the other hand, people like investment thief Bernie Madoff and Enron chairman Kenneth Lay thought only of themselves (and maybe a few cronies), and did great harm in the world.

Politics is similar to business. Though there is more emphasis on manipulating perception and less on power, politicians definitely play to the idea of giving power to their constituents. Not that there is any truth in it. When politicians learn to control the image they project, they become successful. The facts about who a politician really is are almost always there, but a successful politician uses his personal power to affect which parts of his history are considered. I suggest that the politician is able to learn to use his life force to do this. For examples of good and bad politicians I offer Dick Cheney and Barack Obama. You decide which is good and which is bad. It will depend on how much you have been influenced by the collective life force of each side. We can generally agree that Adolph Hitler had a great deal of life force and used it to influence a large portion of the world, not for the better.

Spiritual leaders add promises about teaching their followers about the divine. Whether they actually do or not, they provide the feeling that divine understanding is in their teachings. This is also a life force connection involving the spirit chakra. Although there is some disagreement, we can suggest that the Dalai Lama is generally trying to help make the world better. In the Christian tradition, along with positive leaders, there have been evangelical Christian leaders who have misused their will chakra to deceive their followers and, as far as I can tell, advance the agenda of the devil. The clearest examples may be those who sexually molest children, but there are others who are notorious for taking money from the poor and giving it to themselves. The general theme in the self-enrichment situations is "But those who desire to be rich fall into temptation, into a snare, into many senseless and harmful desires that plunge people into ruin and destruction. For the love of money is a root of all kinds of evils."[69]

Athletics (competitive sports and martial arts) provides one more example of where we train people in using the life force. People are often surprised when the most physically talented athlete is not the winner of a contest. There are ordinary reality concepts such as drive, desire, focus, and concentration that are used to explain the discrepancies. I think a deeper analysis would suggest that in ordinary reality these shouldn't have enough of an effect to make a difference. Physical ability should carry the day. But consider a world where life force exists and these concepts are seen as descriptors of particular aspects of life force processed by the will chakra. They are as much a part of an interaction as the physical abilities, so they will make a difference in the outcome.

There are cases where some people have trained in many of the skills described here. (Oprah Winfrey comes to mind.) These extraordinary folks have trained themselves to use their life force to affect others on many levels including, in Oprah's case, spiritual, perceptual, intellectual, and emotional, while also enhancing her viewers' personal power.

A lack of life force or using life force in ways that are bad for us can also happen. Criminals who attack people on the streets are always looking for the weak to prey on. Self-defense experts emphasize the need to appear confident and prepared. I think that life force is a significant part of what is needed to do that.

Rhonda Byrne's well-known book on manifesting wealth and success, *The Secret*, talks about the power of visualizing good things to improve our lives. This is an excellent concept, but one that is sometimes dismissed by those who ask, "How can wishing for something make it happen?" The answer is life force. Our life force connects with others who have similar desires and people who can help us meet our goals. It's not some mystic wish and coincidence. In soul reality we make connections that affect our ordinary-reality lives.

I want to say here, though, that I don't agree with the belief that there are no such things as coincidences. I think there are. Most of us aren't powerful enough to cause everything that happens to us and there are so many intertwining threads of personal history that I don't think all of their interactions are necessarily part of a greater plan. Sometimes a coincidence is just a coincidence.*

As we can see from the examples, life force can be used for both positive and negative motives. The myth that life force is always positive is just that, a myth. Life force is used for the same reasons as every other force we have available to us. We can use it to do good or to do evil. We can harm or heal. We can bring helpful people and things our way or we can attract ones that will harm us.

In looking at equations that describe the strength of a person's outward ability to send, we need to take into account all of the training the person has had, as well as the results of the experiences during the person's life. We all start with some intrinsic strength. Then we have situations where we train ourselves to send out stronger signals. Some of the places we train are martial arts and healing arts — the same as the places we learn to sense the life force. In addition, we learn to use the life force in places such as training for sales, assertiveness, and public speaking. Our experiences of successes and failures when we try to use life force get added into the mix. What we end up with is a strength at any given time based on the experiences we have had.

We can use the following variables:
OAS is the outward ability to send
IntS is intrinsic strength
LA is learning ability
ST is strength training
PosI is positive interactions
NegI is negative interactions
i is incidents during the person's life
The equation we can use to determine a person's current sending strength looks almost the same as the ability to sense the life force:

$$OAS(t) = IntS$$
$$+ \sum_{i=1}^{life}(LA_i * ST_i) + \sum_{i=1}^{life}(LA_i * PosI_i) + \sum_{i=1}^{life}(LA_i * NegI_i)$$

where learning ability and intrinsic strength may or may not be related. NegI has a negative sign so that negative incidents reduce the sending strength.

---

* It is claimed that Sigmund Freud once said something similar about cigars.

This equation may be more useful than the one for inward ability to accept because the strength training seems to be a strong factor in the equation and we have a pretty good sense of when we are training someone to use the life force, even if that isn't what it is called. This still calls for a lot of information about a person's history. Other techniques to calculate the outward ability to send may be more effective. It is hard to know everything that has happened in a person's life. The next section looks at some of the ways we can measure a person's ability at any given time without having to study all of their past experiences.

Measuring Abilities

Rupert Sheldrake has devised an experiment that has been performed tens of thousands of times called the Sense of Being Stared At.[70] In these experiments one person stares at the back of another person's head. (There are variations using single chakras, but the undifferentiated stare gives us useful information about a person's overall ability. Sheldrake does not use chakras as part of his model.)

About half of the time the person stares. The other half of the time they are looking somewhere else. Whether the person stares or not is determined randomly. The person being stared at tries to feel whether the other person is staring or not. If you would like to try this out, look for the phone app from Pine Winds Press.

In a very large set of trials, with many participants, people are right about 55% of the time.[71] If the results were just chance, they would be right 50% of the time. A pair with a very good sender and receiver can do much better. In another analysis of part of this data Sheldrake found that people who were correct more than half the time outnumbered people who were wrong more than half the time by about two to one.

From the Sheldrake experiments we can see that a history of interaction between two people is not necessary to establish communication. Every person has an intrinsic ability to send and receive life force. However, Sheldrake also found that practicing being stared at (with feedback about whether the answer was correct or not) helped increase sensitivity.*

Finding current ability through experiments is a lot easier than trying to calculate the level by summing up past experiences and personal abilities. The easiest aspects to measure are how well a person can send life force and how well they can receive it.

The most useful concept we have when we are trying to find out how well someone can receive the life force is calibration. Back in the late 1970s I worked on a camera that went into space to observe the sun's atmosphere. This was one of the first times pictures were being taken using a digital receiver in a satellite. We used one of the most sophisticated sensors available — an incredible one million pixels with eight bits of information per pixel. These days the standard camera has about six million pixels and higher end cameras have a few times more — and each pixel has 24 bits of information.

Sensors are now made in huge batches. The surface of the sensor has almost no variation from one part of the sensor to another. If there are too many bad pixels, the whole sensor is tossed out. Not so back in the 1970s. We had one sensor. It was very expensive. And the way it interpreted light striking the surface varied widely from one pixel to the next. Some pixels didn't work at all.

It was a lot like the differences we find when we study how well a million different people sense the life force.

What we did was to subject the sensor to a series of standard light intensities and map how each pixel responded to the light. The graph in Figure 2 shows a couple of pixels that might have been on the sensor.

What we can see from the graph is that pixel 1 is more sensitive to light. A light intensity of about 775 lumens produces an output of 100 and a light intensity of 1130 produces an output of 200. Pixel 2 requires

---

* Sheldrake sums up his finding by saying, "Most people say they have sensed when they were being stared at, and most people also say they have made others turn around by looking at them. The sense of being stared at is taken for granted by most surveillance professionals, security officers, soldiers, celebrity photographers, martial arts practitioners and hunters. The ability to detect makes biological and evolutionary sense. It may be deeply rooted in our animal nature, and widespread in the animal kingdom." (Sheldrake, 2005a)

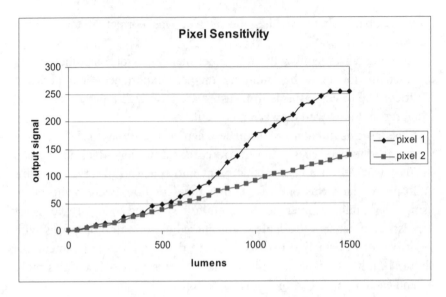

Figure 2: Pixel sensitivity graph.

an intensity of about 1070 to produce 100 and never receives enough light to produce an output of 200. It just isn't as sensitive to the light. (Or you could say it requires more light to produce the same response.)

If you want to apply this to your personal experience, think about pixel 1 as a young person who can practically read in the dark and pixel 2 as an old person who needs a much brighter light for reading. We all have different capabilities for seeing. Similarly, we have different levels of sensitivity for hearing, taste, smell, and touch. What I'm suggesting is that we also have different levels of sensitivity to life force.

In the sensor we were calibrating we also had a few pixels that were totally dead. It didn't matter what intensity of light we used, the dead pixels didn't respond. Conversely, I seem to remember a few pixels that were always on. Even in the dark, they signaled that they were sensing light. People are like that, too. Some people couldn't sense the life force if it bit them and others are sensing something extraordinary even when nothing is going on.

I suggest that we can measure a person's sensitivity to the life force in about the same way we measured each pixel's sensitivity to light. With light, the process is relatively easy. We have standard tools that can measure the intensity of light. With the life force, the problem is more complex.

In the next chapter we'll see that the strongest connections are found in one-time situations where strong emotions, and usually personal harm, are involved. However, it simply won't do to test a person's ability to sense life force by endangering friends, family, or pets. We need a measuring tool that is well researched, is able to discriminate between different levels of ability, is non-destructive, and is repeatable.

Rupert Sheldrake's Sense of Being Stared At is one of the tools we actually can use for standardization. Some of his other experiments, such as knowing who is calling on the telephone, might also be appropriate, but being stared at is about as simple as things get. It also has the advantage of tapping into very primitive sensing. When you are in the jungle or wolf-infested forest, knowing when someone or something is looking at you is a key to survival.

Another advantage of the Sense of Being Stared At is that the experiments clearly demonstrate that some pairs of people are better at sensing than others. Additional experiments show that some people are better senders or receivers regardless of who their partners are.*

We can get a sense of individual abilities by conducting a series of experiments with many different pairs. Let's say that we want to measure the relative abilities of ten people. Here's the procedure.

Conduct tests with each pair. That would be person one sending to person two, then to person three, and so on. Each person would send to the other nine for a total of 90 test runs. We would probably have to run 10 sets of 10 trials to allow for the variability in the test results.

To score each person for sending, calculate the percent of correct answers made by the people he was sending to. To score a person's sensitivity to someone staring at him, calculate the percentage of times he correctly identified whether he was being stared at.†

---

* Twins are more successful, as discussed in Sheldrake (2001). This reference also discusses the idea that who is doing the staring makes a difference.
† This is planned for the Soul Connections phone app, although it was not available yet as I was writing this book.

At this point we know the abilities of each person within this set of ten people. All in all, this isn't very useful. What needs to happen next is to expand the number of people. Mixing a few of the ten in the original study with new people in another group of ten lets us figure out the differences between the two groups. We make the assumption here that a person's ability does not change from day to day. Then if a person scores at 55% in receptivity in group one and 60% in receptivity in group two, we can conclude that there are better senders in group two. Calculating the specific abilities of each sender and each receiver is done through complicated statistical procedures — more than I want to get into here. For now the important concept is that measuring someone's ability requires a standardized set of calibrated people. A random set of ten people will not give us an accurate measure of the abilities of any of them.

Eventually we can build up a large enough population of tested people so that we can calibrate another person's skills relatively easily.

And why would anyone want to go to the trouble? When conducting experiments it is necessary to know the abilities of the people involved. If we don't know the strengths of the senders and receivers, it would be like trying to calculate miles per gallon in a car without being able to measure the miles or the gallons.

Another important question is whether this is so chancy a procedure that it is impossible to trust the results. It certainly is an approximation of a person's ability, but we use approximations all the time.

For example, IQ tests are based on exactly the same kinds of approximations. The tests are devised by giving the test to many people. IQ is determined by arbitrarily setting the average score to 100. Then an IQ of 115 is set so it is one standard deviation above. That means that the number of questions you need to get right to score 115 depends on how well other people do on the same set of questions. The score of 115 or better is achieved by 26% of the population.

The graph on the next page shows the shape of the theoretical IQ curve.

Another interesting piece of information is that IQ tests are renormalized every few years. What has been happening for the past 50 years is that each generation needs to answer more questions correctly to

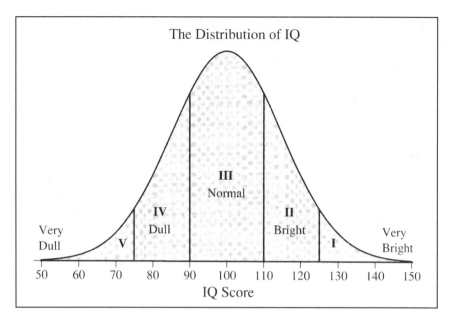

Figure 3: Bell Curve distribution of IQ.

get the same IQ as the previous generation. Put simply, from the perspective of IQ tests, people are getting smarter and smarter by about three IQ points a decade.[72] (The gains tend to be in the lower IQs and the reasons for the change are not obvious.) Some people think the same increase in ability is happening with the ability to send and receive life force.[73]

I am not making any claims that results from the Sheldrake experiment are a consistent measure of a person's ability. Nothing that has to do with people is consistent. Not IQ. Not the ability to solve problems or ride a bicycle. Not the ability to create a tasty and nutritious meal when there are two soccer games and a band concert starting in 20 minutes.

Abilities will vary throughout a person's life and as a result of health, time of the month, emotional state, whatever. Variability will also occur depending on particular partners. Some pairs simply work together better than other pairs. Some of the causes of partner variability will be discussed in the next chapter.

Unlike IQ, which is generally believed to be consistent throughout a person's life,* the ability to sense life force is an ability that can be improved with practice. There may be a maximum ability for each person, but that is something that needs to be explored. Luckily, the way we are measuring ability is based on the number of correct answers. That way we are not comparing abilities between people to determine their score (as we do in IQ tests). If we are using a standardized set of partners, we can accurately determine changes in ability.

The Sense of Being Stared At is a way to measure a person's ability to send and receive life force at any point in time. As we will see later, there are a few more complications, but as a measure of basic ability, this is a good choice.

---

* IQ really isn't consistent and training for any particular IQ test is certainly possible.

12. Building Connections

> The web of our life is of a mingled yarn, good
> and ill together.
>
> — *William Shakespeare*

When we talk about the connection between two souls, we need to discuss four aspects: sending strength, sensing ability, the amount of life force that is being sent at any particular time as a result of the sender's intention, and the connection, which is the amount of what is sent that is actually received. We've already looked at sending strength and sensing ability. In this chapter we will look at the connection.

The connection changes as the situation changes, based on the intentions of the souls involved. The amount of life force going in one direction to make a connection is not the same as the amount of life force going in the other direction, so we always need to keep track of connection in both directions. Connection with life force going from soul 1 to soul 2 will be designated by C_{12}. Connection in the other direction is C_{21}. Each chakra has its own connection to every chakra in the other soul, so the connection for the whole soul is actually made up of the values for each chakra.

The amount of life force that can flow from soul 1 to soul 2 has some limits. At any moment it must be the same or less than the amount of stored life force in each chakra of soul 1. Soul 1 may or may not be able to send all the stored life force at once, so the connection is further limited by the outward ability to send of soul 1. Soul 1 also chooses how much of the life force it wants to send (outward intention). While it may want to send more than its outward ability to send or more life force than it has, it can't, so outward ability to send and stored life force both limit the amount sent.

Soul 2 has two limits. First, it chooses how much life force to receive from each chakra in soul 1 (inward intention). Second, it limited by its inward ability to accept.

The result is that the largest possible connection for each chakra is the lowest value of stored life force, outward ability to send, outward intention, inward ability to accept, and inward intention.

Connection is the minimum of stored life force (SLF), outward ability to send (OAS), outward intention (OI), inward ability to accept (IAS), and inward intention (II).

$$C_{MAX\,12} = \min\left(SLF_1, OAS_1, OI_{12}, IAA_2, II_{21}\right)$$

It is also interesting to look at the ratio between the amount of life force sent and the amount that is actually received (the connection coefficient, CCoef). Life force sent is the minimum of stored life force, outward ability to send, and outward intention. Life force received is the minimum of life force sent, inward ability to accept, and inward intention. The connection coefficient is the ratio of life force received to life force sent. It's a measure of what fraction actually got through.

The connection coefficient (CCoef) is the measure of the life force received relative to the life force sent.

$$LF_{sent} = \min\left(SLF_1, OAS_1, OI_{12}\right)$$

$$LF_{received} = \min\left(LF_{sent}, IAA_2, II_{21}\right)$$

$$CCoef_{12} = LF_{received}/LF_{sent}$$

We have moved a long way from using physical distance to describe interactions between souls. It is mostly soul-related matters that define the interaction. We need to consider how important the two souls are to one another and how well the two souls know one another. There is one way that physical distance has a strong effect on soul connections, but that is because souls in this world are connected to physical bodies.

Measuring Connection

Let's start by looking at the ways we can measure connection. When we are talking about connection in terms of information flow, the closest analogy might be a measure of the quality of signal received compared to the quality of the signal sent. I suggest that when we talk about connection for chakras two through five, we continue to use bits of information as the units. The more accurately two people are able to send information, the higher the connection.

In the previous chapter we talked about a computer analogy for bits of information. There are definitely some issues with what constitutes a bit of information. Let's study the details of what that means by looking at a simple case. This song tells a familiar tale of the ghost of a sailor lost at sea coming back to tell his lover that he has died.

Lowlands[74]

I dreamt a dream the other night,
    Chorus: Lowlands, lowlands, away my John.
I dreamt a dream the other night.
    Chorus: My lowlands, away.

I dreamt I saw my own true love,
His hair was wet, he did not move.

I knew my love was drowned and dead,
He stood so still, no word he said.

All dank his hair, all dim his eye,
I knew that he had said goodbye.

All green and wet with weeds so cold,
Around his form green weeds had hold.

"I'm drowned in the Lowland Seas," he said,
"Oh, you an' I will ne'er be wed."

"I shall never kiss you more," he said,

"Never kiss you more — for I am dead."

My love is drowned in the windy Lowlands,
My love is drowned in the windy Lowlands.

Traditionally the drowned seaman is seen standing, wet and cold, by his lover's bed. He may or may not speak. In this version of the story we have the additional feature of green weeds. So, how much information is required for the woman to understand what is happening?

She needs to know who is sending the message. Throughout their time apart, the woman has received loving energy from the sailor. When the energy stops, the woman senses its loss and feels the break in the connection through the heart chakra. We can see how much energy goes away when we lose someone close by looking at the change in energy we have because of the loss. We usually call this loss of energy depression or grief. I suggest that depression and grief may actually be loss of heart energy. This is consistent with the observation that depression is reduced when we form connections with others and share heart life force with them.

To figure out what has happened to her lover, she needs the visual image of wetness and green weeds. These days we could easily do that with a picture of 300 by 200 pixels, with three colors in the picture and eight bits of information for each pixel. Multiplying these numbers together gives us about 1,400,000 bits.

She needs to hear his words. To record two channels of audio at radio quality (44.1 kHz sample rate with a 16-bit word size), the recording software has to handle about 1,400,000 bits per second.

All of these estimates have much more information than we need to see the image, especially if what is being transmitted lasts for a significant amount of time. We are very good at piecing together a pattern from incomplete information and filtering out static, especially when the heart chakra has increased our intention to receive information through the other chakras. I suggest that one-tenth of the information for about a minute (which turns out to be about how long it takes to sing the song) would be enough to give the woman an accurate understanding of what had happened. That would mean 24 million bits (or less) were required to transmit everything she senses in the song. The corresponding transmission rate would be 400,000 bits per second. (If all the information comes through, we are looking at about 4 million bits per second, which is a significant fraction of the receiving ability we proposed earlier.)

What we need to find is how much information the sailor is actually transmitting. The song isn't detailed enough to give us a clear picture so let's guess somewhere between 400,000 and 4 million bits of information per second. The woman seems to need about 400,000 bits per second to process this kind of information. The connection would be 400,000 bits per second and the coefficient of connection would be 10% to 100%.

There is also an issue about what to do when a person perceives the situation in a way that is either much faster or much slower than normal. When that happens, a soul second doesn't match up with a clock second, but I don't think that is important at this point in the discussion. One person in a couple may be experiencing the situation at a higher clock rate than the other. In this case I suggest that the sailor might be sending 400,000 bits in his soul's seconds, but he could be sending at a much faster rate in clock seconds. If we have extra soul seconds to deal with, we just make sure we count in consistent seconds to measure connection.

Genetic Connections

Let's continue looking at connections by studying ways we are connected. First we will look at folklore and other evidence suggesting a genetic connection between two souls exists. These examples generally deal with the soul as a whole. Usually thinking about individual chakras makes the example stronger, but it is not required.

Many stories about sensing an event occur between two people in the same family. For example, Camille Flammarion tells the following story about two brothers.

> Here is a very remarkable example of vision at a distance, in a dream, of a most unusual accident. I take it from the work "Phantasms of the Living" Volume I, page 338, and from its French translation, "Les Hallucinations telepathiques," page 107.

Canon Warburton of Winchester wrote under date of July 16, 1883:

I had left Oxford to pass a day or two with my brother, Acton Warburton, at that time a barrister. When I reached his home I found a message from him on the table: he excused himself for being absent and told me that he had gone to a ball in some part of the West End and that he intended to return a little after one o'clock. Instead of going to bed I sat and dozed in an arm-chair. At exactly one o'clock I awoke with a start, crying out, "By Jupiter! he has fallen!" I saw my brother, who came out of a drawing-room on to a brilliantly lighted landing, catch his foot on the first step of the stairway and fall head first, breaking the fall with his elbows and hands. I had never seen the house and I did not know where it was. Thinking very little of the accident, I went to sleep again. A half-hour later I was waked up by the abrupt entrance of my brother, who exclaimed: "Ah, there, you are! I nearly broke my neck. As I was leaving the ball-room I caught my foot and fell full length down the stairway."

Such is the canon's tale; he declares, at the same time, that he has never had hallucinations.[75]

Here is a second story about another pair of brothers from Camille Flammarion's book.

Our next case of mental vision is of the same order. Lombroso published the following letter, sent him by his colleague in the university, Professor De Sanctis:

I was once at Rome with my family, which had remained in the country. As the house had been robbed the year before, my brother was in the habit of sleeping there. One evening he told me he was going to the Costanzi Theater. I had come in alone and was beginning to read when I was suddenly seized with terror. I struggled against it and was beginning to undress, but I remained obsessed by the thought that the theater was on fire and my brother in danger. I put the light out; but, growing more and more disturbed, I lit it again, contrary to my usual custom, and decided to await my brother's return before I went to sleep. I was truly frightened, just as a child might be. At half-past twelve I heard the door open, and what was my astonishment when my brother told me about the panic that had been caused by the outbreak of a fire, which had coincided with the hour of my anxiety.[76]

Camille Flammarion tells similar stories about parents and children, too. Here is one of those.

A telepathetic [sic] vision, in a dream, from Strasburg to Paris has been described to me by an old friend, Madame Dobelmann, in the following words:

I do not know, dear Master, whether or not I have mentioned to you an instance of telepathy which I experienced in January, 1901. We were already living in Paris when, at the end of January, we were called to Strasburg, my husband and I, for the funeral of my poor invalid mother. Our son was not able to go also, because of the laws of exception of that place. I was much affected, as can be imagined, by the swarm of memories and by the weather (the air was full of whirling snow), so that I had very agitated dreams at night. One night, especially, I was overcome with sharp distress and dreamed that I saw my youngest son caught between two rows of planks which had fallen on him, unable to free himself and calling me, "Mama!" I spoke of it to my sister, while I was still very much oppressed by this nightmare. But neither she nor I dreamed of attaching any importance to it. A few days later, on our return to Paris, the servant who received us said: "Monsieur Julien is much better, he is at his work." — "What, has he been ill?" — "Why, yes, he had to stay in the house several days, for he hurt his leg. Didn't he write you?"

On my son's return we questioned him, and he told me that he had had an accident, for a pile of boards had fallen on him; but it had been nothing serious, and it would have been useless to frighten us. "But I knew it," I said. "I dreamed about it all one night and the curious thing is that the place did not at all resemble your wood-yard. You were in the midst of planks, unable to get up, in a great unfamiliar yard, and the sun was shining brightly." — "That's correct," replied my son; "the sun was shining on that day and it did not happen in my place but in a neighbor's yard, which is just as you have described it without having ever seen it. But I have no recollection of having called you."

Had my son called me at night in his sleep? It is not impossible, for he was accustomed to dream out loud.

I must add that this is the one and only time that such a thing has happened to me.

Valerie Dobelmann,

(Letter 2320.) 12 rue Linne, Paris.

We see what variety exists among all these sincere, simple, and authentic tales. They reinforce one another and prove to us that our body does not contain all the reality that exists.[77]

The three stories provide a variety of levels of connection. In all three cases there was sufficient connection for the receiver to receive the information.

However, in the first story we have a very detailed view of the location, the accident, and the time it occurred. For the interval of time it took Canon Warburton's brother to fall, the connection was near 100%.

In the second story, we find far less detail about place or actions. In fact, all that was really communicated was the feeling of danger and an impression of fire. If the theater-going brother was transmitting visual and auditory information about the whole scene, it seems like the other brother only got a small part of it. The transmission through the lower chakras seems to have been more effective. The dominant emotion was fear, which would probably be sent by the desire chakra.

With the mother and son we have something in between the first two stories. The mother had a pretty good picture of the accident, but she did not receive it until the night after it happened. We can guess that what she saw was her son's dream the night after he was hurt. So, the connection varied for this pair. It was not strong enough to get the mother's attention when the accident occurred, but they did have a good connection later when the real-world situation of the mother was not as hectic.

The folklore assumption is that the more genes two people have in common, the more connected they are. Identical twins would be at the top of the list.

The excellent quality of the connections described above suggests that the genetic connection is easily at or above the connections described in the analysis of "Lowlands." We need a constant to translate from genetic similarity to connection, which we will call g. I suggest, subject to experimental corrections, that we choose g = 400,000 bits per second.

The equation describing the connection caused by genetic similarity would have the form:

$$GC = g * IG/TG$$

where GC is genetic connection, g is the genetic connection constant, IG is identical genes, and TG is total genes

We will be discussing mutual experiences next, and the question is whether the similarity between twins (or other relatives, for that matter) can be explained by using only mutual experiences. The following research suggests that there is a connection deeper than mutual experiences.

A long-term study by Thomas Bouchard looked at twins who were separated at birth and reared in different families.[78] He found that an identical twin reared away from his or her co-twin seemed to have about an equal chance of being similar to the co-twin in terms of personality, interests, and attitudes as one who had been reared with his or her co-twin. Bouchard concluded that the similarities between twins must be due to genes, not environment. This would be the most likely explanation if one does not allow the possibility of connections between souls. However, saying that genes can exert this kind of control over a whole life seems like an extraordinary claim — I find a soul connection based on similar genetics to be a more likely explanation.

Even more likely is that souls that are already strongly connected decide to be twins. In a reincarnational model the connection causes the twinning, rather than the twinning causing the connection. Similarly, the idea that we reincarnate with the same set of people through many lifetimes means that the genetics are secondary to the established connection that causes us to be genetically similar. The causal relationship is not important, though, as both models lead to a stronger connection between relatives.

One way to test the strength of the genetic connection between souls is to compare non-identical twins separated at birth with identical twins separated at birth. If the identical twins have a closer connection, we have evidence for a genetic component of soul connection. There are ways to study this.* My belief is that we will find a genetic soul connection with the non-identical twins and that there is an added genetic connection between identical twins.

Keep in mind that the similarity of lives can actually be a distraction. The question we need to answer is not whether the lives of the pair are similar. What we need to know is how much of their soul connection at the present time is caused by genetic similarities.

Mutual Experiences

Genetics may play a part, but another aspect closely related to genetic similarity is the number of mutual experiences. Families usually have many mutual experiences that lead to the ability to sense one another, but friends may sense what is happening to one another, too.

---

* If twins separated at birth are not genetically or spiritually connected, then any pair of humans has the same likelihood of having a similar life history. The first task is to create a list of significant life events such as education, profession, details of any marriages, children, health issues. Other important aspects include personality traits, consumer habits, etc. We would also need to look at personal preferences such as food, clothes, colors, etc. Using this similarity index, a large-scale survey of randomly selected individuals could be conducted to gather life and personality information. Then the people in the survey could be matched pairwise to create normative data about similarities between individuals. (Since we are interested in twin similarities, the pairs would need to be matched closely for birth date.) At that point we could search for twins who had been reunited after a long time apart. Comparing their similarity indexes to the norm data would show how likely it is that similarity between twins is a chance occurrence.

How well they sense seems to depend on how emotionally close they feel.

Time spent together is another aspect. Time spent together counts more when there is an intense interaction. Just being in the same office for years is not as important as sharing the birth of a child or climbing a mountain or being captured by rebels in Peru. The kind of connection that translates into souls being close requires life force moving between the people having the experience. The more life force moving during each experience, the more connection the souls will have in the future. At the moment of the experience we can define an experience connection, EC(now).

Sometimes when people meet, they feel an instant connection. It probably means that they spent time together in a past life.

An interesting question is whether it matters if the interactions are positive or negative. Does a child who is being abused by his or her mother form a closer soul connection because of the abuse? I have friends who dearly hope that they did not, but I believe that they actually did form closer connections until they worked specifically to cut them. As they say at the end of one of the episodes of the TV show "Lie to Me,"[79]

> Dr. Cal Lightman: "When someone bashes you around — he's twice your size, does it whenever he feels like it — you learn to read emotions pretty fast. We adapt. To survive. Your abuse made you a natural. He made you what you are."
>
> Ria Torres: Sighing, "Well, I'll be sure to thank him."

If you would prefer a real-life example, here's another one about an abusive father from the work of Elizabeth Lloyd Mayer.

> Beneath [her other concerns] lay far more conventional fears of a child raised by an abusive alcoholic father and a blandly unprotective mother. Home was ugly, unstable, and terrifying. In his drinking bouts, Grace's father was uncontrollably violent. He beat up on Grace, her younger sister, and their mother. Grace learned to find safety in a locked closet where she'd sheltered

herself and her sister. But what scared Grace the most was how she'd known just when to get the two of them inside that closet:

"During the late afternoons, I'd start listening for him. It was a kind of listening. It was like listening with my whole body, not my ears. I don't know how to describe it except to say I was tuned in, vigilant with every part of me. Suddenly I'd *know* — know he was fifteen minutes away and driving home drunk. Then I'd hustle me and my sister into the closet. I couldn't afford to wait and hear him at the door. He'd crash in and grab whoever was in sight, then hit. He grabbed my mother a lot — she just stood there. So I had to be the one to protect me and my sister — I had to learn how. Somehow I just started knowing when he was headed home and when he'd be dangerous. I *knew*. It was like the spooky knowing with my professor but it was different because I *had* to know, I had no choice.

"My dad didn't drink all the time. So there was no predicting. I had to stay tuned in every day, be ready and never trust any pattern. We'd go for weeks and be safe. But I couldn't get lulled into thinking that's how it would stay because suddenly he'd drink again and we'd have to hide again. I'd have to know way before he pulled up at the house. As soon as I knew, I'd start getting ready — turn off the lights in the bedroom, get water for my sister, bring in her blanket, and settle us with pillows to make it cozy.... How did I know when he was on his way and drunk? As a child I accepted it, I thought I just knew because I had to. But now that isn't good enough.... I keep wondering, am I crazy? If I'm crazy, how come I kept being right? It scares me to death..."[80]

I believe mutual connection comes from both positive and negative interactions. I also believe that negative interactions, which almost certainly involve Post-Traumatic Stress Disorder (PTSD), take a tremendous toll. As this example shows, it is terrifying to believe that you are connected to a monster. People who know what their loved ones are doing through positive shared experiences don't feel the same sort of stress and are much less likely to take their stories to a counselor.*

When we are looking at the experience connection, we need to take a time factor into account. Simply put, we often forget about our friends when we don't see them. Given the same number and kind of interactions, we are connected more to the person we saw yesterday than the person we haven't seen for 20 years. One way to take that into account is to give old experiences less weight than new experiences. We could say that experiences half a lifetime ago have half as much impact as experiences now.

Here's one way to implement an age-related calculation for any particular experience. The equation has the characteristics of giving full intensity to what is happening now, half as much intensity to what happened half a lifetime ago, and experiences before birth don't count at all.

$$EC_i(t_{now}) = EC_i(t_{then}) * (1 - ((t_{now} - t_{then})/age))$$

where EC_i is the experience connection for a particular event (i), t_{now} and t_{then} (and other time representations) are expressed in the age of the person ($t_{birth} = 0$) and t_{then} is >= 0.

But, I'm suspicious of this model. I've had the experience of meeting a person I knew a long time ago and having all (or at least many) of the experiences come rushing back. Similarly for Joan Baez[81] in "Diamonds and Rust."

> Well, I'll be damned
> Here comes your ghost again

---

* Mayer looks at this as a case of entanglement in the quantum mechanics sense. It is clear that an entanglement between this woman and her father could develop. However, later in life this woman was able to know things about other people in the same extraordinary way. This is probably not a case of entanglement, although it might be called an example of entanglement that is so messed up that it was formed with minimal contact, at least in one direction. In any case, the woman has an exceptional ability to read the emotions of another person with minimal contact. I think that calling this entanglement is an unproductive use of a physics concept that doesn't really apply. The real test of a concept is whether it adds to our ability to understand and predict what will happen. The concept of entanglement isn't a good enough parallel for me to want to use it, even though others think it is useful.

But that's not unusual
It's just that the moon is full
And you happened to call ...

Ten years ago I bought you some cufflinks
You brought me something
We both know what memories can bring
They bring diamonds and rust.

Perhaps the way to calculate the current connection is to sum up all the connection-producing events from the past and reduce the amount of connection by the last time the pair of people met.

That formula for a particular event would look like this

$$EC_i(t_{now}) = EC_i(t_{then}) * \left(1 - \left(\left(t_{now} - t_{last\,meeting}\right)/age\right)\right)$$

I'm not sure I trust the revised model either. Sometimes those memories don't come rushing back, as in, "Now who did you say you were again?" If we put both factors together, we may be closer to the truth.

Then we have

$$EC_i(t_{now}) = EC_i(t_{then}) * \left(1 - \left(\left(t_{now} - t_{last\,meeting}\right)/age\right)\right)$$
$$* \left(1 - \left(\left(t_{now} - t_{then}\right)/age\right)\right)$$

We can use the adjustments for time to modify the original intensities to come up with the connection two people have. It's as simple as summing up the intensities from every experience the pair ever had together.

In mathematical terms we are looking to measure the sum of the intensity between two people throughout their lifetime:

$$EC(t_{now}) = \sum_{i=0}^{life} \left| \begin{array}{l} EC_i(t_{then}) * \left(1 - \left(\left(t_{now} - t_{last\,meeting}\right)/age\right)\right) \\ * \left(1 - \left(\left(t_{now} - t_{then}\right)/age\right)\right) \end{array} \right|$$

We don't know for sure if positive and negative interactions cancel out or if the absolute value of the intensity should be used. I believe it is absolute intensity.

Keeping track of every interaction is not simple, but at least it gives us a way to think about what we mean by the experience connection.

Another way to calculate the connection is to look at the current relationship. Marriage, family, and friendships with intense experiences all share a common theme: We are interacting with another person in an experience connection over a significant amount of time. A way to measure the connection might be to ask a person to score a relationship on measures similar to the following:

- An assessment with a series of questions, scored on a seven-point scale, including
  - "We are very close." to "We are not close at all."
  - "I can almost read his or her mind." to "I never know what he or she is thinking."
  - "We feel the same thing all the time." to "We are so totally different."
  - "We always finish each other's sentences." to "We don't even talk to the same people."
  - "I know what he or she is doing even when we are apart." to "I don't know what he or she is doing even when I'm right there watching him or her."
- Time spent working or living together. The total amount of time spent actually interacting with the other person over a lifetime. One way to adjust for the quality of the interaction is to require communication (verbal, physical, visual, or whatever) before the time counts. So watching television together would only count the time spent communicating, not the time spent sitting in the same room.
- Number of intense experiences shared. The intense experiences could be divided into categories such as life-threatening, high physical exertion, high emotional impact, high creativity, high spiritual content, difficult situations or opponents to overcome, requiring alternate means of communication. The person would write down the number of times she had each type of intense experience with a particular person.

From a measure like this we can get a sense of how close two people are. The questions in the first bullet give a fairly direct answer to the question of how well information is transmitted between two people in a non-ordinary way.

The other two bullets are measures of past history that suggests how the connections were made. This is the kind of situation where it is possible to get a correlation between events and connection strength by using a large sample of couples. A simple table might look like the table below. By knowing the closeness value, we can look up the connection strength for the top three chakras.

Closeness Score	Experience Connection
Less than 24	0 bits per second
25-32	1,000 bits per second
33-48	10,000 bits per second
49-72	100,000 bits per second

Another factor that may be part of mutual experience is how many friends the person has. It's not clear whether the presence of many relationships has an effect on the strength of a particular relationship. If a person has many friends, is each one less likely to be sensed? Or does having many friends make a person more sensitive to each of them? Since I don't know the answer, I haven't included this factor in the calculation of soul connections between two people.

Up to now we have been looking at mutual experiences in the current lifetime. Since one of the points I'm trying to make is that there may be previous lives, we have to consider the possibility that people may be nearer because they interacted with one another before this life. The same rules of connection apply. The strength of the effect may be reduced by whatever happens between lives. I can't think of a good way to make this calculation, so I will simply note the concern and move on.

Intentional Connections

When putting in electrical wiring for a building, which I have done, it is important to use wires with sufficient capacity. If you don't, the wire heats up too much, melts the insulation, shorts out, knocks out your power, and maybe starts a fire. Your intention is to make a circuit that will effectively carry all of the current you need. You intentionally choose wire that will transmit the required power.

It's easy to see how we can act intentionally on other objects to affect their interactions with us and the rest of the world. What may be more difficult to see is that we can act intentionally on ourselves to change how we interact with the rest of the universe.

Here's one example. When some people play music, they intentionally turn it up so loud that they won't be able to hear by the time they are forty. (Bad choice, by the way.)

The more relevant question in terms of connections between souls is whether we can act on ourselves to change the connection between us and another person. We believe we can by choosing to spend more time and having more experiences with the other person. We covered that aspect in the discussion on mutual experiences. Can we also change the strength of the connection without interactions?

Folklore suggests that we do it all the time. We have one example from the musical *South Pacific*:[82]

> I'm gonna wash that man right outa my hair,
> I'm gonna wash that man right outa my hair,
> I'm gonna wash that man right outa my hair,
> And send him on his way...
>
> Don't try to patch it up
> Tear it up, tear it up!
> Wash him out, dry him out,
> Push him out, fly him out,
> Cancel him and let him go!

Yea, sister!

The intention is to forget the guy — to cut the connections to him. Anyone who has experienced a relationship with a bad person knows that one of the most important aspects of healing is cutting the connections with the other person. All the negative life force that has come through connections with the other person need to be sorted out and removed, hopefully without shutting down all of the good connections with other people at the same time.

We do the same thing on a positive side, too, when we try to increase the connection with another person. In fifth grade I wrote Mary Lee's name over and over. I certainly didn't have the concept of trying to increase that connection, but I think that is what I was trying to do. When we think about somebody, when we care about somebody, when we wonder what they are doing, when we try to understand what they are thinking, these are all ways we intentionally try to increase our connection with another person.

The danger of working in isolation to increase connection is that it can lead to obsession. The bond can seem like a connection, but it may be to an image we have in our head, not to the real person. I know I had a lot more success making a connection with Mary Lee when I talked to her. To strengthen a bond, we need to spend time interacting in real life. Here's a quote that says it all in six words:

> Absence sharpens love, presence strengthens it.
>
> — Benjamin Franklin

For those who prefer the more poetic, I offer:

> But let there be spaces in your togetherness and let the winds of the heavens dance between you. Love one another but make not a bond of love: let it rather be a moving sea between the shores of your souls.
>
> — Kahlil Gibran

To sum up, making a connection stronger is difficult without actually being with the person. Cutting a connection is easier, although having the will to intentionally cut connections can be a huge challenge.

Simply put, your intentional connection to another person is the sum of all the intentions you have had relative to that person throughout your lifetime. The negative intentions are summed based on their strength. The positive intensions are positive only if you are spending time with the person in addition to intending to make a connection with them.

$$IC = \sum_{i=0}^{\text{life}} \left(EI_i * \left(\int_{t=t(i)}^{\text{life}} IDec_i(t)dt + \int_{t=t(i)}^{\text{life}} \left(IInc_i(t) * EC(t) \right)dt \right) \right)$$

Where
IC is intentional connection
EI is event intensity
IDec is intention to decrease
IInc is intention to increase
EC is experience connection
i represents the particular event
t is the time since the event

In terms of the chakra model, the intentional connection is a major component of inward intention. The intention to increase is also part of how we build up the inward ability to accept. The intention to decrease affects our inward ability to block.

I don't think we need a factor that shows intentional connection strength fading for older intentions. What we may need is a calculation for selective memory — where we remember the good things about an old relationship and forget the bad times.

Desire Connections

Intentional connections, as described in the previous section, are between two people who know one another. They happen through the heart chakra, the will chakra, and focused interactions of the desire chakra. In this section we will look at other kinds of desire connections. These are open-ended connections where one person is seeking to connect with someone or something based on a desire, without knowing exactly who or what that might be.

The most common examples these days come from the concept of the law of attraction as described in Rhonda Byrne's books[83] *The Secret* and *The Power*. Byrne says that by using something that sounds very much like life force everyone can have everything they desire.

It's a wonderful wish, but let's look a bit at the concept of fulfilling desires.

I believe that one part of Byrne's claim is true. When we send out life force in an open-ended way through the desire chakra, it can meet with a compatible entity. It is possible to bring things into your life by wishing for them. Unfortunately, the well-known saying, "Be careful what you wish for, it might come true," applies here. Sometimes those wishes have more negative life force attached to them than the wisher realizes and will bring negative things into the person's life along with the positive.

Another part of the claim is not true. The problem with everyone getting everything is that sometimes there are incompatible wishes. For limited resources or conflicting wishes, the stronger get their desire and the weaker ones don't. In some situations, no one gets their desire. The universe, filled with many entities, is simply more powerful than we are. Its chaotic nature means that things happen that can't be controlled by us.

A third point is that having desires, at least according to the Buddha and several other beliefs, can be a serious problem in itself. For Buddhists, desires are the root of unhappiness. Just to want fancy clothes or a new car means that the person is already on the wrong path for enlightenment.

The fourth point is that we need to allow for the possibility of reincarnational promises. There are at least two forms for this promise:

- We make agreements with a person before we are born that we will spend part of our lives with him or her during the next lifetime.
- We vow to get even with a person for something that was done to us.

In either of those cases, if we are born apart from someone we want to be with, it is the desire connection that brings us together. My own thought is that desire, like so many other things, is best to have in moderation.

Regardless of whether having desires is good or bad, we need to look at how desire connections affect our interactions with others. We are more connected to another person when our desires match up. It may be someone we have met in previous lives or someone new. The desire connection pulls us together most strongly when being together will get both of us what we desire.

The desire connection is made up of two aspects: how well the desires match up and how well the desires will be met by being together. First we find the sets of desire for each person and then we combine two sets of desires in this way: If both people have the same desire, we include the desire in the connection. If the desires are both positive or both negative, we include them to make the desire connection stronger. If one desire is positive and the other is negative, we have a negative connection that makes the desire connection weaker. Desires in one person that are not matched in the other are ignored.

Start with the sets of desires (D) from a person

$$\mathbf{D} = \{d_1, d_2, \ldots\}$$

Where d_n is the strength of a particular desire and all possible desires are included in the set **D**.

Combine two sets of desires by applying a <matching> operator. The <matching> operator adds the strengths of desires in this way: If both people have the same desire, we include the desire in the connection. If the desires have the same sign, the absolute value of the desire for each person is included in the desire connection. If the desires have opposite signs, we have a negative connection. In that case the absolute value of both desires is subtracted from the desire connection. Desires in one person that are not matched in the other are ignored.

$$DC = \sum_{d=1}^{\text{all desires}} \left(\mathbf{D}_{p1} \left[\text{matching} \right] \mathbf{D}_{p2} \right)$$

where DC is the desire connection

The desire connection can change with time and interactions between the two people involved. It becomes stronger as two people interact and focus their desires. The connection becomes weaker when the desire is met. Other situations and interactions will also have an effect on the strength of each person's desires, which will affect the desire connection between them.

We'll look at how the connections we discussed in this chapter add together to form a total connection after we look at the role ordinary reality plays in soul connections. The role of ordinary reality is discussed in the next chapter.

13. Ordinary Reality and Connection

Our lives are like islands in the sea, or like trees in the forest, which co-mingle their roots in the darkness underground.

— *William James*

The biggest effect of ordinary reality on connections comes from the current distance between the two entities that are interacting. In this chapter we will look at how ordinary reality and soul reality interact to affect our connection with others.

Physical Distance

How connected souls are does not seem to be a continuous function of distance. By that I mean distance does not affect the strength of life force between souls in the same way as ordinary-reality forces. Gravity, for example, gets weaker in a continuous way ($1/r^2$).

I think the soul experiences physical distances more like zones. If we are a long way apart, a certain kind of connection is possible. The closer a soul gets physically, the more kinds of connections the soul can have. Let's start with the distant connection and move closer to explore the effects of physical distance.

Soul Connection (Far Distance)

One of the interesting observations where physical distance seems to have an effect is found in the 500-mile rule. (For some people this is a 50-mile rule.) The rule states that a person traveling beyond a certain distance doesn't need to be faithful to his or her partner. Traveling salesmen are believed to have invented the rule so they didn't feel as guilty when they were fooling around with the ladies on their sales routes. Of course, it's always possible that it was invented by the salesmen's wives for similar reasons.

For example, from the London Craigslist casual encounters (spelling as in the original posting):[84]

Married guy invoking 500 mile rule - m4w - 35 (Kensington)

OK First off yes I am married but I am invoking the 500 mile rule which says that anything can happen when your that far a part. I am here on business until Friday morning staying at a nice hotel in the Kensington neighborhood, actually I have a huge room since somehow I got upgraded for free. I would love to meet a women who would like to get a drink at the bar and see what happens.

I would say I am average looking standing 5' 11" tall and tipping the scales at 235#. I am 36, have a shaved head and goatee. As far as penis goes I will leave that to the imagination and just say I would consider myself "larger" then average- at least girth wise.

Please contact me if your interested.

I think that physical distance has some effect on how well souls communicate, but I think the effect results more from psychological factors than the actual distance. If a person is fooling around 500 miles away, it's unlikely that the partner is going to find out through any normal means. There can be a connection, however. A friend of mine tells the story of how his wife called to say no fooling around when he was in a tempting situation several thousand miles away. What is important is the connection between the souls, not the physical distance.

Beyond a certain physical distance, souls experience only a long-distance style of connection, as discussed in the previous chapter. This is the connection that is in effect when a mother senses that her son has been in an accident (or a wife knows her husband is being tempted). It's the one connection that is always there. I believe that physical distance has no effect on this type of connection. If the mother can sense the son's accident next door, she would be able to sense the same accident on the other side of the world. This is testable by using something like Sheldrake's telephone experiment with callers from close and distant places.

A truly interesting question is whether the mother could sense the accident from many light years away. It would be even more interesting to know if the mother sensed the accident when it happened* or if the information traveled at a finite, but very fast, speed, such as the speed of light. This is not an experiment we can do.

Another question that comes up is whether we can sense what is happening to another, unrelated entity that is several light years away. I think not. We have almost none of the interweaving associated with genetics or common experiences for connections to exist.†

So whether it's light years or 50 miles, the connection between souls is limited to this long-distance type of connection. The aspects of the souls that define the strength of these connections, as we saw in the previous chapter, are genetic connection, experience connection, intentional connection, and desire connection.

Putting together the pieces of the genetic connection (GC), the experience connection (EC), the intentional connection (IC), and desire connection (DC), we come up with the soul connection (SoC).

$$SoC = GC + EC + IC + DC$$

---

* Relativity introduces some complications into the phrase "when it happened." However, if we could run the experiment, we would be able to decide whether there was approximate simultaneity in many circumstances.

† Some believe the connections are possible and claim to have had contact. At this time, I prefer Patrick Harpur's (2003) explanation, which suggests these are local spirits playing games with us.

It is important to note that this type of connection very rarely gets a message through. The ones that succeed have a very strong force caused by a highly significant event and a close connection between the people involved. Most of the time the noise we have in our daily lives and the loss of signal strength caused by the poor connection means that the signal doesn't reach a threshold where we can recognize the message being sent to us.

A possible way to measure soul connection experimentally was described by Elizabeth Lloyd Mayer in *Extraordinary Knowing*.[85] A series of experiments performed by Dean Radin[86] used a pair of people who knew one another. Both were wired up to detect their physiological signs, including electroencephalogram (EEG). One of the pair was told to send mental instructions to calm or arouse the other person. The two people were in separate rooms and had no ordinary way to communicate with one another.

What Radin found was that the person who was receiving the instructions reacted in response to the instructions at a greater than chance level. The second person was also asked to guess what feelings were being sent. She guessed correctly at a greater than chance level, but not as accurately as the physiological readings. In other words, this set of experiments showed that we sense the connection with another person at the conscious level but we have connections that are even stronger in what Radin calls the subconscious. (To use my soul model: the desire chakra, will chakra, and heart chakra are more reliably connected than the mind chakra and communication chakra.) It's rather like the way Obi-Wan Kenobi sensed a "great disturbance in the Force" when the planet Alderaan was destroyed, except the experiment is a real life phenomenon* and *Star Wars* is an unproven myth.

We can get an estimate of the connection coefficient by looking at how much life force is sent by the transmission. One way might be to divide the strength of the physiological reaction of the second person by

---

* Radin is using a quantum mechanical entanglement model to explain his results, as Mayer did earlier I think the life force, unlike quantum mechanics, explains what is happening in a way that will lead to deeper understanding.

the strength of the physiological change of the first person. It doesn't appear that the experimenters tried that in their experimental design.

This experimental design is not the best way to measure the amount of connection in the mind chakra or communication chakra. We would have to ask exactly what mental pictures (sounds, feelings, etc.) were being transmitted to describe the feelings of calmness or arousal. A more effective design for our purposes might be to have the sender look at a calming or arousing picture and try to send the feelings from the picture to the receiver. Then we could measure the information impressions as well as the emotional/energetic ones.

Informal demonstrations of connection were done by Guy Lyon Playfair.[87]

- For a television show in 2003, Playfair set up a test for twins Richard and Damien Powles. Richard was placed in a sound-proof booth with a bucket of ice water while Damien was some distance away in another studio hooked up to a polygraph machine that measured respiration, muscle and skin response. When Richard plunged his hand into the ice water and let out a gasp, there was an obvious blip on Damien's polygraph that measured his respiration, as if he too had let out a gasp.

- During the same experiment, Richard was instructed to open a cardboard box, from which he expected a nice surprise. Instead, a rubber snake popped out, startling him. At that exact moment, the polygraph recorded a jump in Damien's pulse rate, as if he were having the same experience.

- In a similar experiment before a live TV audience in 1997, twin teenagers Elaine and Evelyn Dove were likewise separated. Elaine was in the sound-proof booth with a pyramid-shaped box while Evelyn was sequestered in another room with the polygraph. When Elaine was sitting relaxed, suddenly the box exploded in a harmless but shocking pop of sparks, flashes and colored smoke. Evelyn's polygraph recorded her psychic reaction at the same moment, with one of the needles running right off the edge of the paper.

As Playfair pointed out, these are not experiments conducted with strict scientific protocols, but in the context of our discussion, they are useful at establishing an amount of connection. As Playfair states, "Telepathy tends to work best when it is needed and when sender and receiver are strongly bonded, as with mothers and babies, dogs and their owners, and those with the strongest bond of all — twins." When we measure the connection demonstrated by the shock, we could compare the physiological reactions of the receiver with the physiological reactions of the sender.

The equation to measure soul connection with these experiments would look like this.

$$SoC = EExp_1 * \frac{R_2}{R_1}$$

where EExp is the energy directed at the sender during the experiment, R_1 is the reaction seen for the sender and R_2 is the reaction seen for the receiver.

Effect and Sense Connection (Middle Distance)

Now let's look at what happens at closer physical distances.

As souls move closer together, other connections occur. There is interaction between the physical world and the soul connection that starts to take effect when the entities containing the souls can sense one another through physical senses. We have three senses that operate outside of touching distance: vision, hearing, and smell.

As Gichin Funakoshi, founder of Shotokan Karate, says[88]

The eyes do not miss even the slightest change.
The ears listen well in all directions.

He doesn't mention smell, probably because it is not a precise sense during combat.

To study how the distance senses operate we can think of the tiger and the human. For the human to have a chance against the tiger, he needs to know the tiger is coming before the tiger leaps. It may be that the connection between the tiger and the man flips into the middle-distance mode at the moment the tiger is close enough to consider going after the man as dinner. It probably matters whether the tiger is hungry or not. With tigers, it is hard to tell. However, we have a story from martial artist Caylor Adkins about humans going after humans* that may shed some light on the interaction.[89]

> A bunch of us were taking part in the segment of a bodyguard training course led by former Green Beret dude Tom Muzila.
>
> Stalking sentries and standing sentry was the exercise. We were taking turns stalking and being stalked and learned that being sharply focused on the sentries soon created uneasiness in them, even when there was a lot of noise from the wind and the birds. They would usually start to seriously look around. We had already learned how to step with minimal noise and with the ebb and flow of the ambient noise. When we defocused our eyes, just keeping the sentry in our peripheral vision, and mentally including the sentry with the surrounding terrain without singling him out, we were increasingly able to complete successful stalks. A few, however, became more difficult to stalk; obviously their awareness was being enhanced... All of us "got it" to a greater or lesser degree.
>
> Tom has also had good success training SWAT team members and sheriffs deputies to sense whether or not there is someone behind a door and, if so, which side they are on. I am very sure that this inherent sensitivity to the attention energy of others is the same that is so successfully trained in various ways by some martial arts experts.

It is not a matter of distance. This kind of interaction is the same at five feet as it is at 20 feet. What counts is that the bodies connected to the souls in the interaction are capable of affecting one another, although they are not in direct physical contact at this moment. When the interaction may be harmful to one of the souls, the level of connection (because of the attention and intention) goes up.

The distance may be even farther in some situations. When a sniper who is capable of shooting several hundred yards is on the attacking side,

---

* Similar experiences are discussed in Sheldrake (2005a).

the connection of the person who is a target should extend to that distance without noticeable change in the effect.*

We can see an increase in connection strength for positive interactions, too. For example, we have the lyrics to "Some Enchanted Evening" from *South Pacific*:[90]

> Some enchanted evening
> You may see a stranger
> You may see a stranger
> Across a crowded room.
> And somehow you know,
> You know even then,
> That somewhere
> You'll see her again and again.
>
> Who can explain it,
> Who can tell you why?
> Fools give you reasons,
> Wise men never try.

While it is not likely that we will be able to run repeatable experiments with snipers and live ammunition (or having someone meet the love of their life for the first time in a repeatable way), there are ways we can test for the effect of distance when two people are within sight of one another. The simplest is to use Sheldrake's Sense of Being Stared At while varying the distance between single sender-receiver pairs. The question is whether the sensing ability changes as the physical distance changes within the range of seeing but not physically touching. My expectation is that it would not change, but I'm open to the other possibility.

---

* The "effect" of the interaction raises some interesting points of its own in this kind of context. I have said that the middle-distance contact is not related to distance, as long as there is sensory contact. Contact adds to the percentage of information that gets through to the receiver. If there is enough information getting through, the danger signal turns on like an on-off switch. Either one feels danger, one doesn't feel it, or one gets that itchy feeling and decides to ignore it. As I noted in the text, this is a testable question.

I would also be interested in the results of an experiment tentatively titled "The Sense of Being Listened To." I think we do sense when our private conversations are being overheard. As for thinking about "The Sense of Being Smelled," I believe I will pass.

Calculating a value for this connection seems to be based on the potential intensity of the possible interaction. People and tigers or stalkers and sentries would have a strong connection. A hundred disinterested people in the same subway car really don't matter. But if one person in the subway is staring at you with malice, you will be much more likely to have a connection. There are two aspects to the malicious stare. It will be strong, as we discussed in the earlier section. The connection aspects are that it is focused on you and that the intent behind the interaction could potentially have a large effect on you. (I've given negative examples here, but I think a potentially positive effect would have the same level of connection as a potentially negative effect.) Stronger focus and larger effects from what might happen make the connection stronger.

The strength of the connection when it is first recognized in the middle distance depends on focus and potential effect. The focus can be found by comparing how much of the person's attention is focused on the target with the amount of attention focused on everything else.

To estimate the strength of the potential effect we can start by looking at how detailed the possible encounter is in the imagination of the entity doing the staring. At some point the hungry tiger decides it's going to do some pretty serious clawing and biting.

The other part of the potential effect is how much change will happen in the life of the entity being affected. Something that won't make any significant change will probably be ignored. We should expect a human about to be eaten by a tiger to get a pretty strong signal.

We can calculate the potential effect of the interaction from the amount of life change and the completeness of the plan. More effect and more complete plans will send more life force to the receiver. We should also note that the strength of the connection probably doesn't depend on whether the potential effect is positive or negative. Either way a strong effect will lead to a strong connection.*

We use the absolute value of the potential effect (PE) because strong positive or negative effects both produce strong effect connections (EffC).

$$\text{EffC} = |\text{PE}| * A_0 / \sum_{a=1}^{\text{all attention}} A_a$$

where A is attention and A_0 is the attention toward the person who will be affected.

Potential effect can be calculated from the completeness of plan (CP) and the amount of life force the plan will direct at the person (LFPlan)

$$\text{PE} = \text{CP} * \text{LFPlan}$$

Notice that we are making the assumption that the person on the receiving end has not connected with the sender with physical senses. When both people in the interaction are aware of each other through physical senses, there is another part to the connection. The connection through the physical senses will often be stronger than the nonphysical connection strength because we usually are better at gathering information from the physical realm. The feedback loop actually is a kind of complete connection. Whether it is sufficient to completely transfer life force from sender to receiver depends on what kind of life force is being transmitted.

The sense connection (SeC) at the initial moment of the interaction is the amount of life force being processed.

$$\text{SeC}(0) = \sum_{s=1}^{\text{senses}} \frac{\text{IAA}_s * \text{LF}_s * A_{s1}}{A_{\text{TOT1}}} * \frac{A_{s2}}{A_{\text{TOT2}}}$$

where IAA is the inward ability to accept the life force sent
LF is life force
A is attention from each person, for the relevant sense and total attention

---

* While the discussion here talks about the soul as a whole, these connections are actually processed by individual chakras. This adds some computational complications dealing with the interactions of different chakras that we will talk about in Part IV. The total-soul model is a good approximation of the situation and is sufficient for understanding the connections that are formed.

Situations in the middle distance have a feedback loop. Let's take the example of that stranger on the subway staring at you. If it is a threatening stare and your reaction is to be scared, the intensity (and connection) will increase. (The person staring at you can see the scared reaction.) If your reaction is to make it clear that you are not afraid, the intensity (and connection) will decrease.

The unafraid reaction has at least two possible modes of operation. One is where you are indifferent to the threat because you know it is not really a threat to you. In that case you have blocked or denied the connection with your inward ability to block. The other possibility is that you send threatening feelings back at the person who is staring at you. That should have the effect of causing the other person to lose strength and focus.

If you're in a bar and see a really attractive person looking at you in a friendly way, the situation is reversed. Being scared makes the connection weaker. Acting indifferent will cause the person to focus on someone else. Acting interested will increase the connection.

The feedback loop in connections seems to be that two complementary (threat-fear or interest-interest) emotions make the connection stronger while two opposed emotions make the connection weaker. We can't rely on any of these connections to be static, which makes experimental tests of connections at this distance a real problem.

The connection in the current time interval is a function of the connection at the previous time and the internal processing of the two souls involved. The positive or negative signs of what is going on matter here.

$$SeC(t) = SeC(t-1) + c1 * PE_1 * PE_2 + c2 * (SCD_1 + SCD_2)$$

where c1 and c2 are constants
PE is potential effect in energy values from each person (PE_2 is the reaction of the second person)
SCD is sense connection damping from each person and comes from the inward ability to block (IAB), the inward intention (II), and the person's analysis of the expected result of a physical interaction

The effect connection can also be changed when both sides are aware of the other. When the original sender notices that the receiver is aware of her, the completeness of the plan and the fraction of attention can both change. When there is an effect connection, as we see in the Sense of

Figure 4: Zener cards.

Being Stared At, the connection often works, even when there isn't a huge soul connection. When we have a sense connection, the odds of recognizing the force being sent go up significantly.

Physical Connection (Close Distance)

The next distance we want to consider is where the two souls are close enough to physically interact with one another. Surprisingly this is not a distance that people think about much when they are studying psychic connection, ESP, or any other kind of communication between souls. I think the lack of interest in touching distances is a telling observation.

The classical research is done outside of arms' length. For example the Zener card experiments* are usually done with physical barriers of some kind between the participants. Often the tests are conducted with the participants in different rooms. The purpose for that is clear, of course. The experimenters needed to ensure that there was no way for the person trying to guess the cards to see a card or receive non-psychic

---

* There are two major kinds of Zener card experiments. In the first the person trying to sense the cards (guesser) is doing it without a partner. The claim is that this is a test of extrasensory perception (ESP). The guesser is trying to read the card through non-ordinary means. In the second type of experiments there is a person looking at the card while the guesser is trying to figure out what the card is. These are considered tests of telepathy (the ability of one person to read the thoughts of another person). Both types of experiments are done in ways that minimize the possibility of information being sent between the participants in an ordinary way. Only the second seems to be a test of soul connection.

signals from the sender. Other experiments with dreaming or visualizing scenes have been done with the participants in separate rooms. Sometimes they have been done with the participants in separate cities.

Sheldrake's recent experimental designs have similar non-touching restrictions. They take great care to avoid any kind of ordinary communication in the Sense of Being Stared At experiments. After much criticism from skeptics, closed circuit television has been used (successfully) so the starer doesn't have to be in the same room as the person being stared at. The telephone and email experiments are done with people far apart. The dogs that know when their owners are coming home are recorded on video with no one in the house at all. If there is a trend, it is to move the participants farther and farther apart to eliminate the claims that the information is being passed through one of the five physical senses.

Luckily, this discussion is not about how to design an experiment that avoids any possibility of information being passed through the physical senses. We are trying to figure out how souls communicate. What we are hoping to find are some testable equations that predict the strength of the communication.

There used to be something magical (and maybe terrifying) about sitting in a movie theater and wondering if it is all right to put an arm around your date for the first time. I wonder if that is still an issue today. Holding hands across the table at a restaurant has the same kind of tension.

Tension is a really good term to use here. The feeling is somewhat similar to the surface tension of water. We have our personal space. Some people are invited inside that space, but we want most of the world to stay outside it.* There is often a conscious decision to change a relationship — to go from a nod to a handshake or from a handshake to a hug. For those outside of the United States, let me suggest that air kisses to the cheek are roughly equivalent to handshakes. Both air kisses and

---

* Different cultures have different sizes for personal space. While I think it would be interesting to look at the relationship between personal space, the cultural beliefs of kinship, and how the life force is perceived, this is beyond what I want to do in this book.

handshakes are culturally accepted methods of greeting and provide evidence that it is possible to keep barriers up even when we are in physical contact.

The question we are trying to answer is how much the connection between souls is changed when bodies are in contact and which chakras are affected the most. The first aspect to consider is how compatible the two people are. With some people a touch is welcome. With others it just feels creepy. When we are talking about the connection, it becomes stronger when the touch is welcome. The connection might even be reduced when someone's touch makes us feel creepy.

My martial arts instructor once told a group of us that, if we were touching our wives or girlfriends, we would know if they were telling the truth. (He forgot to mention that this works well only when we are also telling the truth.) What he was saying is that our souls are connected better when we are in physical contact. This is another channel (or if we use a chakra model, several channels) that can transmit information.

Connection should be roughly equivalent to the amount of physical sensing that is coming from the body associated with the soul we are interested in. One observation is that we will have less soul contact with a particular soul when there is a lot of contact from many different sources. We need to be paying attention to the contact for it to create connection between souls.

If we are rejecting the touch, we will probably also be rejecting the soul connection as much as possible. However, a powerful person can affect us more easily when he or she is closer to us. Physical contact reinforces the message. It's one reason politicians feel that it is very important to shake as many hands as possible.

The equation for calculating contact connection (CC) takes into account the feelings between the two people (how much of the touch or taste they choose to accept) and the amount of information that is being passed through touch and taste.

$$CC = \sum_{c=1}^{contacts} \left(CA_c * LF_c * A_{c1}/A_{TOT1} * A_{c2}/A_{TOT2} \right)$$

where CA is the ability of a contact sensor to feel the life force sent
LF is life force
A is attention from each person, for the relevant contact and total contact

One important point about contact connection is that connections between souls can be going on even when connections between bodies are also going on. It isn't a case of one or the other. The physical sensations may be much stronger, but the soul connections can be pretty strong, too, when physical contact is made. It's usually clear that a message is being sent, and most of the time the message is also understood.

Total Connection

To find the total connection between two people we add up the connections from all the distances that apply. If the people are not able to sense one another with physical senses, we include only the soul connection, which is made up of the genetic connection, experience connection, intentional connection, and desire connection. If they are able to sense one another, we add up both the soul connection and the sense connection. If the two people are touching, we also include the contact connection. Note that the soul connection is relatively stable. It doesn't change much during a short encounter. The other connections can have very different strengths from one moment to the next, depending on what is happening in the encounter.

When we add up the connections, we come up with a value for how much life force can move from the sender to the receiver. How much actually moves also depends on how much life force the sender is trying to send and how much life force the receiver is willing to receive.

The equation for calculating connection needs to take into account the three zones of contact: beyond physical sensing, physical sensing but not in contact, and in contact.

$$C = SoC + [\text{if in middle zone or close zone}](EffC + SeC)$$
$$+ [\text{if in close zone}]CC$$

where
C is total connection
SoC is soul connection
EffC is effect connection
SeC is sense connection
CC is contact connection

14. Sending a Message

The test of all knowledge is experiment.
Experiment is the *sole judge* of scientific "truth."
— *Richard Feynman*

When we are trying to calculate the likelihood of a transmission between two people, we need to take into account the abilities of the two people involved. One possibility is to average the probability that a sender can send a message of sufficient strength and the receiver can receive a message of the same strength. That would suggest that a really strong sender (or a sender in a really energetic situation) could make up for a weak receiver. It also suggests that a very talented receiver could pick up signals from almost anyone.

The probability of transmission in this case would be the average of the probability that a sender can send a strong enough message and the probability that a receiver can receive that message. We are assuming the same kind of controlled experimental situation that was used to determine the abilities in the first place.

$$P_{transmit} = (P_{sender} + P_{receiver})/2$$
where P is the probability

I don't expect this result to be correct, though. The probability of a very weak receiver (say 10%) sensing a strong sender (say 90%) doesn't seem likely to be 50%. (Experiments may prove otherwise.) The weakness of the receiver seems to have a much stronger effect. I suggest that a better model is to multiply the abilities of the two people involved.

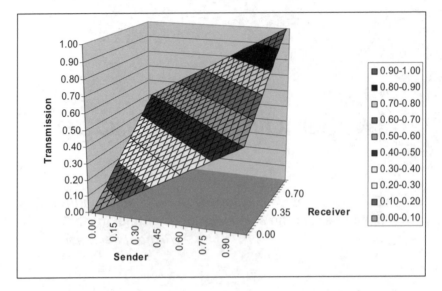

Figure 5: Transmission probability based on averaging the abilities.

That gives the weakness of one of the people a stronger effect on the outcome of the transmission attempt.

The probability of a successful transmission is based on the probability of a good sender and the probability of a good receiver.

$$P_{transmit} = P_{sender} * P_{receiver}$$

Using this equation we would expect that the probability of transmission between a sender of 90% and a receiver of 10% would be 9%. That makes sense because neither of the people is perfect, so either of them could cause a failure of the transmission. The graphs above and on the next page show how likely it is to have a successful transmission based on the probabilities of the sender and receiver. The first graph (Figure 5) shows the predicted transmission success based on an average. The second graph (Figure 6) shows what we expect when we multiply the abilities.

The important thing to note is that the ability to transmit a life force signal goes up in a linear way for averaging and a non-linear way for multiplying. The strikingly different predictions in the lower ability ranges

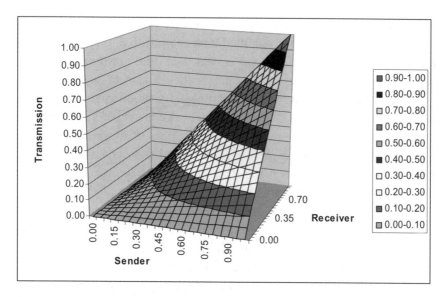

Figure 6: Transmission probability based on multiplying abilities.

show that there is much less chance of transmission when multiplying the abilities.

We can see that if one of the pair is not skillful, the averaging equation still means there can be a good chance of a successful transmission. When we multiply the abilities, the prediction is that there is very little chance of a transmission. Deciding which method of combining abilities is more accurate is something that should be relatively easy to test.

One place where we have seen the importance of the sender's ability was in the attempted replication of the Sheldrake experiment by John Colwell.[91] They changed senders and redid the experiment when they were getting results that seemed to be supporting Sheldrake's position. Using the equation that multiplies abilities, we can see how easy it is to get chance results in the Sense of Being Stared At experiments by just using a sender who has no ability to send.

Blocking

Some people seem to block communication with others. Anger, a negative form of closeness, is one of the big issues. Emotional closeness has both positive and negative aspects. We need to ask which is a better representation: the negative summed with the positive to create a single number or the positive as one aspect and the negative calculated separately to act as interference for the positive. I suspect the latter.

One reason I have for thinking that negative emotions act as a block is based on observations of skeptical debunking, where situations that destroy life force are often created. The creators of these situations are exceptionally talented at causing emotional upsets, uncomfortable situations, and trick experiments that prove little beyond the fact that sensing life force can't occur in every situation.

Beyond that, the skeptics themselves seem to be strongly armored against the life force. To many people, they appear to be soulless. Others see them as some evil, other kind of creature that is an enemy of true human beings. Robert Morgan describes them as Soul Snatchers.[92]

Less evil influences may also block signals or decrease the likelihood of sensing a transmission. Here are some examples.

Influences from other people do not have to have evil intent to block the signal. Other people's thoughts may be picked up by the receiver. One way to reduce the interference is to find a way to tune the sender and receiver so that they are more able to pay attention to one another. We discussed this in the chapter on Connection.

As with any stimulus, other external stimuli may overpower the signal from a sender. We have trouble hearing a conversation in a noisy restaurant. Talking on a cell phone while driving significantly reduces our ability to drive safely because information coming in from the road isn't being processed well. Similarly, it is hard to receive a signal through the life force when our other senses are being bombarded.

It's not just external thoughts or sensations that interfere. Internal thoughts or feelings may reduce the abilities of the receiver. If she is thinking about what to have for dinner, picking up a life force signal is less likely to happen. Unless, of course, it's a life force signal from an animal that is going to *be* dinner. A hungry person out on the hunt is more likely to pick up that kind of signal.

Especially in experimental conditions, the receiver (and the sender, too, for that matter) may be bored. One of the disappointing problems with the early ESP experiments on sensing Zener cards was that spectacular results at the beginning almost always fell off with time. Skeptics suggested that these were normal, random events. I suggest that there is also a boredom factor.

Many experiments have been done to show how well people can attend to important stimuli for long periods of time — not very well. As a result, air traffic controllers are required to take frequent breaks[93] and pigeons are more accurate than humans when it comes to watching for defects coming down an assembly line. We, as humans, are just not good at long-term attention to the same stimulus.

Another problem with experimental design occurs when scientists specifically choose test methods that eliminate emotion. Zener cards are a good example of this. They are transmitted by the communication chakra, which is one of the weakest senders of life force.

We know that the most dramatic cases of connection between people occur when there is a strong emotional connection already in place from the heart chakra or will chakra. Trying to work with non-emotional stimuli is a nearly fatal flaw in the experimental design, which comes about from the error of reducing the ESP concept to specific components and indicators that do not match the concept being studied.[94]

Being worried about success may have a negative effect. This is the kind of concern we see in baseball pitchers who aim the ball instead of throwing it. Intense concentration and effort help (as in throwing), but hesitant actions (aiming) are often ineffective. Another place this shows up is test anxiety. Knowing a subject cold is not enough if you are too worried to remember what you know during a test.

A similar effect comes from trying too hard to interpret the signal with our consciousness. When we look at the chakra system, we see that there are many paths that connect two people together. Consciousness may not even be one of them, depending on how you interpret the chakra centers. (It may be brain rather than the mind chakra.) We need to be open to the connections between all of the centers and not rely on consciousness alone to be optimally aware of the life force.

Not believing that sensing the life force is possible or being very afraid of sensing the life force are certainly sufficient to block a signal that is not being forced on us. We are very good at not sending, processing, or retaining sensory input that is at odds with our belief system. For example, here's a reason one of the staring experiments failed to show an effect:

> [Wiseman] later said that he found staring 'an enormously boring experience' and that in most of the trials he was 'pretty passive about it.'[95]

Passive signals (those sent with no energy behind them) simply don't get through. It's kind of like trying to send smoke signals when you have no fire or turning on a flashlight with a dead battery.

If we don't believe it is possible to sense soul signals, we just dismiss what we receive as silliness and forget it was received. That we forget what we received is important. We can't notice that we got information in a non-ordinary way if we don't remember it long enough to check it out. Forgetting accurately received signals is the converse of the skeptical claim that we only remember times we have correct premonitions. It explains how positive instances of soul messages can be lost.

There are other physiological and psychological states that make a signal harder to sense. These are just some of the ones that are especially relevant to experimental conditions.

Enhancing

Many of the enhancements are the opposite of blocks. We sense signals better when we are in a calm situation with no negative influences. It helps if we accept the possibility of receiving signals through soul connections.

We saw several possible enhancements in the previous two chapters. Signals are easier to receive when we have a strong connection with the sender, either positive or negative. We are more likely to receive signals that will have a significant effect on us. Being in the middle zone or close zone of sensory perception increases the connection strength.

It is also important that the sender puts out a strong signal. That usually happens when the sender is facing significant danger. We hear about it less often with a strongly positive experience, but that may be a reporting effect. There is a threshold effect in transmitting a message.

The signal needs to break through all of the other noise (ordinary and soul) that surrounds us before we can sense a message coming to us.

The final enhancement is the state of mind of the receiver. We've talked about a situation where there are no other distractions, but even beyond that, it helps if the receiver is in a receptive state. One of the best times to receive signals is in the twilight mental state while transitioning between being awake and being asleep. Many authors talk about this as the most receptive time including Bryon, Mayer, and Castaneda.[96]

I think that a large part of what is happening at this time is that the brain is shutting down. Then the mind can be more aware of non-sensory events and the rest of the chakras are not as overshadowed by the power (and static) of the brain.

A state of meditation has many of the same effects. In meditation we can work with the specific aim of shutting the brain off and paying attention to other signals from other non-ordinary sources.

Time Factors

We've talked about how the strength of a life force signal can vary between senders. In the section on Blocks, we looked at some of the effects that can reduce the likelihood of a signal being sensed. One additional effect that we need to look at when we try to predict the success of a signal being sent between two people is the length of the signal.

Signals are not instantaneous. For example, the stare in The Sense of Being Stared At lasts up to twenty seconds.[97] The question we need to ask is how the chance that the signal will be received and recognized is affected by the length of time that the life force signal is being sent.

We know from other studies in perception that there is a lower limit to the length of time required for a signal to be sensed. In visual studies a typical length of time for flashing a subliminal signal is 24 milliseconds.[98] (Subliminal means that the signal is not consciously recognized, but some part of the brain is affected so that some behavioral difference can be observed after being exposed to the signal.) Signals that are longer and signals that are stronger have a better chance of being consciously recognized.

The length of the signal is important because a longer signal gives whatever is sensing the signal longer to lock onto the signal and gives the mind more opportunities to become aware of something happening. We might miss the first drip from a leaking faucet, but most of us are very aware of each and every drip after we notice one. Similarly, we might not notice when someone glances at us, but a prolonged stare is more likely to get our attention.

I suggest that given a constant strength of life force signal and a constant receptivity, the probability of sensing a signal is proportional to the length of the signal.

$$P_{transmit} \propto T$$

where T is the duration of the signal

We also can look at this from the perspective that we need to receive a certain amount of energy before we recognize a signal. (This is true for both ordinary and soul signals.) At each moment there is a threshold level of energy that needs to be exceeded before we tune in to what is happening. The threshold changes depending on what is going on around us.

We can calculate the amount of energy we have received by multiplying the sending strength by the duration.

Life force received is the sending strength times the duration.

$$LF = SS * T$$

where SS is sending strength

Alternatively we can come up with a better answer for variable signals if we integrate the signal over time.

$$LF = \int_{t=signalstart}^{signalend} SS(t)dt$$

Once we know the amount of life force received, we can compare it to the current threshold. As we noted in the sections on Blocks and Enhancements, the threshold is lower when we are in a calm situation and are attending to information from non-ordinary sources.

Directionality

Another important finding of the Sense of Being Stared At experiments, and something you have probably noticed yourself, is that people are pretty good at knowing the direction the stare is coming from. The survival advantages of that ability are clear. When the tiger is staring at you from behind a bush, it's really helpful if you can tell which bush it's hiding behind.

This ability to sense direction leads to two possibilities for the physics of the soul. One is that life force forms a field with a gradient that is roughly analogous to gravity. The other is that we have an extended field that knows where life force sources are within the field.

The first possibility means that life force forms a field with different amounts of force in different locations. This is a relatively simple concept when we are talking about gravity. As we move on the earth, gravity is always pulling us down toward the center. We know which way gravity wants us to go because we can feel the pressure against gravity on the parts we are sitting, standing, or lying on. We also have the ability to sense the slight difference in pull between the top of our head and our feet when we are standing or sitting.

When we shift to talking about life force, things get more complicated. We don't have exactly the same concept of distance, having changed it to connection. Movement (velocity) takes on a different meaning when we are talking about change in connection strength rather than change in location.* However, we can see some similarities when we think about the tiger that is trying to move us in a direction so it can connect its teeth with us. We need some kind of life force to resist.

The relevant spatial gradient is that the closer we get to the tiger, the more power the tiger has over us. Farther away is safer. This should be enough of a gradient to tell us the tiger's location. Remember also that

---

* When we are "falling" in love using a gravitational analogy, we accelerate toward a stronger/closer connection. That means we are moving together faster and faster. Something eventually slows us down because we don't (usually) crush both souls into one. As a side note, I point out that the physics term for a change in acceleration is "jerk." And we all know that someone being a jerk is a pretty good way to stop falling in love.

we may operate in soul time in stressful situations and probably have the ability to sense the future. The charge of the tiger combined with our potential path to escape, as seen in the time dimension, also provides a gradient for danger that will point to the tiger.

The second possibility is that we sense the location of the source of the life force in the same way we sense a touch on our skin. For the sense of touch a single touch is enough. No gradient is required. What is required is that our life force sensing receptors are spread through space all the way to the entity that is affecting them. Then we know what location in space is being touched because we have spatial coordinates in the sensing receptors, just as we have spatial coordinates on our skin. Sheldrake's works with phantom limbs supports the idea of life force sensing receptors being spread out in space.

Experiments can be set up to test which of these possibilities is correct. (There may be effects from one or both of them.) One question we need to ask is whether we can sense direction when the sender is a long ways away. In this case we need to be beyond the middle distance we talked about in the last chapter so that there is no possibility of ordinary sensing. If we can tell direction at far distances, we are probably sensing direction because there is a field with a gradient. If we can tell the direction of the sender only in the middle or close distance, it is more likely that our life force receptors are spread throughout the middle distance.

There is a lot more to be said about sending and receiving messages. We'll take a look at other aspects of this topic in Part IV.

15. Extremely Powerful Life Force

Music in the soul can be heard by the universe.

— *Lao Tzu*

For most of the discussion in Part III we have been using human examples. Contact with other entities is much the same as contact with other humans. I believe that the equations we have discussed should be approximately correct, but humans are not strong broadcasters of life force, nor are they especially sensitive to it. When we are in contact with entities who are powerful broadcasters of life force, we need to see if the equations can predict the effects that have been observed. If they can't, we will need to modify them to handle more powerful transmissions.*

Let's look first at the most common effect of contact with other types of entities: sensing something that isn't physically there. In Part III we have talked about the Sense of Being Stared At. Between strangers there

---

* Isaac Newton's equations of gravity work well as long as things aren't extremely dense and aren't moving extremely fast relative to one another. But our universe does have situations where dense and fast make a big difference. That's where Einstein's relativity and other tweaks to his equations are needed to explain what is observed. It may be that the life force equations need some modifications when the strength of the life force is extreme. Please note that I am not suggesting any connection between life force and relativity. I am only suggesting that the physical world may shed some light on how we need to think about the life force world when we are looking at extreme life force conditions.

isn't anything like an image of the starer being projected into the staree's mind. When we sense a loved one in trouble, we may get an image of the loved one. Sometimes an indication of what has happened is part of the image. With phenomena such as ghosts and angels,* the observer has sounds and often a clear visual image of a being. I suggest that what is happening is that the input from the life force causes the mind (if not the brain) to sense the life force entity as a physical manifestation.

To do that the life force information needs to be stronger than the information coming from the physical senses. We have talked about the concept of daytime eyes and nighttime eyes. Earlier we were talking in human terms. The "light" hitting the daytime eyes needed to dim before the nighttime eyes could see. In this case we are suggesting that the information the nighttime eyes gather can increase in strength enough so that the nighttime eyes take over even in the "daytime."

We know that humans are capable of seeing things that aren't there with extreme (and often frightening) clarity. We have examples of that happening because of PTSD flashbacks, as described by Eric Newhouse in his book, *Faces of Combat, PTSD & TBI.*

> Grant Leland, an Iraqi vet who earlier saw combat in Somalia and Bosnia, tells of driving his car down a three-lane urban highway, looking down at what appeared to be a pothole, then looking up again to find himself in the middle of a convoy going up the same dusty road he had patrolled in a Humvee a year before. He said he knew where he really was — he could hear traffic on both sides of him — but he couldn't see where he was going. So he had to slow his car down and stop in the middle of the highway until the flashback passed. But the worst flashback was when Leland lost his sight altogether. "I thought I'd gone blind," he said. "After a while, I could see again. Then I figured out I was having a flashback of a night battle where they were dropping mortars on us and we were firing back. But that was when I realized I really needed to get help."[99]

---

* UFOs, fairy folk, and Bigfoot may be the same kind of life force entity. Whether they are ordinary or non-ordinary, they certainly qualify as having extremely strong life energy.

These were total takeovers of the sense of sight. I am not suggesting that seeing other creatures happens because of PTSD. The examples are presented only to show that the physical senses can be overwhelmed by other effects if the effects are strong enough.

We have some numbers about the amount of sensory input we receive, which is somewhere in the range of 20 million bits per second. Our estimates for the life force transmissions we have been discussing so far have been less than two million bits per second. That is barely enough to get them noticed. To completely overwhelm the physical senses we probably need to have about ten times the usual sensory input level, or a life force signal that is about 100 times what we encounter in daily life.

Humans are probably not capable of that level of transmission. Entities that are strong enough seem to be rare (or else they are so good at it that we don't even notice they are here). We're not going to talk about these kinds of entities in this book, but the possibility of extremely strong life forces needed to be pointed out.

Other Pathways

There may be other pathways for transmitting life force besides the connection between two people. Here is the math behind some of the possibilities we have discussed earlier.

Angels may serve as a pathway between two people. I believe we can simply add the effect of the angel transmission to the effect of transmission that normally would be there. I also think that the angel effect is usually much stronger than what people can produce. The problem is in getting the angel's attention.

The connection taking the angel effect into account would look like this:

$$C = C_{angel} + C_{human\ pair}$$

The probability of a signal getting through is based on the total force of the transmission. Pathways with other entities have similar equations.

With that I think we have covered as much as we can with the simple model of the soul. In the next part we will look at the complications that arise when we look at a more complicated model of soul connections.

Part IV. Complex Soul Connections

The storm and the earthquake have no soul.
Soul cannot command no soul. Only God can.
But elephants have souls. Anything that can get
drunk...must have some soul. Perhaps this is all
"soul" means. Events between soul and soul are
not God's direct province: they are under the
influence either of Fortune, or of virtue.
— *Waldetar (Thomas Pynchon, V.)*

In Part II of this book we looked mostly at individual chakras. We've seen a lot of information on how a chakra functions and how chakras act together to form a soul. Part III looked at the basics of connections between souls. In the final part of the book we will look at how the soul interacts with the physical body, and how we actually accomplish the process of connecting our soul with another's.

16. Soul-Body Connections

> You don't have a soul. You are a Soul. You have
> a body.
>
> — C. S. Lewis

We are a soul and we are a body. The soul operates on life energy and the body operates with electromagnetic energy. I'm pretty sure I understand why souls like to be in bodies. I'm not as clear on how it is done. Let's start by looking at the why.

Purpose of Bodies

Souls have spent billions of years (or more) evolving bodies so they can act in the physical world. The problem they were having is that life force is not strongly coupled with physical matter. It seems to take a whole lot of life force to move even an atom or two.*

The fundamental idea of conservation of momentum, which probably applies to the life force, means that to change the momentum of one thing, you also need to change the momentum of something else. We can throw a ball with our bodies by pushing against the earth. (The earth hardly notices.) But what can a soul push against if it wants to throw the same ball?

Souls, being very clever, figured out that they needed an amplifier to increase their influence on the physical world. Souls needed something

---

* When I was young, my friends and I tried to move small rocks with our minds. Once out of dozens of attempts we said that we thought we might have succeeded. Even then we were pretty sure it was just wishful thinking.

that had the properties of needing very little input in, say, an electromagnetic field to produce a large effect. Single-celled creatures were a start. Dinosaurs were a pretty good step, but jumbo jets and trips to the moon are even better. Souls influence the brain, the brain moves the body, and the body moves whatever tool it controls. Now we are looking at two-stage amplification of the life force.

So one purpose of adding a body to our souls is to explore and change the physical world more effectively.

A second reason for continuing the experiment with bodies is that bodies are fun. Some folks who believe in reincarnation say uncomplimentary things about those who come back lifetime after lifetime for the current equivalent of sex, drugs, and rock and roll. One group thinks our purpose on earth must be greater than that and the other group just wants to *PARTY*.

I believe that we really do have a greater purpose here, but that doesn't mean that a good party, with lots of positive life force running around, is a bad idea. It's when the negative side of sex, drugs, and rock and roll appears that there is a problem.

There are downsides to having bodies, but overall the good seems to outweigh the bad for many people. If it didn't, why would so many people choose to come back?*

A third reason for bodies is that thinking and creating are great accomplishments. Humans see themselves as the top of the list in thinking, but I often wonder if there aren't other species with high accomplishments that we don't fully recognize. Whale songs come to mind immediately, but we have to consider the mockingbirds who sang outside my window as I was growing up in Southern California. They composed their songs all night and I never caught them repeating. Dragonflies are magic in their own way, and the advantage of looking at

---

* Some believe it's a lottery (as in the draft lottery of the 1970s). Your number gets called and you get the next body (or report for an army physical). Then there are days when I think that many of us are just moving up from being mosquitoes. That makes me wonder if I'm being fair to the mosquitoes. (I've decided that I am.)

this from a soul perspective is that we don't have to worry about the size of the brain. Feel free to add your own examples.

I think, though, that human brains were developed for their ability to reason and make effective use of symbols. The whole arc of human development seems to point in that direction. Early humans drew representations on cave walls. We invented symbols and alphabets to preserve and share our words. The continuing fascination we have with creating computers that are better and better at matching (and sometimes exceeding) human capabilities is further evidence that this is one of the purposes of bodies with large brains. They can calculate, cogitate, and compare.

I read somewhere, and I don't remember where, about channelers. These are people who say they allow wise spirits to enter their bodies and speak through them. (Mediums are similar, but they don't make a claim that all the spirits they are in contact with are wise.) What I read was that the messages from channelers are spoken as Truths. It's not maybe this or I think that. What these wise spirits say is clear, precise, and said in a way that approaches absolute fact.

Some people say that what the wise spirits say is banal and obvious. Both groups actually are saying almost the same thing. The spirits don't have brains. They don't see the myriad possibilities of real life. But they do have this distilled wisdom. (Distilled wisdom is, in fact, obvious.) Having a brain to go with our soul gives us an advantage and the ability to come up with something new, whenever we choose to use our brains.

Incarnational Way

David Spangler[100] of the Lorian Institute presents a related viewpoint on why we choose to mix our soul with a body. His view has more of an altruistic flavor than mine, but I fully support the idea that we need to work to increase the positive life force in our world. As we will see in his discussion, he works with non-incarnated spirits to understand and explain how and why our souls and bodies interact. Spangler calls his point of view the "incarnational way."

> My colleagues in the non-physical realms, the ones who presented me with this worldview in the first place and have

been my partners in its articulation and expression ever since, have a simple purpose: they want us all to live well and prosper, to paraphrase the Vulcan greeting from Star Trek, and to do so in a way that enhances the wellbeing and prosperity of all life. They wish us to live our lives on the earth in a manner that blesses us and creates a future that blesses the world. With their view of our better natures, they see us as quite capable of doing so.

They see this because to them we are spiritual beings as fully as they are. We are not in their eyes "spiritual beings having a human experience," as if that human experience were divorced from spirit in some way; in short, we're not "down here" slumming. We are spiritual beings having an experience of spirit in a particular form that we call the physical world.

If we think of incarnation at all, we usually think of something transpersonal and spiritual inserting itself into something personal and physical. A familiar metaphor for incarnation is that our souls enter our bodies the way a driver gets into a car. But this is a flawed image both in its perception of a duality between soul and body and in its portrayal of how an incarnation takes place.

It would be more accurate to think of incarnation as akin to a chemical reaction that combines several different elements to produce a new alloy, a reaction that in the process generates energy. In incarnation the elements that come together may be thought of as energies or presences. They include the energy and intentionality of the soul, the energies of the world and of nature (which collectively I think of as the World Soul), the energies of spirit and the non-physical realms, and the energy of sacredness. The "alloy" they co-create through their relationship is an individual — you, me and everyone else. We are each a unique manifestation of this relationship which at its heart is enabled and empowered by love. Love is at the heart of every incarnation as that which brings and holds the diverse elements together so that the alloy of individuality can emerge.

Like physical chemical reactions, this spiritual "reaction" generates a unique spiritual energy, one that does not come from somewhere else but emerges from the incarnational process itself. It is a spiritual force and energy that emerges from our intent to be part of this physical world and the process that implements that intent. The act of incarnation itself is a dynamic relationship that makes each of us spiritually radiant, a source of spiritual energy.

Many, if not most, spiritual traditions acknowledge that there is an inner light within us and that we possess a spiritual component. This is what [Abraham] Lincoln referred to as the "angels of our better nature." But most would see this light and spirit as coming from somewhere else or would identify it as "the God within" or the "Divine Spark," a part of us that is separate and distinct from the physical world around us. Such a transpersonal light, spirit or energy does exist within us; in fact, it's one of the elements that is necessary for the "chemical reaction" of incarnation to take place. But the radiant energy that actually is produced by the act of incarnation is a unique spiritual force, an "angel" or a "better nature" in its own right. It doesn't come from anywhere else; it comes from the incarnational process itself. It is a product of our being here, and its generation is one of the reasons we take incarnation in the first place.

I call it our self-light. Think of a light that comes on automatically in a room when you enter it. Our self-light is a radiant, spiritual force that "comes on" when we incarnate; it manifests as our individuality. And because incarnation is a process, not a onetime event, this light has the potential to develop and grow throughout our lives.

Over fifty years, since I was first introduced to the existence of this incarnational radiance and spiritual force, I have sought to understand it with the help of my non-physical allies and colleagues. While we often see such non-physical beings as radiant sources of spiritual blessing, this is precisely how they see us as well. This incarnational light that emanates from us is a vital part of the world, a gift to the cosmos; we are spiritual energy sources in the world and not just energy recipients or energy consumers.

This should not be too unusual a thought if we think about it. Our bodies take in food and convert it into the substance of those bodies, releasing biological energy in the process. We are all generating life energies all the time; why not see ourselves as generating and radiating spiritual energies as well?

What is important to this perception is that this self-light is a part of this world, a product of the act of taking on embodiment and being a physical human being. We are sources of spiritual energy *because* we are in the world and not because we are in some way apart from it. It is not a light or spiritual energy we bring from somewhere else. It is a spiritual force we generate by being here and making this world, this dimension, our home. It is "indigenous," so to speak. Realizing this can be wonderfully liberating and uplifting, giving a whole new meaning and value to being human and being in a physical body.

When I had my original vision about this self-light when I was seventeen, I was told that a spiritual practice would emerge that would honor and work with this incarnational light, this spiritual radiance of our personhood. Over the years I have worked to explore and give voice to what this practice might be like. The incarnational spirituality I teach through our Lorian classes is a result of that exploration, an exploration that is ongoing and evolving.

There are different kinds of spirituality, and each attunes to one of the important and contributing elements of the "reaction" that manifests as incarnation. The mystical path usually focuses on the spiritual experiences and qualities that come directly from the Sacred. Esoteric or magical paths focus on spiritual energies and forces that come from the non-physical worlds and from the beings within them — what I call the Second Ecology. The shamanic and earth-based spiritualities such as Wicca or Druidism work with the spiritual powers and energies coming from the land, from nature, and from life itself, as well as dealing with invisible beings.

What I think of as the "incarnational way" focuses on the spiritual power of our incarnational light, the light that "comes on" and is generated by the incarnational process itself. It is a spirituality of individuality and personhood, which are the fruits of incarnation and the mechanism for bringing this incarnational light to the world. It is this personal light that is often overlooked in the quest for transpersonal experiences and contacts. Yet it is in the understanding and cultivation of this incarnational self-light that we connect with that angel of our better nature that is most attuned to our personal wholeness and also most concerned with and able to serve the wellbeing and wholeness of the earth itself.

The incarnational way is a way dedicated to creating wholeness in all aspects of life. It could hardly be otherwise. Incarnation is an act that occurs in partnership with the sacred, with the soul, with the world and nature, and with the non-physical realms. Our self-light is not independent from these other forms of spiritual energy but integrates them in an ecology of blessing and radiance. The generative spiritual energy of incarnation is a force for wholeness in the world because it emerges itself from an act of wholeness.

In other words, the incarnational way is one of blessing ourselves but also blessing the life we all share as part of this world. Incarnation is about partnership and relationship.

Further, because it is indigenous to this world, it can usually make connections with earthly matters and produce an effect of blessing more efficiently and gracefully than can a transpersonal or transcendent force, which may be too subtle to be readily perceived or felt. It has certainly been true in my experience in working with people for many years that where a person may have a challenge in connecting with the transpersonal or transcendent forces in their lives, he or she can more readily connect with the spiritual energies that emerge from his or her own personhood and incarnation once they grasp that such energies exist.

There are important implications to this for all kinds of subtle energy work such as energy hygiene, manifestation, prayer, and the emerging field of subtle activism. It has been my work and the work of Lorian to explore and develop these implications to find additional ways in which we may serve the planetary needs of our time.

The incarnational way affirms that we have "better natures" and that they exist in us not simply because there is something in us that is "higher" and "more spiritual" than the world around us but because there is a light in us that is part of the world and at home in the world, a product of our loving choice and act to be here in this world. As incarnate persons possessing and generating an incarnational light, we are ourselves the physical angels who create these better natures. If we understand this, we discover we have an innate spiritual resource to tap that is completely natural and indigenous to us as citizens of the earth. And when we tap it, we can become the blessing from which a better history, a better future, can emerge.

Most of this discussion stands on its own, but there is one point that I would like to emphasize and expand on: "This incarnational light that emanates from us is a vital part of the world, a gift to the cosmos; we are spiritual energy sources in the world and not just energy recipients or energy consumers."

We saw earlier that none of the manifestations of soul force took more that a few hundred calories of energy. Perhaps we are literally sending energy that we get from eating food to the spirit world. We have many science fiction stories that look at the possibility of creatures using humans as food. The writers of those stories might be tapping into some subconscious knowledge of the spirit world as they write their stories. The Spangler model is a more pleasant one than many of those stories in that we benefit from the exchange when we are in the spirit realm. If the energy transfer goes from humans to entities in the spirit world, it is yet another reason for having bodies.

Connections between Body and Soul

I have some observations, but I don't have a definitive proposal for how bodies are connected to souls. In trying to provide a comprehensible explanation, David Spangler says it is akin to a chemical reaction. I think it is more complicated (so does David). A chemical reaction is electromagnetic. The joining of a soul and body involves finding a way to couple two different kinds of fundamental forces.

We know that fundamental forces couple with one another. Gravity and electromagnetism interact to produce bending of light in gravitational fields. What we are looking for is a coupling between life force and the electromagnetic forces in the body.

Luckily we don't have to explain how the coupling works, just as physicists don't have to explain how gravity bends light. They have to predict what will happen and the predictions need to be expressed in an equation that covers a large range of conditions, but this is not the same as saying how. For those who know enough to say that the how is that gravity bends space, we move the question up a level and ask how does gravity bend space? We can say in what way space is bent, but the mechanism for bending it is not all that important a question.

I don't have the equations that describe the coupling between life force and electromagnetic force, but we can look at some things that might point in the right direction.

One thing that is said is that intelligent people have more convolutions in their brains.* Some people also say we see more convolutions in human brains than in brains we consider evolutionarily† less advanced. When electrical engineers hear about convolutions, they think about the resonance cavities the convolutions create in the brain. In resonance cavities a small, but coherent energy input (or weak energy coupling) can cause a large effect as the cavity acts to amplify the signal. I'll leave this as a possibility.

One really good question that gets asked is why an injury to the brain causes a change in what a person can do. If there is a soul that isn't hurt by the brain injury, why doesn't it keep the person functioning?

I think the answer is that we need all of the parts working together. There is a connection between soul and body, but part of that connection

---

* It's probably an old wives' tale. See Simms (1898 — yes, one of those years before the invention of the television)
† Also probably an old wives' tale, Simms (1898). In addition, the topic of evolution is best left for another book.

goes through the brain. Damage there, or anywhere else for that matter, will reduce functioning for the system.

People who have brain injuries show effects in all the areas covered by chakras, not just in thinking. There are at least three possibilities. One is that the mind chakra loses energy trying to keep the brain functioning and that all the other chakras send their energy to the mind chakra, reducing their functioning. Another is that the energy levels of the other chakras are reduced (or even made negative) because of the emotional effect of the brain damage. A third is that all the chakras connect to the body through the brain and all of the connections to the brain are damaged. The third possibility is not the mechanism I prefer, but I'm still searching for the equation that works.

Another observation is that there are brain experiments where electrodes touch certain portions of the brain and particular, very vivid memories are stimulated. One set of experiments was written up by Penfield and Perot in 1963.* These experiments don't go on for very long. They are usually just a secondary procedure for brain surgery, and keeping the brain exposed for longer than necessary is not considered best practice, especially since the patient is usually conscious for the operation. No one that I know of has tried to repeat the procedure to see if the same point has the same memory forever.

I suggest that what we are seeing in these experiments is not necessarily evidence of the brain's method of storing memories. What we may have instead is a connection point between the mind chakra and the

---

* More details on the procedure: The stimulus was provided to "the temporal lobe using a 1.5 mm square silver ball electrode providing square-wave pulses of 2-5 ms at 40-100 Hz, 1-5 volts, delivering a stimulus current of 50-500 micro-amperes."

"The region that gives rise to auditory epileptic experiences and electrocortical experiential responses is the superior temporal convolution, with some differences between left and right" "there is a sharp functional frontier between the sensory and the interpretative areas ... in the auditory cortex (the electrode may elicit) a ringing, humming or rumbling ... but then, if the electrode is moved only a few millimetres away into the neighbouring cortex around these sensory areas, a response of a totally different order of neuronal organisation may result. There is no longer a sound but a voice, no longer a rumbling but music." Compston, 2005.

brain. The electrical stimulation would be increasing the ability of the brain to access a memory from the mind.

None of these observations leave us with a clear indication of the connection between soul and body. Another problem we face is that the body does not clearly divide into the segments described by the chakras. There is a real sense when I practice karate that the energy and connections is centered in the tanden (lower abdomen) region. When I'm involved in a serious confrontation, it's best if the brain is not involved, and it feels like the reactions are not part of a thinking process of either the mind or the brain. However, I do need to use legs and arms to make movements. Those same arms are used by my communication and mind chakras as I am writing this book.

It makes sense that the body follows the most active chakras. It also makes sense that the body follows more strongly when the chakras all agree on what should be happening. When athletes speak of being in the zone, it probably means that all the parts are working together well.

Without suggesting a complete equation, let's put together the pieces that we have.

First we can look at actions. Higher energy in the chakras leads to more power in the body. High chakra energy brings physical (mental) energy to the part of the body the chakra is associated with. The arms and legs can follow nearby chakras well and more distant chakras to some extent. (Arms and legs both work well with the will chakra. Arms work well with the mind chakra, but legs are barely connected.) When the chakras do not have a unified intention, the body cannot act effectively. We cause changes with both our life force and electromagnetically based forces.

Next we can look at perception. In sensing what is happening in the outside world, the mind needs to reach out to be able to effectively take in information. It's easy to miss something if we are not fully tuned in. We sense by receiving both life force and electromagnetically based forces.

Finally we can consider existence. We maintain our health, well-being, and emotional stability more effectively when we have positive energy in all of our chakras.

The nice thing about these suggestions is that each is testable (once we agree on a measure for the amount of energy in a chakra). We can see how much influence chakras have on actions, perceptions, and health. Armed with that information we can make better models of the connections between soul and body.

17. Soul Interactions

Make everything as simple as possible, but not simpler.

— *Albert Einstein*

It would be so nice if people were simple. Two people could fall in love and share all that wonderful heart life force back and forth. They could fall in lust and share desire life force. Or they could do both. Why even bother with the other chakras when all that is going on. Life (and calculations of soul interactions) would be simple.

Unfortunately, that's not how the world works. We also have situations like the supervisor who coerces a subordinate into sexual activity. The supervisor is using the will chakra to force the subordinate to provide desire life force (at least the physical manifestation of it) and allow the supervisor to release unwanted (probably negative) desire life force in the subordinate's direction. When the situation is truly coercive, we can expect a lot of negative heart life force flowing both directions. You can bet a lot of mind and communication life force will also be wasted by the supervisor who is trying to not get caught and the subordinate who is trying to get the supervisor's ass busted.

The reality is messy, In this chapter we will develop calculations of interactions between people that can handle the complications we find.

Connections between Souls

What we are trying to describe first, when we look at the connections between souls, is the amount of life force that is flowing between them.

It looks to me as if every chakra in one soul can send life force to every chakra in the other soul. That means there are potentially 49 streams of life force flowing from one person to another and 49 streams of life force flowing back. Let's start by looking at the amount of life force that will flow along one of these connections.

To calculate the life force flow for the whole soul we need to combine two things we discussed earlier in the book: connections between souls and elements in the structure of the chakra. Each chakra in one soul will have its own value for its connection to each of the chakras in the other soul. There will be 49 values to represent all of the connections between the chakras in the two souls.

Connection between a pair of chakras is represented by C_{ij} where i is a chakra in soul A and j is a chakra in soul B.

It shouldn't be surprising that each chakra pair has its own value for connection. Most of us have probably experienced a situation where a relationship changes (for example, from friend to lover or from an email contact to meeting in person). It can feel like starting the interaction all over again as different chakras hook up in different ways. The connections represent the amount of life force that flows between the chakras during each time interval. A higher connection means that more life force is flowing.

When we looked at the structure of the chakra, we named eight aspects that described the connections between chakras in two different souls: inward ability, inward set point, inward intention, internal set point, outward ability, outward set point, outward intention, and external set point. We can use these to calculate how much life force the soul wants to transfer out and how much life force the soul wants to allow in.

On page 101 we calculated the outward life force that a particular chakra wanted to send along a particular connection. This is the starting point for the calculation of how much life force actually flows.

It is important to remember here that life force in made up of energy and information. The information component allows a chakra in one soul to tell each chakra in the other soul what it wants done with the energy.

Each connection between each chakra will potentially be sending many sets of information and the energy flow associated with each of them.*

Life force moving between a pair of chakras in different souls (LF_{ij}) is composed of experience and energy.

$$LF_{wish\ ij} = set[e]\{LF_{wish\ ij}^{e}(e)\}$$

where e is the set of experiences currently active in the chakra and $LF_{wish\ ij}^{e}$ represents the amount of life force the chakra wishes it could send with experience e.

It is possible that the energy associated with some of the experiences will be positive, while other experiences will carry negative energy. We need to total up the energy correctly because negative and positive energy both take up "space" in the connection.

The energy flow for the connection is the absolute value of the sum of the energy flows for each experience. We are assuming that both positive and negative energy flows can occur along the same connection, and they both take up "space."

$$LF_{wish\ ij} = \sum_{e=1}^{active\ experiences} \left| LF_{wish\ ij}^{e}(e) \right|$$

where e is the number of experiences currently active in the chakra.

The details of the math suggest that sending positive and negative energy associated with different memories will reduce the strength of both messages, if there are any limits on the amount of life force that can be transferred. I believe this is an accurate representation of reality. We also find that sending many possibilities with divided life force is less effective than sending one possibility with all the life force available.

Once we know the strength of the connection, the outward intention of the first soul, and the inward intention of the second soul, we can calculate the limits on the life force flow between the chakras. We use the smallest of these values to find how much life force flows.

---

* This might not be as bad as it seems, although it can get pretty complicated. The saving realization is that the mind chakra, with the help of the brain, can hold about seven experiences at a time. I don't think that each chakra on its own can hold more than one or two.

Maximum life force flow (LF $_{max}$) is the minimum of strength of the connection (C $_{ij}$), the outward intention of the first soul (OI $_i$), and the inward intention of the second soul (II $_j$).

$$LF_{max} = [min](C_{ij}, OI_i, II_j)$$

If the energy the chakra wants to send is greater than the maximum amount of energy that is allowed, the amount of energy associated with each memory is reduced proportionately.

The energy flow for each experience may be reduced.

if $LF_{wish\ ij} \leq LF_{max}$ then

$$LF_{ij}^e(e) = LF_{wish\ ij}^e(e)$$

$$LF_{ij} = LF_{wish\ ij}$$

else

$$LF_{ij}^e(e) = (LF_{wish\ ij}^e(e)) * \frac{LF_{max}}{LF_{wish\ ij}}$$

$$LF_{ij} = LF_{max}$$

endif

We can put the whole energy flow together as a matrix. It will look a lot like the matrix we had for energy going internally between the chakras in one soul. The biggest difference is that the diagonal of the matrix is not zero here because one soul can transmit energy from a chakra to its counterpart chakra in the other soul. (Within a single soul that would be saying a chakra was sending energy to itself.)

We can represent the life force (LF) from soul A to B with a 7 by 7 matrix of life force movement to represent connections between each chakra. LF $_{12}$ would represent the flow from chakra 1 of soul A to chakra 2 of soul B.

$$\mathbf{LF} = \begin{matrix} LF_{11} & LF_{12} & LF_{13} & LF_{14} & LF_{15} & LF_{16} & LF_{17} \\ LF_{21} & LF_{22} & LF_{23} & LF_{24} & LF_{25} & LF_{26} & LF_{27} \\ LF_{31} & LF_{32} & LF_{33} & LF_{34} & LF_{35} & LF_{36} & LF_{37} \\ LF_{41} & LF_{42} & LF_{43} & LF_{44} & LF_{45} & LF_{46} & LF_{47} \\ LF_{51} & LF_{52} & LF_{53} & LF_{54} & LF_{55} & LF_{56} & LF_{57} \\ LF_{61} & LF_{62} & LF_{63} & LF_{64} & LF_{65} & LF_{66} & LF_{67} \\ LF_{71} & LF_{72} & LF_{73} & LF_{74} & LF_{75} & LF_{76} & LF_{77} \end{matrix}$$

Once we have this matrix, there are a few other calculations we can make to help us understand the relationship between the souls. One is the concept of net life force change (NC). The idea here is to measure how much life force moves between the two souls. We can figure this out by starting with the movement from A to B and subtracting the movement from B to A.

Calculating net life force change (NC) through each connection.

$$NC_{ij} = LF(AB)_{ij} - LF(BA)_{ji}$$

The net life force change for the whole system is the sum of each of the elements in the net life force change matrix.

$$NC = \sum_{i=1}^{7} \sum_{j=1}^{7} NC_{ij}$$

This provides one kind of information, but it is important to notice that a net life force change near zero can result from two very different conditions. In one case there is little life force moving either direction. In the other case there is a great deal of life force moving in both directions. The first case is a disconnected and unimportant connection, while the second case represents a significant, balanced connection. With anyone we care about (as long as the life force flow is positive) the second case is better. In addition to the net life force change, we can calculate a net life force flow (NF) by adding the flows in both directions.

Calculating net life force flow (NF) through each connection.

$$NF_{ij} = LF(AB)_{ij} + LF(BA)_{ji}$$

The net energy flow for the whole system is the sum of each of the elements in the net life force flow matrix.

$$NF = \sum_{i=1}^{7} \sum_{j=1}^{7} NF_{ij}$$

Life force flow can be both positive and negative. When there is positive and negative flow in the same interaction, the net life force flow will be reduced when the two are added. It can also be useful to calculate the total life force flow (TF, both positive and negative). We can do that by taking the absolute value of each flow and adding those together.

Calculating total energy flow (TF) through each connection.

$$TF_{ij} = \left| LF(AB)_{ij} \right| + \left| LF(BA)_{ji} \right|$$

The total life force flow for the whole system is the sum of each of the elements in the total life force flow matrix.

$$TF = \sum_{i=1}^{7} \sum_{j=1}^{7} TF_{ij}$$

These three numbers (NC, NF, and TF) are very important as characteristics of a relationship between two souls. They show us the depth and balance of the relationship and whether it is making the people in the relationship more or less healthy. The healthiest relationships are balanced (NC close to zero when averaged over time), powerful (NF a large positive value), and healthy (NF positive and almost equal to TF).

There is one more useful value we can calculate. This looks at the ratio between the life force transmitted through the same chakras (for example, from one heart chakra to another) and the amount of life force transmitted between different chakras (for example, the will chakra to the spirit chakra). Straightforward relationships transmit much more between the same chakras. Whenever a lot of life force is transmitted between different chakras, we can expect to find relationship problems or relationship imbalances. We'll talk about this more in the next two sections.

The energy that flows through the same chakras (SCF) is the sum of the diagonal of the matrix.

$$SCF = \sum_{i=1}^{7} \left(|LF(AB)_{ii}| + |LF(BA)_{ii}| \right)$$

The ratio of flow through the same chakra (SCR) to flows through different chakras can be calculated by dividing SCF by the flow through the rest of the chakras (TF - SCF)

$$SCR = \frac{SCF}{TF - SCF}$$

Connections between Matching Chakras

I believe that the majority of interactions and the majority of life force flow occur between matching chakras. However, this is an area where we need to conduct studies to verify whether my belief is correct or not.

The advantage of connecting with matching chakras is that each chakra understands the type of energy and the kinds of information that are being transferred. The aspects of each chakra are usually able to handle life force coming from the same kind of chakra, so the outward and inward intentions will usually be kept within the desired levels.

Connections between Different Chakras

Connections between different chakras can cause problems. The kind of situation we are talking about here includes cases such as parents who try to force a child to love them. Similar situations involving heart chakras include supervisors who force sexual relationships and relationships where a person is talked into a friendship even when it isn't in the person's best interest.

I believe, for the most part, relationships based on connections between non-matching chakras are unhealthy. They often use negative life force from one person to force the other person to give back positive life force in return.

John Gottman[101] has studied this problem in marriages. He has found that relationships fail when there is too much negative. They succeed when there are positive emotional connections.

Interactions between different chakras are relevant to the question of whether it is possible for one entity to force the other entity to give up or take life force in a particular chakra. For specific examples: Can one person steal another person's will? Can one person force another person to feel loved when the second person is convinced he is unlovable? I believe the answer is not usually when only a single chakra is involved. Usually there will be more than one chakra involved in the interaction before an entity can be forced to give up positive life force.

Couples and Groups

So far we have been talking about connections between individual souls. The question arises, how do we calculate connections with a group?

The simplest example of this would be a person dealing with a couple. There seem to be two possibilities for the connections between the single person (P) and the two people in the couple (C1 and C2). The first possibility is that we can calculate everything of importance by looking at the three pair-wise connections (P-C1, P-C2, and C1-C2). The other possibility is that there is a virtual entity called the couple (C), so that we need to include connection with the couple as a separate entity in the calculations. Then we have the pair-wise connections P-C1, P-C2, P-C, C1-C2, C1-C, and C2-C.

I believe that the couple is, in fact, a separate thing for the purpose of understanding soul connections. People often act one way with one person in a couple (P-C1) and quite differently when both people are there (P-C becomes more important than P-C1 or P-C2). Since how people act is pretty much the definition of the connection between them, understanding interactions with a couple is probably best calculated by adding the couple entity. The stronger the bond between the couple, the more important the couple entity will be.

Another way to decide on whether to consider a couple entity is to ask whether it meets the criteria for an entity. Is it made up of one or more chakras? Do the chakras have the expected characteristics? Let's look at the central five chakras. I believe we can find couples that have thoughts that are different from the thoughts of the individuals, although there are certainly similarities. Communications can be different. (George never talks when Martha is around, but he's really interesting when you talk to him alone.) They share feelings differently as a couple than they do as individuals. What a couple tries to accomplish can be different from what each does separately. Sexual encounters with a couple fall under quite different rules than sexual encounters with either member of the couple individually. In addition, couples have memories that are different from the memories each person has separately and members of a couple can be putting life force into or taking life force from the couple in ways that they might not be able to take it from each other. (People will put up with a lot of grief from their partner for the sake of the couple when they wouldn't put up with a tenth as much from anyone else.) I think it's clear that a couple needs to be added to calculations.

In the couple case the solution seems more complicated. When we extend this idea to groups of more than two people, we find that it can actually simplify the calculations. What can happen is that the group becomes so dominant that the individual connections can mostly be ignored.

This can be seen in interactions between countries. There is some personal contact, but the diplomats are more easily thought of as communication chakras for a country than for their individual contact with the diplomats of the other country. Other chakra equivalents are pretty easy to figure out.

Looking at smaller groups, labor negotiations are usually between management and the union. City councils argue among themselves, but they usually present themselves to the public as a small set of entities. (In the US that would be the conservative bloc and the liberal bloc.)

Large groups (G) allow us to simplify the connection calculations to P-G. As groups get smaller, we need to consider some of the connections between individuals, for example P-G, P-G5, P-G12. However, the rest of the P-Gn calculations can, perhaps, be ignored. The connections between group members and the group may or may not need to be considered depending on the type of understanding we are trying to reach.

Collective Consciousness

We also combine in ways that would probably not be considered a group. We are very much creatures of our society here in the Western world. The consensual reality we live in is pervasive. Even if we know that there is more to the world than ordinary reality, finding a way to escape from it can be difficult.

We often have to go high into the lonely mountains of Peru to talk with the gods. Shamanistic training involves going deep into the non-ordinary earth to find sources of power. It's hard to do either of those driving down a freeway in rush hour traffic or while playing video games.*

The nearly seven billion people in the world, almost all part of the same consensual reality, are currently having a strong effect on keeping things solidified. Some may be able to find a fluid reality. Castaneda claimed that his group did. Shamanic healers say more about their ability to affect reality in non-ordinary ways than they say about causing changes in ordinary reality through their power to shape chaos. Creating something out of chaos is difficult, at best.

In fact one of the few groups who seem able to create something from the chaos below, apparently after praying long and hard to their gods above, are the physicists. They seem to have created the mystery of quantum mechanics, relativity, quarks, black holes, dark energy, and other marvels out of the chaos by following their equations and dark rites

---

* The virtual reality in video games still seems pretty ordinary, even when ogres and troll bosses are involved. Non-ordinary reality will probably not be found in computers or software — not even when running in the cloud. Studies have shown that video games are most effective at training the brain (and perhaps the mind) to react more quickly and accurately to a particular set of stimuli. The number of areas stimulated in the brain, as shown in fMRI studies, is reduced to a small number of areas by these games. Shooter games are especially effective at reducing the number of areas. See, for example, Gentile (2009).

of experimentation.* They are currently saying they have found a Higgs boson. For quite personal reasons I hope they are wrong.†

Regardless of the fact that this collective consciousness affects our lives very deeply, I suggest that no separate entity is required in our calculations. Perhaps that is because the collective consciousness is too big to connect to. It's as if we are more swimming in it than connected to it.‡

---

* Biologists wish they could create new structures and processes in the same way, but they are tied much closer to the consensual reality because everyone can mostly see what they are talking about.

† And you're not going to find an explanation of that down here.

‡ Here's another of those places where I will welcome the next generation of thoughts.

18. Non-Living Interactions

A good book is the purest essence of a human soul.

— *Thomas Carlyle*

I used to think that it was a silly idea when people said that ghostly visitations were because of energy stored in the surrounding environment. For example, the stone walls of Ackergill Tower are supposed to hold the memory of the death of a young woman who killed herself there.[102]

Ackergill Tower has had a stormy history over the last 600 years. At one time it was owned by the Keith family who had frequent fights with the Gunns and Sinclairs who came from the same part of the country. The castle is said to be haunted by the ghost of Helen Gunn who was kidnapped by one of the Keith family who brought her back to Ackergill Tower. She threw herself from the battlements of the tower rather than submit to her captors.

How could that be, I asked? Don't memories require a living substance, perhaps some part of the dead person's soul stuck forever in the horror of being killed?

I've come to a different conclusion after working through the implications of souls being made up of chakras. I now think that it is possible for non-animate objects to hold the same kind of life force, with both memories and energy, that chakras hold. The difference is that non-living objects are just that — non-living. They are not capable of changing the information or energy they hold. Living entities can change them by, for example, rewriting a book, but left to themselves non-living entities are only repositories or recording devices.

In this part we will take a brief look at examples where this happens. You will notice that the line between living and non-living is not clear-cut when we look from the outside. We have to study the inner workings before we can decide the question.

Mind and Communication Interactions

I talked earlier about books holding energy. There will almost certainly be communication life force. Depending on the type of book there may also be life force from the mind, heart, will, or desire chakras. When we read the book, we connect with what the author left there. While the book may not change from one reading to the next, the connections are alive because the reader is. With an important book (however we define important) we may find new information with each rereading. I believe that is because we change the connection we have with the book as we change personally.

Other expressions that share the ability to connect with our communications chakra include movies, TV, and art. In these we can see how someone in the past chose to communicate with others. We can feel the same communication ourselves.

It is interesting to note that the concept of nearness that we discussed in Part III of this book plays an important role in how much we get out of a particular item. In the soul's terms, to be near something means that we have an understanding of it. Art or old movies that aren't part of our world do not have a lot to tell us.

Heart and Will Interactions

There are many things that can hold heart and will energy. They can be both positive and negative. Sometimes the object is quiet and non-reactive, but I'll include some objects that behave more like an entity.

Mementos from loved ones often hold a special significance. It is almost as if we can feel the person when we are holding the object. In fact, there are people who claim to have the ability to tell us about a person just from holding an object he or she owned.

In a similar vein, the Japanese value many things based on who the previous owners were. An important owner makes items more significant, according to the Japanese, because something of the owner is left with the object.

Wills and bequests are excellent ways for people to impose their will after they die. Negative and positive life force can both be expressed.

It's not just things passed from people we know that seem to hold life force. We can find other examples of souls that become something considered non-living but still retain soul-like attributes.

Terry Pratchett in *The Light Fantastic* talks about old trolls who get tired of moving around and sit down to have a long philosophical think. They turn into rocky hillsides. After enough time they never move again. In this book the bad guys light a fire in the troll's mouth (thinking it was a cave) and the troll wakes up. Pratchett's books are generally regarded as fiction.

Of course, we find the same kind of story in the tales of Dreamtime in Australian Aborigine stories. Dreamtime was the time before ordinary time started when the earth was forming itself. Here's one story: [103]

> Gagai'yeibmi or Gagai'mi, a *yariyaning, nagamarang* man, came from Gubugoidj, in Gunwinggu territory, high up in the escarpment country. He was crying out there [hence the place name], but no one answered. He went on to Malbangandi waterhole, covered with lilies, and stood there, calling out. He went on to Mirong and sat there, calling out, but no one answered. 'Where are all the people?' he asked. He continued to Mabina, calling out, with the same result. 'I'll have to go on farther!' he thought. He went on to Luli — but again no one answered his cries. He walked farther and found some caves. 'I'll stay here,' he said. He called out from morning to sunset, but no one answered. He was becoming hoarse and his tongue lengthened itself, like a dog's. He tried to call out again, but found he could only whisper. He sprang up and 'jumped', making himself a rock among those caves. In one of them he put

himself as a 'picture' [transformed himself as an ochred painting]. He named that country Gagai'mi, after himself, because he was calling out but no other people were there.

Some Aborigines keep the old ways enough to still be able to tap into Dreamtime and connect with the souls that have gone into another form of existence. While this is not the same as ordinary reality, they do not consider this to be fiction. It's Dreamtime, which is, in my view, an example of the reality of the soul. The Aborigine practice of taking care of these sacred places is an example of connection with them through the heart chakra.

In the final analysis I now think that chakras are part of everything. They are vital for understanding the connections between people and every other living thing. They also seem to be the conduits/connections (whatever that means) between all of the things, including the non-living, that are part of our reality, whether ordinary or non-ordinary.

There is a lot more to say regarding souls and how they are connected, but I'm going to leave that for later. This book is intended to provide a foundation for future study. How the studies proceed and where they lead is not part of this discussion.

19. Wrapping Up, Moving On

If the person you are talking to doesn't appear to be listening, be patient. It may simply be that he has a small piece of fluff in his ear.
— *A. A. Milne,* Winnie-the-Pooh

Thank you for reading all the way back to here.

By now, at the end of the book, we have developed a fairly complex system of interactions between pairs of people and groups of people. The model is based on the idea that each of us has a soul and that the souls connect with one another.

We started with souls with seven distinct parts and seven distinct functions. We looked at how these souls connected to one another and found seven times seven ways a pair of people can interact. My definitions of the parts looked like this:

- Spirit Chakra — Connection with God or the gods and other soirit entities
- Mind Chakra — Senses and thoughts
- Communication Chakra — Passing information between entities
- Heart Chakra — Connection to other entities
- Will Chakra — Personal power
- Desire Chakra — Creation, destruction, and personal desire
- Chaos Chakra — Connection with chaos and primal energy

Within each chakra we found a structure and a set of values for each element in the structure. The proposed structure of the chakras looked like this:

Life Force
> maximum internal, internal set point, internal level, leakage, goal

Outside the soul
> inward ability, inward set point, inward intention, outward ability, outward set point, outward intention, external set point

Inside the soul
> to other chakras, from other chakras

We connect within ourselves using the parts labeled inside the soul. We connect to others using the parts labeled outside the soul. We have levels of life force that we try to maintain. And each chakra remembers what has happened to it, either perfectly or with some emphasis on keeping important events and discarding memories of events that are not as significant. If experiences are lost, they may be lost in some chakras, but not in others.

An indispensable part of this chakra model is the concept of life force. Many of us have had experiences that can't be explained with the four forces of ordinary reality. It is impossible to run a chakra model without having life force as part of the explanation.

Now the question is, once we accept a life force and a chakra model for the soul, what does it do for us?

While I have not emphasized it, along the way I have proposed a few places where using this model offers an explanation or, at least, a deeper understanding of some things many of us have experienced, which are puzzling — or perhaps impossible — with an understanding of the world based only on ordinary reality.

We touched on knowing what is happening to someone closely connected with us even when we are far apart. We talked about seeing a little way into the future. Angels and ghosts were mentioned as entities that could exist in a reality that includes life force and souls. We also proposed life force and chakra-like structures in inanimate objects as a possible explanation for some types of hauntings. All of these are within the realm of what is often called the paranormal. For people who have had these experiences and have struggled to explain them in ordinary-reality terms, this book and soul reality should provide a better model for figuring out what happened.

Another area that had brief mention is that the chakra model can provide a framework for many of the important theories in psychology. When we are forced to use the brain as the explanation of everything, important observations by a number of very intelligent people are forced to fight for territory in a rather small and not very complicated lump of neurons. When souls with chakras are allowed into the conversation, we can find places for a lot more observations. We can give Freud and his followers the desire chakra. The gestalt psychologists can have parts of the mind chakra and communication chakra. Jung can have the chaos chakra or the spirit chakra and probably a bit of both. Rogers and the other humanists can have the heart chakra. Maslow's hierarchy fits pretty well with the chakras from bottom to top. It may be time to stop fighting for dominance and welcome everyone to the metaphorical table.

Energy psychology, which has proven to be quite effective, now has what I consider to be a better model to explain what is happening. Any model that is limited to the single concept of the unconscious mind will find a lot more room to spread out when there are five or six distinct chakras beyond the one or two we usually think of as conscious (mind and perhaps communication). The idea that each chakra holds its own experiences provides a mechanism for what is seen to happen during energy work: Negative experiences that created negative energy levels in the desire, will, and heart chakras are being filled with positive energy. Paul Ekman describes his heart chakra filling with positive life force when all he did was sit with the Dalai Lama, although he didn't use exactly those words.[104] Methods to treat PTSD and some other psychological conditions are easier to comprehend when souls are considered.

Let me be the first to point out that this model of soul connections will need revisions, corrections, and additions. I believe the core ideas of souls and life force will survive to improve our understanding of the world and each other.* The details of the connections and ways to use this understanding will be the topics of our ongoing research.

---

* I'm less certain that this increased understanding will be a positive thing. As with most new understanding — think of atomic energy as an example — there are positive and negative uses. That's just what the entities in this universe are like.

20. Apologies

What men are poets who can speak of Jupiter if he were like a man, but if he is an immense spinning sphere of methane and ammonia must be silent?

— *Richard Feynman*

I want to include in this book an apology that has three parts. This book was written because I needed to figure out souls and the life force. Since I wrote it for me, it has not served the needs of all its readers as well as it might have.

First, I want to apologize to all who were hoping I would write a book about souls and life force that was a delightful, touchy-feely discussion. (Of course, you should have been warned by this book's title. I promise the next book will be totally delightful and as touchy-feely as you could possibly desire.) I'm stepping on one of the major beliefs about these topics — that they can't be measured or calculated.

Not being able to measure soul experiences is what makes discussions about souls so comfortable. People who believe in souls can say, "It's a matter of faith." They can hide behind the insubstantiality of the subject. No matter if a strange twist or turn is proposed. It can't be measured anyway, so it *might* be true.

Others in the observer community are happy to record examples of strange events. They don't see the need for an overall, consistent system. In fact, they often clearly state something like, "We can't start to create a theory about all of this until we have more information." If you want to see where that leads, look at the spiritualists in the early 1900s. There were thousands of reports, many of them extremely credible, and the spiritualists were laughed out of the scientific community.

Of course skeptics (in the sense of anti-believers), who don't allow for the possibility of souls or other such nonsense, can point to the lack of precision in the discussions. Their rallying cry is, "If it can't be measured and replicated, it can't be real!" They get to live in their comfortable ordinary reality without worrying about this mumbo-jumbo.

So I apologize to you whether you are a believer, an observer, or a skeptic. By creating a theory of soul reality that can be measured, I have made all of your worlds less comfortable.

Second, I want to apologize specifically to Patrick Harpur, whose book on daimonic (soul) reality[105] is one of my inspirations. One of the things he warns against is trying to apply scientific thinking to soul reality. When you try to measure it or quantify it, all you will get is tricked by the beings in charge of it.

Patrick, you're probably right.

For Patrick's take on explaining the functions of the soul see Appendix 1 about the journey of Heracles (Hercules) into Hades to capture Cerberus, the three-headed dog who guards the entrance to the underworld. (I hope I don't fare as badly as Heracles, and luckily my children are not living at home any more.)

Understanding these concerns I still made a try, and that requires an apology. The reason I am taking the chance is that I think it is possible to use both daytime eyes and nighttime eyes at the same time. I think that events can be looked at from both perspectives. Patrick Harpur discusses that very issue.[106]

> "...do you not see a round disk of fire somewhat like a Guinea*? O no, no, I see an Innumerable Company of the Heavenly host crying 'Holy, Holy, Holy is the Lord God Almighty.'"[107]

---

* A guinea is a gold coin.

The percipient is of course the visionary poet and artist William Blake; the "disk of fire" is the sun. Blake insisted that his poems were not mere figures of speech but true accounts of the natural world, transformed (invariably personified) by the power of the creative imagination. He could see the sun perfectly well as everyone else does, as a golden Guinea; but he could also see its deeper reality, as a heavenly host. He distinguished between seeing *with* the eye and seeing *through* it.

I think that's another way of talking about daytime and nighttime eyes. I'm looking more for a deep initiation into the workings of the soul reality, rather than an attempt to try to control it. I think that the measurements I propose will not damage the underlying mystery. They will just make the mystery a little more predictable in controlled situations, much as shamans learn to control their shamanistic journeys — and much the same as the developers of quantum mechanics created accurate equations without really understanding what was going on behind the scenes. (And, as you will have noticed, what I am proposing has nothing to do with quantum mechanics.)

I deeply hope, in agreement with Patrick's wishes, that the book will lead more people to directly experience the reality of the soul.

Third, I want to apologize to anyone who is non-mathematical. The math is in there for four reasons: One is that it clarifies what the words are saying. Two is that it allows us to put a whole lot of information in a compact form. Three is that it provides something to measure when we test the quality and accuracy of the model. Four is that sometimes the equations point to results that we didn't anticipate and can lead to new insights. I have tried my best to make the text understandable even if the equations were more than you wanted to attempt.

If you did look at the equations, thank you.

I want to make two things clear. The equations are an early attempt to write down relationships for soul reality. I welcome improvements. More important is that most of the equations have some kind of factor that describes rate of change, for example, how quickly connection between two souls strengthens. We each have our personal rates of change. We also make personal decisions about how much of our past experience we go through again when we have new experiences. Studying these factors will help us to better understand ourselves and the range of human possibilities.

For the non-mathematical, the equations are difficult, and I thank you for reading a book that was filled with them. You have made it possible for me to give people who are interested in continuing the research a place to start from. I hope many people continue on from here.

Appendix 1.
The Heraclean Ego

From Patrick Harpur's *Daimonic Reality: A Field Guide to the Otherworld.* [108]

Every perspective of spirit which seeks to stand outside soul in the form of an ego can be represented by a god or goddess, but, above all — as we have seen — by a mythological hero. Each hero has a different style of approaching the Otherworld; each is paired — that is, both determining and determined by — a different aspect of soul, anima, like mutually reflecting mirrors. Aeneas has his Dido, for example; Odysseus his Circe, Calypso, and Penelope; Orpheus his Eurydice; Perseus his Andromeda; and so on. Thus we may ask: is there a hero analogous to that special, singular perspective of spirit I have called the rational ego? The answer is yes, and his name is Heracles (Hercules) who, above all, represents the pattern of heroic ego that predominates in modern Western culture. [109]

What is Heracles' attitude to soul, to daimonic reality, to the Underworld? It is eccentric, to say the least. He visits the Underworld of Hades in the course of his twelfth (and last) labor — which is to capture the guardian of Hades itself, Cerberus, the three-headed dog. [110] Where other heroes go to be initiated or instructed, Heracles goes solely to take. Club in hand, he bludgeons his way in, intimidating Charon to carry him across the river Styx. The shades of the dead flee from him in terror, just as the daimons run from our own hard-nosed rationalism. Throughout his visit, he treats the shades (the images, the daimons) as literal. Confronted by the shade of Meleager, he aims an arrow at him and has to be told that there is nothing to fear. Faced with the shade of Medusa the Gorgon, he draws his sword, before Hermes (who has of course accompanied him down) reassures him that she is only a phantom. Here, Heracles commits two crass errors: he not only mistakes the image of the Gorgon for the real Gorgon, but he also thinks that the real Gorgon can be vanquished head-on — in fact, brute force is useless against her because she turns all who look on her face to stone. (We shall be meeting the Gorgon again.) And so it goes on: Heracles muscles his way through the Underworld, wrestling Hades' herdsmen, slaughtering their cattle in order to feed the shades with blood — as if to literalize them back into life — and, finally, choking and chaining Cerberus before dragging him up into the daylight land of the living. In short, Heracles behaves just as the waking rational ego behaves in dreams, when it usurps the imaginative perspective of the daimonic ego. He seems, in fact, incapable of imagining. Rather than die metaphorically, as initiation demands, he kills literally, even attacking death itself (he wounds Hades in the shoulder). He embodies that myth within mythology itself which denies myth, just as our rational egos, grounded in soul, deny soul.

Because of the difficulty and danger of his last labor, the capture of Cerberus, Heracles asked if he might partake of the Eleusinian Mysteries before undertaking it. This, of course, would have initiated him into the secrets of death and rebirth, enabling his smooth passage into the Underworld. But he was either refused permission or, as other variants of the myth claim, permitted only to partake of the Lesser Mysteries (which were especially founded on his account). This lack of initiation implies exactly what I have been maintaining — that our rational egos remain uninitiated and thus ignorant of, and inimical to, the nature of daimonic reality.[111] The consequence of this is dire: Heracles, alone of all the heroes, goes mad (and kills his sons). "The initiation of the heroic ego...is not only a 'psychological problem'... It is cultural, and it is vast and crucial. The culture-hero Hercules, as well as all our mini-Herculean egos mimetic to that Man-God, is a killer among images. The image makes it mad, or rather evokes its madness, because heroic sanity insists on a reality it can grapple with...or bash with a club. Real equals corporeal. So it attacks the image, driving death from his throne, as if recognition of the image implies death for the ego."[112] (For "image," we can, of course, read "daimon.")

Too much of our recent history has been soul-slaughter, imagining the past as merely primitive and, muscle-bound with technology, bulldozing the sacred places, hunting the daimonic animals with high-velocity rifles, dispatching the jets to shoot down the UFOs, violating the moon-goddess with phallic rockets, and so on. Having severed all connection with the gods and daimons, we reckon we are getting away with it. But we aren't. The victory over the daimons is hollow; we simply make a hell of our world. And, as we drive out the daimons before us, they creep back in from behind, from within. We compel them to seize and possess and madden us. If we want to know our own fate, we would do well, perhaps, to look at the fate of Heracles. He neglected his wife, his soul, who, in order to rekindle his attention, sent him a shirt soaked in what she had been told was a love potion. But the potion was a poison that coursed over his body, corroding his too-solid flesh. The more he tore at the shirt, the more he tore himself to pieces. He was glad to find death on a burning pyre. (His wife killed herself out of remorse.)

This is a warning of what happens to spirit when it becomes divorced from its soul pairing, when it ceases to find its reflection in soul — and loses it. It becomes the solitary heroic rational ego which deludes itself into believing that there is no soul. It creates a correspondingly delusional world for itself which, deprived of its connection with a personal and personified counterpart, opens onto the soul's depths, as abysmal as deep space and as impersonal as the subatomic realm.

Appendix 2.
Operators and Variables

Operators

The following operators are used in the equations in this book:

[abslim] sets limits such that the value of the preceding calculation can't be greater than the absolute value of the following calculation or less that the negative absolute value of the following calculation

[if in…] the following calculation is included if the operator is true

[from] looks at energy moving out from each chakra in the chakra set

[lim] sets a limit such that the value of the preceding calculation can't be greater than the value of the following calculation

[matching] tests for equivalent items in a pair of sets and uses the corresponding values

$[max]_c$ (value) takes the maximum for the values in the list (value $_1$ to value $_c$)

[min] (list) takes the minimum value from the following list

[pair dif] selects all pairs of chakras that are different from one another

[sign] shows whether the value has a positive or negative sign

[to] looks at energy moving into each chakra in a chakra set

$\left[\text{weighted average}\right]_{t=\text{from}}^{\text{to}}$ creates an average value with more importance placed on the values closest to the to interval.

Variables

The following variables are used in the calculations of chakra and soul values.

a is a constant

A is attention

Amp is an amplitude curve; specific to an individual's characteristic response to a situation

b is a constant

BV is body vitality

c_{ic} is a constant that represents how much an experience changes a particular component of chakra i

C is connection

CA is contact ability

ChC is a chakra component

CC is contact connection

CCoef is the connection coefficient

CEC is the conversion factor for converting energy between a pair of chakras

CIC is the conversion factor for converting information between a pair of chakras

CLFC is the conversion factor for converting life force between a pair of chakras

CP is completeness of plan

CS is connection strength

CSB is current state of being

CT is time to cause a change

d is a counter for desires a person has

D is the desire vector

DC is the desire connection

EC is experience connection

EExp is energy directed at the sender

EffC is effect connection

EI is event intensity

ELR is energy leakage rate

g is the genetic similarity constant

GC is genetic connection

i is a counter for incidents during the person's life

IA is inward ability

IAA is inward ability to accept

IAB is inward ability to block

IC is intentional connection

IDec is intention to decrease

IG is identical genes

II is inward intention

IInc is intention to increase

IntA is intrinsic ability

IntS is intrinsic strength

IntSP is internal set point

InwSP is inward set point

LA is learning ability

LF is life force

LFA is the life force a chakra has available

LFC is life force a measurer is capable of seeing

LFF is life force from another chakra in the same soul

LFL is life force leakage

LFO is life force we allow a measurer to observe

LFP is life force pathway

LFPF is life force pathways from other chakras

LFPlan is life force the plan will direct at the person

LFPT is life force pathways to other chakras

LFT is life force to another chakra in the same soul

M is momentum

MLF is maximum internal life force (with energy and information components)

NC is net life force change

NF is net life force flow

NegI is negative interactions

OA is outward ability

OAB is outward ability to block

OAS is outward ability to send

OD is outward draw

OI is outward intention

OSP is outward set point

P is probability

PE is potential effect

PF is a single energy pathway from a chakra

PosI is positive interactions

PT is a single energy pathway to a chakra

R is reaction strength

S is success

SCD is sense connection damping

SCF is same chakra flow

SCR is same chakra ratio

SeC is sense connection

SLF is stored life force (with energy and information components)

SLFM is the change in stored life force caused by measuring the stored
life force

SoC is soul connection

ST is strength training

t is a time counter for the soul reality equivalent of time

T is time

TF is total life force flow

TG is total genes

V is velocity

WLF is the life force in the world

Endnotes

1. Mayer. E. L. (2007).
2. Feynman, Leighton, & Sands. (1963). p. 4-2.
3. Feynman, Leighton, & Sands. (1963). p. 4-1.
4. Teresa of Avila, 1957.
5. Strieber, 1988.
6. See, for example, D.D. Home's Incidents in My Life, (1864).
7. Magnetic Field Lines of a Bar Magnet.
   http://scripts.mit.edu/~tsg/www/demo.php?letnum=G%202. Accessed 11/18/2009.
8. Schulte, M. & Schulte, J. (29 May 2003) Private communication.
9. Spirit + Self. (2009).
10. Singh, J.B. (2008).
11. Goswami (1999), p. 15
12. The discussion of the chakras is taken from Goswami (1999), Shumsky (2003), Rin (2009), Spirit + Self. (2009), and Singh, J.B. (2008).
13. Drumheller (2012).
14. Institute of Physics (2011).
15. Fox (2011). Impressions on Mind.
16. Lawrence, M. (2011). Market Newsletter. February 25, 2011. The particular experiment is in Blackiston, et al. (2008).
17. Ekman (2003).
18. Suicide. (2011). http://www.medicinenet.com/suicide/article.htm. Accessed 2 April 2011).
19. Smith, D. W. (2001), p. 169.
20. Lennon (1967).
21. Merrill (1961).
22. Buckminster Fuller (1981).
23. Eight superpowers (from Shumsky, 2003, pp. 160-161):
24. D. D. Home (1864).
25. Pratchett (1999).
26. "Defenses." www.psychpage.com. Retrieved 4 April 2011.
27. Bryon (2012).
28. See for example, Padmasambhava (2004) or Head and Cranston (1967).

29. Shumsky (2003), p. 106.
30. Llewellyn Encyclopedia, 2011.
31. See for example Jung (1981).
32. Wikipedia, (2011). Archetype.
33. Castaneda (1974), pp 219-222. (Different editions of the book will be on different pages. It's in the chapter "Three Witnesses to the Nagual.")
34. See Adkins' (2011) book, Iron Ball, Wooden Staff, Empty Hands for a comparison of the power centers described by Liu Wen Wei and Ida Rolf.
35. Adkins (2011).
36. Adkins (2011).
37. Whitfield (1995).
38. Ekman and Friesen (2003).
39. Atkinson and Shiffrin (1968).
40. Dubuc (2011).
41. Dubuc (2011).
42. Dubuc (2011).
43. From a set of quotes in the Guardian (2011).
44. See, for example, Children Who Remember Previous Lives: A Question of Reincarnation by Ian Stevenson (2000).
45. Pahl, et al. (2010).
46. See Newton (1994), Newton (2000), Newton (2004).
47. Newhouse, 2008, pp. 117-118.
48. Singer, 2001.
49. Newhouse, 2008.
50. Squat and deadlift. Powerlifting Watch (2011).
51. See Ekman, P. (2003).
52. See Ekman, P. (2003).
53. EFT (2011).
54. Liang and Yang. (1996). p 4.
55. Reninger (2011a).
56. Reninger (2011b).
57. Dalai Lama and Ekman (2008).
58. Wikipedia (2011), Human Nature.
59. Aristotle, Nicomachean Ethics.
60. Aristotle, Politics
61. Aristotle, Ethics
62. Mayer (2001), Mayer (2009).
63. Steinbach, Diane. (2009). Personal communication.
64. Stevenson, 2000, for example.
65. For Edwards, see Edwards (2010). For Van Praagh, see Van Praagh (2009). For Anderson, see Martin and Romanowski (1988).
66. Dolen, Carolyn. (2010).
67. Centers for Disease Control and Prevention (2011).

68. Wikipedia. Shannon-Hartley Theorem (2012).

69. Bible, English Standard Version, 1 Timothy 6:9-10

70. Sheldrake, 2004.

71. Sheldrake 2005a, 2005b.

72. Flynn Effect. (2009) and Raven (2000).

73. Drewes (2010).

74. Hugill, S. (1970).

75. Flammarion and Brooks. (1921). pp 148-149.

76. Flammarion and Brooks. (1921). p. 139.

77. Flammarion and Brooks. (1921). pp 143-144.

78. Bouchard, et al (1990).

79. "Lie to Me" episode 5, season 1.

80. Mayer. E. L. (2007). p. 100.

81. Baez, 1975.

82. Hammerstein and Rodgers (1949).

83. Byrne, 2006 and 2010.

84. http://london.craigslist.co.uk/cas/1009856995.html. retrieved 21 Aug 2008.

85. Mayer, E. L. (2007).

86. See, for example: Radin, D. (2006) or Radin, D. (2009)

87. Wagner, 2011, p. 2.

88. Funakoshi (1973), p. 248.

89. Adkins, 2010, pp. 60-61.

90. Hammerstein and Rodgers (1949).

91. See Colwell et al. (2000), Baker (2000), Shermer (2005), and Sheldrake (2011).

92. Morgan, 2008. Also see Livingston, 2004.

93. Associated Press, 2011.

94. Ragheb, 2011. See especially Chapter 16, Formal Steps in Measurement Construction.

95. Watt et al., 2002.

96. Mayer, E. L. (2007), Castaneda (1972), and Byron (2012).

97. Sheldrake, 1995.

98. for example: Karremans, et al., (2006).

99. Newhouse, Eric. (2008). p. 118.

100. Spangler (2009).

101. Gottman and DeClaire, 2001.

102. Haunted Scottish Castles (2011).

103. Berndt and Berndt (1994), p. 39.

104. Dalai Lama and Ekman (2008)

105. Harpur, 2004.

106. Harpur, 2004. p. 108.

107. "A Vision of the Last Judgment," in Blake (1966), p. 617.

108. From Harpur, P. (2003). pp. 259-261.

[109.] Hillman (1979), pp. 110-17.
[110.] Graves, vol. 2, pp. 153f. ibid.
[111.] Hillman (1979), p. 112.
[112.] Hillman (1979), p. 115.

References

Adkins, Caylor. (2010). *Iron Ball, Wooden Staff, Empty Hands: Understanding Structure, Flow, and Maneuver in Martial Arts.* Enumclaw, WA: Pine Winds Press.

Akemi. (2009). Starseeds: Alpha Centaurians. Real Life Spirituality. http://reallifespirituality.com/starseeds-alpha-centaurians. retrieved 6 October 2011.

Aristotle. Nicomachean Ethics, VIII. http://www.perseus.tufts.edu/hopper/text?doc=Perseus%3Atext%3A1999.01.0054%3Abekker%20page%3D1162a

Aristotle. Politics. http://www.perseus.tufts.edu/hopper/text?doc=Perseus:text:1999.01.0058

Aristotle. Poetics. http://www.perseus.tufts.edu/hopper/text?doc=Perseus%3Atext%3A1999.01.0056%3Asection%3D1448b

Aristotle. (1887) *The Politics of Aristotle: With an Introduction, Two Prefactory Essays and Notes Critical and Explanatory*, Clarendon Press.

Associated Press. (2001). US air traffic controllers given longer breaks to prevent fatigue. The Guardian. http://www.guardian.co.uk/world/2011/apr/18/air-traffic-controllers-breaks-fatigue. retrieved 13 Sep 11.

Atkinson, R.C. and Shiffrin, R.M. (1968). Human memory: A proposed system and its control processes. *Psychology of Learning and Motivation 2*: 89-195.

Baez, J. (1975). "Diamonds and Rust." *Diamonds and Rust.* A&M Records

Baker, R.A. 2000. Can we tell when someone is staring at us? *Skeptical Inquirer* 24 (2): 34-40

Blackiston, D.J., Silva Casey, E., Weiss M.R. (2008). Retention of memory through metamorphosis: can a moth remember what it learned as a caterpillar? *PLoS One*, *3*(3):e1736. http://www.ncbi.nlm.nih.gov/pubmed/18320055. retrieved 14 Sep 11.

Blake, William. (1966). *Complete Writings*, ed. Geoffrey Keynes. London: Oxford University Press.

Berndt, R.M. and Berndt, C.H. (1994). *The Speaking Land: Myth and Story in Aboriginal Australia.* Rochester, VT: Inner Traditions International.

Bouchard, T.J. Jr, Lykken D.T., McGue M., Segal N.L., Tellegen A. (1990). Sources of human psychological differences: the Minnesota Study of Twins Reared Apart. *Science 250*(4978): 223–228.

Bord, J. and Bord, C. (2006). *Bigfoot Casebook Updated: Sightings and Encounters from 1818 to 2004.* Enumclaw, WA: Pine Winds Press.

Bryon, Deborah. (2012). *Lessons of the Inca Shamans: Piercing the Veil.* Enumclaw, WA: Pine Winds Press.

Buckminster Fuller, R. (1981), *Critical Path.* New York: St. Martin's Griffin.

burlingame, j. & Blaschko, T. (2010). *Assessment Toole for Recreational Therapy and Related Fields, Fourth Ed.* Enumclaw, WA: Idyll Arbor.

Byrne, R, (2006). *The Secret.* Hillsboro, OR: Atria Books/Beyond Words.

Byrne, R, (2010). *The Power.* Hillsboro, OR: Atria Books/Beyond Words.

Castaneda, Carlos. (1972). *Journey to Ixtlan.* New York: Simon & Schuster.

Castaneda, Carlos. (1974). *Tales of Power.* New York: Simon & Schuster.

Centers for Disease Control and Prevention (2011). Concussion and Mild TBI. http://www.cdc.gov/concussion/index.html. retrieved 9 Sep 2011.

Colwell, J., Schröder, S., & Sladen, D. (2000). The ability to detect unseen staring: A literature review and empirical tests. *British Journal of Psychology, 91*, 71–85.

Compston, A. (2005). From the Archives. *Brain 128*(3): 449-450.

Conger, C. (2011). Can a person remember being born? Discovery Fit and Health. http://health.howstuffworks.com/mental-health/human-nature/perception/remember-birth.htm. retrieved 8 Aug 11.

Cook, G. and Van Horn, J. (2011). *How Dirty is your Data? A Look at the Energy Choices that Power Cloud Computing.* Amsterdam: Greenpeace International.

Dalai Lama and Ekman, P. (2008). *Emotional Awareness: Overcoming the Obstacles to Psychological Balance and Compassion: A Conversation between the Dalai Lama and Paul Ekman.* New York: Times Books.

Dębiec. J., Díaz-Mataix, L., Bush. D. E. A., Doyère, V., and LeDoux. J. E. (2010). The amygdala encodes specific sensory features of an aversive reinforcer. *Nature Neuroscience 13*, 536-537.

Dolen, Carolyn. (2010). *Brain Injury Rewiring for Survivors: A Lifeline to New Connections.* Enumclaw, WA: Idyll Arbor.

Drewes, A. (2010). Kids Who See Ghosts — Athena Drewes Responds. The Perceptive Children Support Forum. http://www.perceptivechildren.org/resources/research-psychic-children-athena-drewes/kids-who-see-ghosts-athena-drewes-responds/. retrieved 9 Sep 11.

Drumheller, J. D. (2012). *The Subconscious, The Divine, and Me: A Spiritual Guide for the Day-to-Day Pilgrim.* Enumclaw, WA: Pine Winds Press.

Dubuc, B. (2011). The brain from top to bottom. Canadian Institutes of Neuroscience, Mental Health, and Addiction. http://thebrain.mcgill.ca/flash/a/a_07/a_07_cr/a_07_cr_tra/a_07_cr_t ra.htmlretrieved 8 Aug 2011.

Edwards, J. (2010). *After Life: Answers from the Other Side.* New York: Sterling Ethos.

EFT (Emotional Freedom Techniques) (2011). http://www.eftuniverse.com/. retrieved 2 Aug 2011.

Ekman, P. and Friesen, W. V. (2003). *Unmasking the Face: A Guide to Recognizing Emotions from Facial Expressions.* Los Altos, CA: Malor Books.

Ekman, P. (2003). *Emotions Revealed: Recognizing Faces and Feelings to Improve Communication and Emotional Life.* New York: Times Books.

Evans-Wentz, W.Y. (1994). *The Fairy Faith in Celtic Countries*. New York: Citadel Press.

Experience Project. (2011). I Can Remember Being Born. http://www.experienceproject.com/groups/Can-Remember-Being-Born/218567. retrieved 8 Aug 2011

Feynman, R. P., Leighton, R. B., & Sands, M. (1963). *The Feynman Lectures on Physics: Volume 1: Mainly Mechanics Radiation, and Heat.* Reading, MA: Addison-Wesley Publishing.

Flammarion, Camille and E.S. Brooks (trans.). (1921). *Death and its Mystery Before Death: Proof of the Existence of Souls*. New York: The Century Co.

Flynn Effect. (2009). Wikipedia. http://en.wikipedia.org/wiki/Flynn_effect. Accessed 18 July 09.

Force. (2007). *Wikipedia*, http://en.wikipedia.org/wiki/Force. retrieved 17 May 2007.

Fox, P. (2011). Impressions on Mind. http://peterfox.com.au/meditation_samskara.htm. retrieved 4 April 2011.

Funakoshi, Gichin. (1973). *Karate-Do Kyohan: The Master Text.* (translated by Tsutomu Ohshima). New York: Kodansha International.

Gentile, D. A. (2009).Video Games Affect the Brain — for Better and Worse. Dana Foundation. http://dana.org/news/cerebrum/detail.aspx?id=22800. retrieved 12 Oct 2011.

Gleick, J. (1987). *Chaos: Making a New Science*. New York: Viking Penguin.

Goswami, S.S. (1999). *Layayoga: The Definitive Guide to the Chakras and Kundalini.* Rochester, VT: Inner Traditions.

Gottman, J. H. and DeClaire, J. (2001). *The Relationship Cure: A 5 step guide to Strengthening Your Marriage, Family, and Friendships.* New York: Three Rivers Press.

Graves, R. (1955). *The Greek Myths*. London: Penguin.

Gray, J. (2004). *Men Are from Mars, Women Are from Venus: The Classic Guide to Understanding the Opposite Sex.* New York: Harper Paperbacks.

Guardian. (2011). The Body Beautiful: Is it possible to remember being born? http://www.guardian.co.uk/notesandqueries/query/0,5753,-2899,00.html. retrieved 8 Aug 11.

Hammerstein. O. & Rodgers. R. (1949). *South Pacific.*

Harpur, P. (2003). *Daimonic Reality: A Field-Guide to the Otherworld.* Ravensdale, WA: Pine Winds Press.

Harpur, P. (2010). *The Secret Tradition of the Soul.* Berkeley, CA: Evolver Editions.

Haunted Scotland Castles. (2011) http://www.rampantscotland.com/features/haunted.htm. Retrieved 7 Aug 11.

Head, J. and Cranston, S. L., Eds. (1967). *Reincarnation: A Living Study of Reincarnation in All Ages; Including Selections from the World's Religions, Philosophies and Sciences, and Great Thinkers of the Past and Present.* New York: Causeway Books.

Hillman, J. (1979). *The Dream and the Underworld.* New York: William Morrow.

Home, D. D. (1864). *Incidents in My Life.* Reprinted 2009. Ithaca, NY: Cornell University Library.

Hugill, S. (1970). *Shanties from the Seven Seas (Maritime).* Mystic, CT: Mystic Seaport Museum.

Institute of Physics. (2011).Could you power a city with lightning? http://www.physics.org/facts/toast-power.asp. retrieved 18 Oct 2011.

Judge, W. Q. (1971). *The Ocean of Theosophy.* Los Angeles: The Theosophy Company.

Jung, C.G., Adler, G., and Hull, F. C. (1981) *The Archetypes and The Collective Unconscious* (Collected Works of C.G. Jung Vol. 9, Part 1). Princeton, NJ: Princeton University Press.

Karremans, Johan C., Stroebe, Wolfgang, Claus, Jasper. (2006). "Beyond Vicary's fantasies: The impact of subliminal priming and brand choice", *Journal of Experimental Social Psychology 42* (6): 792-798.

Lawrence, M. (2011). Mark's Market Blog, 2-25-11: Libya in flames. http://investing.calsci.com/blog2-26-11.html. retrieved 27 Feb 11.

Lennon. J. (1967). "All You Need Is Love." *Magical Mystery Tour.* London: Apple Records.

Liang, Shou-Yu and Yang, Jwing-Ming. (1996). *Hsing Yi Chuan, Theory and Applications.* Wolfeboro NH: YMAA Publication Center, Inc.

Livingston, J. G. (2004). *Adversaries Walk Among Us: A Guide to the Origin, Nature, and Removal of Demons and Spirits.* Fort Bragg, CA: Lost Coast Press.

Llewellyn Encyclopedia. (2011). Muladhara — The Root Chakra. http://www.llewellyn.com/encyclopedia/article/252. retrieved 1 December 2011.

Martin, J. and Romanowski, P. (1988). *We Don't Die: George Anderson's Conversations with the Other Side.* New York, Berkley Books.

Mayer, E. L. (2007). *Extraordinary Knowing: Science, Skepticism, and the Inexplicable Powers of the Human Mind.* New York: Bantam Books.

Mayer, J. D. (1995). A framework for the classification of personality components. *Journal of Personality, 63,* 819-877.

Mayer, J. D. (2001). Primary divisions of personality and their scientific contributions: From the trilogy-of-mind to the systems set. *Journal for the Theory of Social Behaviour, 31* (4), 449-477.

Mayer, J. D. (2003). Structural divisions of personality and the classification of traits. *Review of General Psychology, 7,* 381-401.

Mayer, J. D. (2009). Personality Psychology: A Systems Approach. http://www.thepersonalitysystem.org/index.htm. retrieved 11 Aug 11.

Merrill, B. (1961). "Love Makes the World Go Round." *Carnival!*

Morgan, Robert W. (2008). *Bigfoot Observer's Field Manual.* Enumclaw, WA: Pine Winds Press.

Morgan, Robert W. (2008). *Soul Snatchers: A Quest for True Human Beings.* Enumclaw, WA: Pine Winds Press.

Newhouse, Eric. (2008). *Faces of Combat, PTSD & TBI: One journalist's crusade to improve treatment for our veterans.* Enumclaw, WA: Issues Press.

Newton, M. (1994). *Journey of Souls: Case Studies of Life between Lives.* Woodbury, MN: Llewellyn Publications.

Newton, M. (2000). *Destiny of Souls: New Case Studies of Life between Lives.* Woodbury, MN: Llewellyn Publications.

Newton, M. (2004). *Life Between Lives: Hypnotherapy for Spiritual Regression.* Woodbury, MN: Llewellyn Publications.

Padmasambhava. (2004). *Dakini Teachings*. Berkeley, CA: North Atlantic Books.

Pahl M, Tautz J, & Zhang S. (2010). Honeybee Cognition. In: *Animal Behaviour: Evolution and Mechanisms*. Kappeler P (Ed). New York: Springer Verlag.

Penfield, W. and Perot, P. (1963). The brain's record of auditory and visual experience. A final summary and discussion. *Brain 86*, 595-696.

Powerlifting Watch. (2011). Men's Raw World Records http://www.powerliftingwatch.com/records/raw/world. retrieved 12 May 2011.

Pratchett, T. (1999) *Hogfather*. New York: Harper.

Pratchett, T. (2000). *The Light Fantastic*. New York: Harper.

Radin. D. (2006). *Entangled Minds: Extrasensory Experiences in a Quantum Reality*. New York: Paraview Pocket Books.

Radin. D. (2009). *The Conscious Universe: The Scientific Truth of Psychic Phenomena*. New York: HarperOne

Ragheb, M. (2011). *Measurement for Leisure Services and Leisure Studies*. Enumclaw, WA: Idyll Arbor.

Rampant Scotland. (2011). Haunted Scottish Castles. http://www.rampantscotland.com/features/haunted.htm. Retrieved 22 August 2011.

Raven, J. (2000). The Raven's Progressive Matrices: Change and Stability over Culture and Time. *Cognitive Psychology 41*, 1–48. http://eyeonsociety.co.uk/resources/RPMChangeAndStability.pdf

Reninger, Elizabeth. (2011a). How Does Qigong Work? About.com. http://taoism.about.com/od/practices/a/QigongWorks.htm. retrieved 27 July 2011.

Reninger, Elizabeth. (2011b). Mai. About.com. http://taoism.about.com/od/glossaryoftaoistterms/g/Mai.htm. retrieved 27 July 2011.

Rin. (2009). The Chakra System. Under the Bodhi Tree. http://under-the-bodhi-tree.com/category/chakras/, retrieved 13 Dec 2010.

Ronson, J. (2004). *The Men Who Stare at Goats*. New York: Simon & Schuster.

Rowling, J. K. (2004). *Harry Potter and the Order of the Phoenix.* New York: Scholastic Paperbacks.

Scott, D. (2005). Mother Teresa's Hunger for God. *Saint Anthony's Messenger* (internet edition, September 2005). http://www.americancatholic.org/Messenger/Sep2005/Feature2.asp. retrieved 14 Sep 2011.

Sheldrake, Rupert. (1995). *Seven Experiments That Could Change the World: A Do-It-Yourself Guide to Revolutionary Science.* New York: Riverhead Books.

Sheldrake, R. (2001). Experiments on the sense of being stared at: The elimination of possible artifacts. *Journal of the Society for Psychical Research, 65*, 122-37.

Sheldrake, Rupert. (2004). *The Sense of Being Stared At: And Other Unexplained Powers of the Human Mind.* New York: Three Rivers Press.

Sheldrake, Rupert. (2005a). The Sense of Being Stared At Part 1: Is it Real or Illusory? *Journal of Consciousness Studies, 12*(6) 10-31.

Sheldrake, Rupert. (2005b). The Sense of Being Stared At Part 2: Its Implications for Theories of Vision. *Journal of Consciousness Studies, 12*(6) 32-49.

Sheldrake, Rupert. (2011). Follow-up Research on the Feeling of Being Stared At. http://www.sheldrake.org/Articles&Papers/papers/staring/followup.html. retrieved 6 Sep 2011.

Shermer, M. (2005). Rupert's Resonance, *Scientific American,* October 24, 2005. http://www.scientificamerican.com/article.cfm?id=ruperts-resonance. retrieved 6 Sep 2011.

Shumsky, S.G. (2003). *Exploring Chakras: Awaken Your Untapped Energy.* Pompton Plains, NJ: New Page Books.

Simmons, D. (1990). *Hyperion.* New York: Spectra.

Simms, J. (1898). Brain Weights and Intellectual Capacity. *Appleton's Popular Science Monthly, 54*(11), 243. From GoogleBooks. http://books.google.com/books?id=sCUDAAAAMBAJ&pg=PA243&lpg=PA243&dq=intelligence+more+convolutions&source=bl&ots=1vG4uwHvgl&sig=PdzI3XDB49-qxhX2njYO-T7eTTE&hl=en&ei=9ypMToj_JeLmiALDoZl6&sa=X&oi=book_result&ct=result&resnum=7&sqi=2&ved=0CE0Q6AEwBg#v=onepag

e&q=intelligence%20more%20convolutions&f=false. Retrieved 17 August 2011.

Singer, I. (2001). *Emotional Recovery after Natural Disasters: How to Get Back to Normal Life.* Enumclaw, WA: Idyll Arbor.

Singh, JB. (2008). Third Eye Health. Bright Eyes Blog. Chakra Chart: Chakras versus Endocrine Glands. http://blog.thirdeyehealth.com/chakra-chart-chakras-versus-endocrine-glands/. retrieved 13 Dec 2010.

Smith, D. W. (2001). *To Rome with Love.* Eugene, OR: Harvest House Publishers.

Spangler, D. (2009). David's Desk #20. Issaquah, WA: Lorian Assoc. email 3 Feb 2009.

Spirit + Self. (2009). The Seven Chakras. http://www.spirit-self.com/2009/03/the-seven-chakras/. retrieved 13 Dec 2010.

Steinbach, D. (2009). Personal communication.

Stevenson, I. (2000). *Children Who Remember Previous Lives: A Question of Reincarnation.* Jefferson, NC: McFarland & Company.

Strieber, W. (1988). *Communion: A True Story.* New York: Avon.

Teresa of Avila (1957). *The Life of Saint Teresa of Avila by Herself.* trans. J. M. Cohen. London: Penguin.

Thompson. H. S. (1995) *Better Than Sex.* New York: Ballantine Books.

TopTenz.net (2011). Top 10 Things Better Than Sex. http://www.toptenz.net/top-10-things-better-than-sex.php. retrieved 5 Aug 2011.

U.S. Department of the Interior. (2005). Hydroelectric Power. www.usbr.gov/power/edu/pamphlet.pdf. retrieved 11 Oct 2011.

Van Praagh, J. (2009). *Ghosts among Us: Uncovering the Truth About the Other Side.* New York: HarperOne.

Von Schlippe, W.B. (2003). The Two-Body Problem in Classical Mechanics. http://www.phys.spbu.ru/content/File/Library/studentlectures/schlippe/twobdy.pdf. retrieved 7 Oct 2011.

Veda. (2011). The Chakras. http://veda.wikidot.com/the-chakras retrieved 28 June 2011

Wagner, S. (2011).Twin Telepathy: Best Evidence. http://paranormal.about.com/od/espandtelepathy/a/Twin-Telepathy-Best-Evidence_2.htm. retrieved 12 Sep 2011.

Watt, C., Wiseman, R., & Schlitz, M. (2002). Tacit information in remote staring research: The Wiseman-Schlitz interviews. *The Paranormal Review, 24*, 18–25.

Whitfield, B. (1995). *Spiritual Awakenings: Insights of the Near-Death Experience and Other Doorways to Our Soul*. Deerfield Beach, FL: HCI.

Wikipedia, (2011). Archetype. http://en.wikipedia.org/wiki/Archetype, retrieved 4 April 2011.

Wikipedia. (2011). Human Nature. http://en.wikipedia.org/wiki/Human_nature retrieved 11 Aug 11.

Wikipedia (2012). Shannon-Hartley Theorem. http://en.wikipedia.org/wiki/Shannon%E2%80%93Hartley_theorem. retrieved 27 July 12.

Wolfe, Tom. (1982). *The Electric Kool-Aid Acid Test*. New York: Bantam.

Index

1

1 Corinthians 13:8, 42

A

ability, 197, 237
  lost, 183
Aborigines, 61, 279
abuse, 113
access, 86
Adkins, Caylor, 66, 227
Aeneas, 289
affection, 55
affiliation, 41, 42
agape, 41
ajna chakra, 31
akashic records, 26
Alderaan, 224
Amadeus, 102
Amaru, 64
amplification, 254
amygdala, 90
anahata chakra, 41
Andromeda, 289
angels, 26, 248, 249
anger, 84, 118, 239
anima, 289

anorexia, 113
anxiety, 94
Apucheen, 65
archetypes, 61
Aristotle, 157
artists, 56
athletics, 190
attention, 84, 135
attraction, 54, 105
  intense, 176

B

baby
  cranky, 143
bad vibes, 121
Baez, Joan, 211
battery, 76, 80
bee, 92
behaviorism, 10
being of two minds, 162
belly, 64
betrayal, 42
biology, 33, 88
birth memories, 91
Blake, William, 287
blocking
  external, 240

internal, 240
blocks, 154
bodies, 4, 253
   purpose of, 253
   working with chakras, 263
body language, 37
books, 278
boredom, 241
Bouchard, Thomas, 207
boundaries, 110, 124
Brahman traditions, 27
brain, 32, 163, 261
   memories, 88, 90
brain injury, 184, 261
brain surgery, 262
Braveheart, 51
Bryon, Deborah, 51, 64, 243
bubbling over, 114
Buddha, 104, 218
Buffet, Warren, 189
bummer, 121
burn out, 80
burning out, 125
business, 188
butterflies
   learning, 32
Byrne, Rhonda, 217

C

calibration, 193
California Institute of
   Technology, 12
capacity, 214
care package, 129
Carlin, George, 113

Carnegie, Dale, 188
Castaneda, Carlos, 6, 43, 49, 65,
   243, 274
castes, 27
caterpillars, 92
   learning, 32
Cerberus, 289, 290
chakra, 5, **21–66**, 282
   access, 86
   ajna, 31
   anahata, 41
   as flower, 23
   change mechanisms, 72–74
   changing focus, 153
   chaos, 49, 56, **59–63**, 59, 60,
      61, 62, 71, 78, 283
      life force processing, 62
      openness, 62
   colors, 24
   communication, **36–40**, 36,
      37, 38, 39, 45, 55, 57, 65,
      76, 77, 97, 99, 109, 143,
      146, 155, 164, 179, 181,
      185, 224, 225, 241, 273,
      283
      life force processing, 38
      openness, 39
   connections outside, 70–71
   control, 162
   desire, 41, 51, **54–58**, 54, 55,
      56, 57, 64, 78, 79, 84, 98,
      105, 143, 160, 179, 188,
      206, 217, 224
      life force processing, 56
      openness, 57
   energy, 75

energy leakage, 93
energy oscillations, 150
energy set point, 82
equivalents, 64
external connections, **101–37**
external set point, 71
finding solutions, 162
from other chakras, 72
gender differences, 98
genital, 54
goal, 69, 98
guru, 26
heart, 39, **41–47**, 41, 44, 45,
    46, 48, 50, 55, 64, 65, 77,
    99, 105, 106, 109, 116,
    117, 126, 143, 144, 146,
    151, 154, 155, 168, 177,
    179, 188, 202, 217, 224,
    241, 270, 271, 280, 283
    healing and, 97
    life force processing, 44
    openness, 46
    superpowers, 42
hrit, 41
inconsistent set points, 155
indu, 31
information, 76
information exchange, 143
information leakage, 95
information set point, 84
integration, **157–64**
intention, 103
interaction, 162
internal connections, 71–72,
    139–56
internal energy level, 85–88

internal level, 69
internal set point, 68, 81, 127
internal transfer, 147–53
inward ability, 70, 122, 124–
    26, 127
inward flow, **120–33**
inward intention, 70, 122,
    129–33
    variation, 131
inward set point, 70, 112,
    116, 126–29
leakage, 69
life force, 68
manas, 31
manipura, 48
maximum capacity, 121
maximum internal energy, 79
maximum internal
    information, 81
maximum internal level, 68
mind, **31–35**, 31, 33, 34, 41,
    65, 76, 77, 84, 88, 91, 95,
    97, 99, 103, 112, 143, 145,
    154, 155, 163, 164, 177,
    181, 185, 224, 225, 241,
    262, 263, 283
    life force processing, 33
    openness, 34
muladhara, 59
negotiations, 143
nirvana, 26
outward ability, 70, 102, 108–
    12
outward flow, **101–8**
outward intention, 71, 116–
    20, 129

as a function of time, 118
outward set point, 71, 112–16, 112, 116
pathways between, 145–47
rating, 25
relative importance, 161
root, 59
sahasrara, 26
self-regulation, 80
spirit, 26–30, 27, 28, 33, 36, 59, 60, 61, 62, 77, 79, 106, 189, 270, 283
life force processing, 28
openness, 29
storage, **75–100**
stored energy, 85
structure, 68
structure basics, **67–74**
structure overview, 68
svadhisthana, 54
systems, 21
talu, 36
to other chakras, 72
vishuddha, 36, 37
will, 48–53, 48, 49, 50, 51, 52, 55, 64, 78, 103, 106, 109, 126, 151, 154, 160, 179, 188, 189, 190, 217, 224, 241, 263, 265, 270
life force processing, 51
openness, 52
chakras
Hindu model, 23
channelers, 255
chaos, 59, 62
chaos chakra. *See* chakra, chaos

Chen, William C. C., 65
Cheney, Dick, 189
chi, 5, 49
channels, 139
Chocachinchi, 64
Christians, 27
Circe, 289
clocks, 170
coefficient, 203
cognitive-behavioral therapy, 10, 156
coincidence, 190
collective consciousness, 274
Collective Unconscious, 60
Colwell, John, 239
communication
non-ordinary, 181
ordinary, 182
time factors, 243
communication chakra. *See* chakra, communication
Complete Guide to the Soul, 62
connection, 121
abuse, 209
between souls, 265–71
blocking, 239
body and soul mechanism, 260–64
building, **199–219**
calibration, 195
changes without interactions, 215
close distance, 232
coefficient, 200, 203
complete chakra model, 268
complex, **251–84**

deep, 59
desire, 217
different chakras, 271
directionality, 199, 245
distance, **221–35**
EEG measurements, 224
effect of distance, 226
effect of time, 211
energy threshold, 244
enhancing, 242
example, 203, 204, 205, 209
experience, 208, 211
extraterrestrial, 223
far distance, 222
feedback, 230
genetic, 203
groups, 272
instant, 209
intentional, 214
interpersonal, **265–75**
life force, 169
life force strength, 209
limits, 199
matching chakras, 271
measuring, 180, **199–219**
measuring ability, 192
measuring relationships, 213
message, **237–46**
middle distance, 226
non-living, **277–80**
non-ordinary, **167–78**
ordinary, **167–78**
ordinary reality effects, **221–35**
other pathways, 249
physical, 168

physical distance, 232
physiological signs, 224
probability, 237
reincarnational, 207
sensing distance, 226
soul-body, **253–64**
strong emotions, 241
through all chakras, 241
total, 235
twins, 207
conscious executive, 159
consciousness, 33
consensual reality, 274
conservation of energy, 13
conversion
    energy, 141
    information, 142
    life force, 139–56
convolutions (brain), 261
Cosby, Bill, 113
counseling, 144
countries, 273
couples, 272
Craigslist, 222
creation, 54
crown chakra, 26

D

daimonic
    ego, 290
daimonic reality, 289, *See*
    reality, soul
Dalai Lama, 189, 283
danger, 242
De Sanctis, Professor, 204

death, 4
Death (Terry Pratchett's version), 44
debunking, 240
decisions, 50
dementia, 95
depression, 155, 202
desire, 217
desire chakra. *See* chakra, desire
destruction, 54, 55
devil, 27, 189
Diamonds and Rust, 211
dissociation, 95
distance, 168
  physical, 221
divine, 27
Dobelmann, Valerie, 205
domination, 48
Dove, Elaine, 225
Dove, Evelyn, 225
dreams, 164
Dreamtime, 279, 280
dripping faucet, 244
Dubuc, B., 89

E

eating disorders, 113
Edison, Thomas, 28
ego, 158, 289, 290
Ekman, Paul, 37, 84, 118, 131, 153, 283
electromagnetic energy, 76
electromagnetism, 12, 168, 172
Eleusinian Mysteries, 290

emotion, 241
Emotional Freedom Techniques, 10, 136, 154
emotions, 37
energy, **12–16**, 59, 75
  capacity, 79
  conservation of, 15
  electromagnetic, 76
  enough, 86
  flow, 45
  healing, 10, 283
  leakage, 93
  measuring, 75
  stale, 94
  transfer, 148
energy lattice, 158
energy vampire, 110
energy-information interactions, 133–37
enlightenment, 218
Enron, 189
equations, 287
eros, 41
ESP experiments, 240
Eurydice, 289
experience, 72, 79, 82, 134, 162
extended field, 245
extended mind, 18
external set point, 71
Extraordinary Knowing, 224
Eye Movement Desensitization and Reprocessing, 10
eyes
  daytime, 6, 248, 287
  nighttime, 6, 248, 287

F

Faces of Combat, PTSD & TBI, 248
faith, 285
families, 181
feelings, 41
Feynman, Richard, 12, 13, 113
fields, 15
five-hundred-mile rule, 222
Flammarion, Camille, 203, 204, 205
flashbacks, 95, 96
fluid dynamics, 178
focus, 119, 132, 153
followers, 188
force, 11, 13
    fundamental, 11
forgetting, 242
Fox, Peter, 32
Franklin, Benjamin, 216
Freud, Sigmund, 10, 56, 158
Freudian tradition, 55
friends, 73, 130, 214
    needy, 117
friendship, 74
from other chakras, 72
Fuller, R. Buckminster, 42
Funakoshi, Gichin, 226
future
    sensing the, 171

G

Gagai'yeibmi, 279
Galileo, 104
gay rights, 105

gender differences, 98
genital chakra, 54
ghosts, 45, 201, 248, 277
Gibran, Kahlil, 216
goal, 69
God, 4, 26, 55
    working through humans, 106
good cop, bad cop, 151
Gorgons, 289
Goswami, 22
Gottman, John, 271
grace, 5
gradient, 245
gravity, 12, 13, 167, 168, 172, 221, 245
grief, 202
groups, 272
guru chakra, 26
gut reaction, 50
guts, 49

H

Hades, 289, 290
Harpur, Patrick, 6, 62, 286, 289
Harry Potter, 81
hate, 38
healers, 42, 61
healing, 140
health care, 48
heart, 64
heart chakra. *See* chakra, heart
heaven, 286
Hepburn, Audrey, 188
Heraclean ego, 289–91
Heracles, 286, 289–91

Hermes, 290
heroic ego, 290, 291
Higgs boson, 275
higher pleasures, 55
Hindu religion, 27
hippocampal/mammillothalamic
     tract, 89
Hitler, Adolph, 38, 189
Hogfather, 44
holographic fields, 32
Home, D. D., 14, 43
Homer, 57
hrit chakra, 41
Hsing Yi Chuan, 139
Hyperion, 57

I

id, 158
imagination
     creative, 287
     perception and, 287
Inca shamans, 64
incarnation, 255
incarnational light, 260
Incarnational Way, 255
indu chakra, 31
information, 12, **16–17**, 33, 75,
     76, 180
     desire, 16
     emotional, 16
     leakage, 95
     symbolic, 16
     transfer, 141, 152
information-energy interactions,
     133–37

initiation, 290
inspiration, 26
intellect, 31
intention, 103
interconnectedness, 41
internal connections, **139–56**
internal energy level, 85–88
internal level, 69
internal memory level, 88–93
internal set point, 68, 81
inward ability, 70, 124–26
inward flow, **120–33**
inward intention, 70, 129–33
     variation, 131
inward set point, 70, 126–29
IQ, 196

J

Jacob, 48
Jedi warriors, 44
Jesus, 43, 104
Jung, Carl, 10, 60

K

Kali, 55
ki, 5
Kinect, 23
kinetic energy, 14
knowledge works, 159
kundalini energy, 71, 139

L

labor negotiations, 273
labor union, 273

Lawrence, Mark, 32, 49
Lay, Kenneth, 189
Layayoga, 22
leaders, 188
leakage, 69, 93
learning, 78
Leland, Grant, 96, 248
Lennon, John, 42
Lessons of the Inca Shamans, 64
Lie to Me, 209
life, 4
life energy, 12, 13
life force, 5, 12, **17–18**, 68, 101,
   168
   ability to sense, 181
   calibration, 195
   capacity, 120
   complete flow, 268
   conversion, 139–56
   draining, 102
   filtering, 185
   in non-animate objects, 277
   in the chakra model, 282
   in Western culture, 188
   lack of, 155
   limits, 199
   maximum, 107
   measuring, 180
   measuring ability, 185, 192
   net change, 269
   net flow, 269
   outward flow, **101–8**
   pathways, 145–47
   positive or negative, 105, 177
   powerful, **247–49**
   same chakra flow, 270

sending, **179–98**
sending strength, 187
sensing, **179–98**
sensitivity, 194
sent, 266
stealing, 112
total flow, 270
transfer, 103, 147–53
transmission, 173, **237–46**
world, 107, 123
Light Fantastic, The, 279
Lightman, Cal, 209
Lincoln, Abraham, 257
Liu Wen Wei, 65
Loki, 27
Lombroso, 204
long-term memory, 88
long-term relationship, 176
Lorian Institute, 255
love, 38, 41, 42
love of money, 189
lover dying, 201
Lowlands, 201

M

Madoff, Bernie, 189
magicians, 44
magnetic field, 168
management, 273
manas chakra, 31
Manet, Édouard, 56
manipura chakra, 48
Marshall, S. L. A., 160
martial arts, 51, 65, 139
mathematics, 287

maximum internal energy, 79

maximum internal information, 81

maximum internal level, 68

Maxwell's Demon, 62

Mayer, Elizabeth Lloyd, 6, 209, 224, 243

Mayer, John D., 158

meditation, 243

Medusa, 289

memory, 32, 33, 34, 76, 79, 81, 135, 156, 262, 267
    brain functions, 90
    long-term, 88
    process, 89
    short-term, 88
    theory, 90

Men Who Stare at Goats, The, 160

message, **237–46**

mind, 32, 64

mind chakra. *See* chakra, mind

mockingbirds, 254

Mohamed, 104

momentum, 169, 253
    soul, 172

Morgan, Robert, 240

morphic resonance, 33

mosquitoes, 254

Mother Earth, 64

Mother Teresa, 28

mouth, 36

Mozart, Wolfgang Amadeus, 56, 102

muladhara chakra, 59

multiple-soul problem, 177

munay, 64

N

Native Americans, 183

near death experience, 81, 84, 170

negative image, 127

neural network, 32, 50

New Age, 31, 139

Newhouse, Eric, 96, 248

nightmares, 96

nirvana chakra, 26

noise, 243

non-ordinary reality. *See* reality, soul

Noriega, Manuel, 96

Norse gods, 27

nutrients, 60

O

Obama, Barack, 189

Obi-Wan Kenobi, 224

Odysseus, 57, 289

one-night stand, 176

operators (in equations), 293

ordinal scale, 87

ordinary reality. *See* reality, ordinary

organization chart, 78

Ormand, Julie, 188

Orpheus, 289

Ouija board, 182

outward ability, 70, 108–12
    to block, 110
    to send, 108

outward intention, 71, 116–20
  as a function of time, 118
outward set point, 71, 112–16

P

Pachamama, 64
Papez's circuit, 89
Pappas, Sam, 96, 135
paranormal, 283
pathways, 145
patterns, 33
pecking order, 78
performers, 188
Perseus, 289
personal power, 188
personal space, 233
Peru, 64
Phantasms of the Living, 203
phantom limbs, 246
phonemes, 182
physical matter, 253
physical reality. *See* reality,
  ordinary
physical strength, 108
physics, 167, 274
Picasso, Pablo, 56
platonic love, 41
Playfair, Guy Lyon, 225
pleasures
  higher, 55
  sexual, 55
politics, 38, 78, 189
positive people, 121
post-traumatic stress disorder,
  80, 210, 283

potential energy, 13
power, 48
Power, The, 217
Powles, Damien, 225
Powles, Richard, 225
prana, 5
Pratchett, Terry, 279
precognition, 171
psychology, 10, 88, 283
psychopathic personalities, 161
purpose on earth, 254

Q

Q'ero shamans, 51, 64
qi, 5
Qigong, 10, 49, 140, 142
quantum mechanics, 287
quest, 183

R

radiation, 15
Radin, Dean, 224
rational ego, 289, 290, 291
rationalizing, 145
reality
  consensual, 274
  daimonic. *See* reality, soul
  non-ordinary. *See* reality, soul
  ordinary, 6
  physical. *See* reality, ordinary
  soul, 6, 282, 287
receiver
  non-ordinary, 186
  ordinary, 186
receptive state, 243

rehearsal effect, 164
Reiki, 10, 179
reincarnation, 55, 109, 181, 207, 218, 254
relationships, 44, 270
   health of, 270
religion, 189
remembering, 33
rite of passage, 183
Rolf, Ida, 66
romantic love, 41
Ronson, Jon, 160
root chakra, 59
Rowling. J. K., 81

S

sacred places, 280
sahasrara chakra, 26, 60
salesmen, 222
salesmen's wives, 222
Sasquatch, 48
Second Ecology, 258
Second Law of Thermodynamics, 62
Secret Tradition of the Soul, 62
Secret, The, 190, 217
self-awareness, 163
self-reflection, 122
self-sabotage, 115
senior-junior relationship, 10
Sense of Being Stared At, 192, 195, 228, 232, 233, 239, 243, 245, 247
senses, 6, 31
sensitivity, 194

sentry, 227
sexual addiction, 126
sexual energy, 55
sexual pleasure, 55
sexuality, 54, 55
Shakespeare, 57
shamanism, 61, 287, *See also* Inca Shaman and Q'ero shaman
Sheldrake, Rupert, 18, 33, 192, 195, 228, 233, 246
short-term memory, 88
Shotokan Karate, 226
Shumsky, Susan, 42, 60
Simmons, Dan, 57
single-cell creatures, 55
sirens (of the Odyssey), 57
skepticism, 4, 9, 240
skeptics, 241, 286
Smith, Debra White, 42
sniper, 227
social actor, 159
social psychology, 10
society
   effects of, 183
solar plexus, 65
Some Enchanted Evening, 228
sonqo, 64
soul, 4, 5, **19–164**, 281
   complex connections, **251–84**
   connections between, 265–71
   integration, **157–64**
   interactions, **265–75**
   loss of, 291
   momentum, 172
   multi-soul interactions, 177

physical amplifier, 253
physics, 245
self-awareness, 163
simple connections, **165–249**
structure, **21–66**
time, 171
soul reality. *See* reality, soul
Soul Snatchers, 240
South Pacific, 215, 228
Spangler, David, 255, 260
Spirit + Self, 22
spirit chakra. *See* chakra, spirit
spirit energy, 62
spirit journey, 61
spirits, 44
spiritualism, 286
St. Teresa, 14, 43
Star Wars, 224
staring, 229
static electricity, 167
Steinbach, Diane, 181
Stevenson, Ian, 92, 182
stimulus, 180
strong nuclear force, 12
Structural Integration, 66
subliminal signal, 243
subtle body, 67
superego, 158
superpowers, 42, 45, 50
surface tension, 233
surroundings, 119, 132
svadhisthana chakra, 54
symbology, 33

T

Tales of Power, 65
talu chakra, 36
tanden, 65
telepathy, 226
tension, 233
Teresa of Avila. *See* St. Teresa
texting, 38
the zone, 171
thermal energy, 14
thinking, 33
third eye, 31
Third Eye Health, 22
Thompson, Hunter S., 78
thought, 23, 32, 41
throat, 36
throat chakra, 36
Tiger in the Jungle, 184, 226, 245
time, 170
   variable, 170
to other chakras, 72
too much information, 122
Torres, Ria, 209
training, 191
transformation, 46
transformation (instant), 134
transmission, **237–46**
   probability, 237
trauma, 95, 154
trauma counseling, 97
Trojan Wars, 57
trolls, 279
Truths, 255
Twain, Mark, 55

twins, 207
two-body problem, 167
two-soul problem, 168
    calculations, 172
    solution, 173

V

vampire, 44, 110
variability, 197
variables (in equations), 294
velocity, 169
vishuddha chakra, 36
Vulcan mind meld, 177

W

Wallace, William, 51
Warburton, Acton, 204
Warburton, Canon, 204, 206
*We All Have Souls and I Think I
    Can Prove It*, 4
weak nuclear force, 12

whale songs, 254
will chakra. *See* chakra, will
win friends and influence
    people, 188
Winfrey, Oprah, 190
world life force, 123
World Soul, 256

X

Xbox, 23

Y

yachai, 64
yoga, 22, 32

Z

Zen Buddhism, 32, 43
Zener cards, 232, 240, 241
zone, the, 171

About the Author

Tom Blaschko earned a Bachelor's degree in astronomy from the California Institute of Technology, where he learned something about science. He earned a Master's degree in developmental psychology from the State University of New York at Buffalo, where he learned several seemingly contradictory things about the inner workings of people. He earned a third degree black belt in Shotokan Karate, where he learned about the martial arts aspects of the life force called ki.

He has been interested in paranormal phenomena since grade school and went on his first (unsuccessful) ghost hunt in the 1970s. Scientific influences include research by Rupert Sheldrake on morphic fields, Ian Stevenson's studies of people who remember past lives, analysis of the effects of Emotional Freedom Techniques and other energy healing, and research on ki by Kuo Kanshin and Shigeru Egami's group.

Beyond the scientific research there are thousands of stories from seemingly credible people who have talked with angels or fairy folk or apus or djinn, seen ghosts, and lived in Dreamtime. Dozens of people have witnessed D. D. Home and St. Teresa of Avila, among others, floating in the air. Hundreds of reports are available describing how someone knew at the moment it happened that a loved one was hurt or sensed something that was going to happen in the future.

Rather than try to discredit all of these reports, Tom asked the question: What is the least that needs to be added to Western science to make these research results and reported events possible? It turned out to be a two-item list: souls with chakras and a fifth force he calls the life force. Both of these are well accepted in many cultures, so nothing really new was needed.

Calculating Soul Connections is the result of working out the details.